Trees and Shrubs for Flowers

Glyn Church

Photographs Pat Greenfield

FIREFLY BOOKS

A FIREFLY BOOK

Published by Firefly Books Ltd. 2002

Copyright © 2002 Glyn Church (text), Pat Greenfield (photographs) and David Bateman Ltd.

Originated in 2002 by David Bateman Ltd.,
30 Tarndale Grove, Albany, Auckland, New Zealand

First Printing

National Library of Canada Cataloguing in Publication Data

Church, Glyn
    Trees and shrubs for flowers
(Woody plant series)
Includes bibliographical references and index.
ISBN 1-55297-631-9 (bound)
ISBN 1-55297-630-0 (pbk.)
1. Flowering trees. 2. Flowering shrubs. I. Greenfield, Pat
II. Title. III. Title: Flowers. IV. Series: Church, Glyn. Woody plant series.

SB435.C482 2002   635.9'7713   C2001-903297-8

Publisher Cataloging-in-Publication Data (U.S.)

Church, Glyn.
    Trees and shrubs for flowers / Glyn Church ; photographs by
Pat Greenfield. – 1st ed.
[160] p. : col. photos., maps ; cm. (Woody Plants)
Includes bibliographic references and index.
Summary: An illustrated gardening guide to over 100 trees and shrubs
selected for their flowers.
ISBN 1-55297-631-9
ISBN 1-55297-630-0 (pbk.)
1. Flowering woody plants. 2. Flowering trees. 3. Flowering shrubs.
I. Greenfield, Pat. II. Title. III. Series.
635.976 21   CIP SB435.C58   02002

Published in Canada in 2002 by
Firefly Books Ltd.
3680 Victoria Park Avenue
Willowdale, Ontario
M2H 3K1

Published in the United States in 2002 by
Firefly Books (U.S.) Inc.
P.O. Box 1338, Ellicott Station
Buffalo, New York
14205

Printed in Hong Kong through Colorcraft Ltd

Above: *Sophora tetraptera*

Opposite top: *Plumbago auriculata*

Below right: Rose 'Flower Carpet'

Page 1: *Michelia yunnanensis*

Pages 2 and 3: *Bougainvillea* 'Scarlett O'Hara'

Contents

Introduction

Flowers are the "stars" of the garden—they are what we often notice first, and for many of us, they are the main reason for selecting a particular plant. We tend to think of flowers as our reward for all our garden labors, and with many species we can extend this reward by bringing blooms inside to brighten our homes. Their myriad colors and forms allow us to "paint" with our plants and create the garden's mood, whether it be soft cool blue, hot orange red or the exuberance of a multicolored meadow garden. The passing of the seasons in the garden is marked by the flowering of specific species and we feel elated when the first spring flowers appear, often before any leaves, letting us know a long winter is coming to an end. Many flowers also add the extra dimension of fragrance to our garden environment.

While we can enjoy their blooms, plants flower for very selfish reasons—as a means of reproduction. Once this is understood, along with the energy a plant puts into this most vital aspect of its life cycle, it can be used to the gardener's advantage. Some plants flower in one huge burst, while others tend to flower over a long season. As soon as a flower is pollinated, it has performed its task and it starts to fade as the plant now puts its energies into producing seeds. We can persuade many plants, such as roses, to keep producing blooms by cutting off the spent flowers. This prevents the bush from making seeds and so it tries again, making new flowers. Some plants like mophead hydrangeas have sterile flowers that can never be pollinated and so the flowers last for months and months. Pruning at certain times of the year can also encourage repeat flowering and extend the flowering season. Where applicable, I have noted techniques for encouraging flowering under the species descriptions. This may include pruning and training techniques. For example, training a plant in a horizontal fashion will increase the number of flowers. This is because the internal hormones in a horizontal stem are saying "make flowers," whereas a vertical or upright stem has different

Left: *Brachyglottis perdicioides*
Opposite: *Camellia* x *williamsii* 'Donation'
Below left: *Magnolia campbellii*

hormones saying "grow to the sky." Orchardists are very familiar with this phenomenon and thus train apples and other trees with lots of horizontal stems. It is also very obvious in climbers like wisteria, which produce masses of flowers when trained horizontally but few flowers when allowed to grow up in a tree. In fact, nearly all woody plants act like this, but you do need a balance between new vigorous growth and older flowering wood or the bush may lose impetus and fade away.

A woody plant is one with a permanent woody structure. Some woody plants die back to some extent in the winter but there is always some woody part visible throughout the year. My own garden has well over 2,000 different woody plants, and many of the photographs in the book were taken there. I have used this garden and also my experience of growing plants in windy, dry or cold climates to explain the likes and dislikes of the plants. Zones are given to show how cold a climate a plant will cope with, but they are only guides. When a plant does not like warm or hot regions, I have included an upper as well as a lower limit.

It is very hard to generalize about the climate a plant needs in order to thrive. Within any region and even within a garden there are microclimates—places that are warmer or colder than the surrounding area. Even planting a shrub next to a wall where it gets the reflected heat can make the difference between success and failure. Similarly with soil, we can improve it and irrigate if necessary. The type of soil is critical to the well-being of some plants and irrelevant to others. Over the years I have gardened on heavy clay soils with a pH of 7.0, on rocky soil with a pH of 6.0, and currently a free-draining acidic loam of pH 5.5, so I have used my experience regarding soil types when writing the plant descriptions.

I have also included plants that may have naturalized in your region. The more I travel the more I find that what is regarded in one region as a weed is a treasure somewhere else. Sometimes this is based on the plant actually self-perpetuating in that region and sometimes it is just plain bias against a certain plant or group of plants.

In this book I've tried to find as many outstanding flowering woody plants as I can. For some, your climate may be too cold, for others too hot, but there will still be hundreds to choose from, with a huge range of shape, color and size. I invite you to come with me on a journey of the wonderful flowers that I have grown and enjoyed over the years.

How to use this book

The plants presented in this book are organised alphabetically by genus. If you know the common name only, you can find the botanical name entry through the index, where both botanical and common names are listed.

Each entry has a variety of information laid out in the format illustrated below, so you can quickly find what you need to know about a particular plant. The text includes not only notes on cultivation, but anecdotes and historical information, making this a fascinating book to browse through.

The table at the back of the book will help you to find plants by hardiness zone, flower color and flowering season, as well as those native to North America. An extensive glossary covers the botanical terms used throughout the book.

Genus

Common name

Family
Taxonomic grouping of genera to which this genus belongs.

Elaeagnus

THORNY ELAEAGNUS
Elaeagnaceae

Elaeagnus is a large genus of plants with a widespread distribution from southern Europe through to Asia and over to North America. Some are deciduous while others are super-hardy evergreens, though few of them have enough merit to be brought into our gardens.

The most useful aspect of these plants is the wind-hardiness of *E. pungens* and *E. macrophylla* and the dazzling variegated leaf forms of *E. pungens* and *E.* x *ebbingei*.

Elaeagnus = wild olive (from Greek *elaeagnos*, in reference to the fruits).

Elaeagnus angustifolia
OLEASTER OR RUSSIAN OLIVE
Oleaster makes a large deciduous shrub or small tree with a billowy habit, reddish stems and hidden spines. The tiny, fragrant, creamy yellow flowers appear in summertime. However, the prime reason for growing this is the silvery willow-like leaves, and it is often confused with a *Pyrus salicifolia*. It is found native in southern Europe to central Asia. Height x width 20 ft (6 m). ZONE 3.

'Quicksilver' is an excellent silvery leaf form grown for its consistency. Height x width 12 ft (4 m).

Angustifolia = narrow leaf.

Description of genus

Meaning of botanical name

Species description and cultivation notes

Hardiness zone
These zones are guides only (see page 9). The zone range is given at the end of each species entry. If no upper limit is given, the plants will grow to zone 10, though possibly with some change to habit, e.g., some deciduous trees can become semi-evergreen. Unless otherwise stated, cultivars grow in the same zone range as the species.

Approximation of size
Height and width can be an approximation only as it varies enormously depending on your climate. If you are concerned about something growing too big, check with a local garden center to find out how they grow in your area.

Species name

Common name
These names vary from place to place. To be sure of what you are buying, always check the species name.

Cultivar or form
Cultivated variety, usually bred but can be a natural variety, then often called a "sport." Can only be propagated true from cuttings.

Right: *Prunus serrulata* 'Shogetsu'
Far right: *Metrosideros excelsa*

Hardiness zone map

This map has been prepared to agree with a system of plant hardiness zones that has been accepted as an international standard and range from 1 to 11. It shows the minimum winter temperatures that can be expected on average in different regions. Where a zone number has been given, the number corresponds with a zone shown here. That number indicates the coldest areas in which the particular plant is likely to survive through an average winter. Note that these are not necessarily the areas in which it will grow best. Because the zone number refers to the minimum temperatures, a plant given zone 7, for example, will obviously grow perfectly well in zone 8, but not in zone 6. Plants grown in a zone considerably higher than the zone with the minimum winter temperature in which they will survive might well grow but they are likely to behave differently. Note also that some readers may find the numbers a little conservative; we felt it best to err on the side of caution.

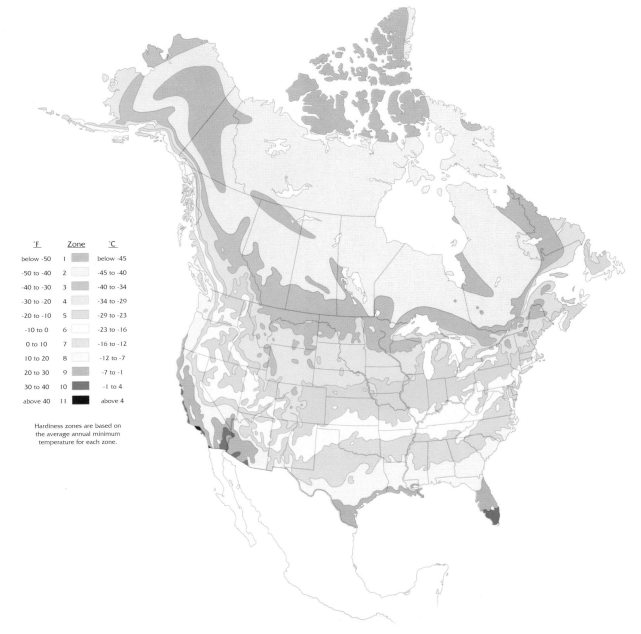

°F	Zone	°C
below -50	1	below -45
-50 to -40	2	-45 to -40
-40 to -30	3	-40 to -34
-30 to -20	4	-34 to -29
-20 to -10	5	-29 to -23
-10 to 0	6	-23 to -16
0 to 10	7	-16 to -12
10 to 20	8	-12 to -7
20 to 30	9	-7 to -1
30 to 40	10	-1 to 4
above 40	11	above 4

Hardiness zones are based on the average annual minimum temperature for each zone.

Left: Floribunda rose 'Playboy'
Far left: *Olearia phlogopappa* 'Blue Gem'

Abutilon

FLOWERING MAPLE, INDIAN MALLOW, PARLOR MAPLE,
CHINESE LANTERNS
Malvaceae

Abutilons or "Chinese lanterns" are marvelous evergreen
shrubs and when they are in bloom, from spring to fall,
there is a flower at every leaf, and sometimes three or
four. Not even roses can produce as many flowers in a summer.
The showy flowers are usually an open bell-shape, though a few
species are more tubular. If you are lucky enough to live in a
region with nectar-feeding birds, you will have the birdlife as a
bonus in your garden.

While it is true that these plants are a bit frost-tender, they
will grow in shade, giving you the chance to shelter them from
the cold. And if you have a mild climate, they will provide you
with a riot of color nearly all through the year. They will, of
course, grow in full sun as well as shade and for gardeners in
cool climates there is always the option of planting them against
a warm wall. Abutilons are ideal for the back of a mixed or
herbaceous border and also look fine in a woodland dell.

Abutilons are soft shrubs, where the stems remain green
even on quite old specimens, so they never become truly woody.
In cold climates the tops may be frosted, but if the plant is
established it is highly likely it will regenerate from the base. In
these environments the trick is to plant one in the spring and
water it regularly to get it as big as possible by the first frosts of
winter. The bigger the plant by frost time, the better its chances
of survival. Transplant them when they are young, as they
quickly become container-bound. You can move larger plants to
a new location if you prune them drastically, but it is easier to
grow some cuttings and start afresh.

These plants are not fussy about soil as long as it is free-
draining, and being alkaline or acidic makes no difference to
them. Being soft shrubs they are thirsty plants and need
sufficient moisture to keep them lush and healthy. The soft,
luxuriant foliage needs protection from wind: either planting as
a wall shrub or in a sheltered woodland garden is ideal. Both
situations will help protect them from winter cold as well as
wind.

Abutilons need regular pruning to keep them tidy. Left
unpruned, they will start to climb through neighboring shrubs
and the lower stems will trail along the ground, putting out new
roots to form a thicket. Most of the cultivated plants come from
South and Central America.

Abutilon = mallow.

Abutilon hybridum, syn A. globosum

The flowers of these abutilons come in an amazing range of colors,
including white, reds, orange, apricot, pink, lavender, gold, yellow
and maroon. Good handsome reds include **'Ashford Red'** and
'Strawberry Crush', while **'Golden Fleece'** is the best of the
goldy yellows. The flowers are bell-shaped, 2–3 in (5–8 cm) long,
and appear from spring through to fall.

The name *Abutilon hybridum* covers a multitude of hybrids and
selected clones. While breeders diligently keep notes about the
parentage of orchids and roses, when it comes to abutilons no one
keeps track.

Depending on the species or hybrid, the leaves can be small
and dainty, right up to enormous leaves bigger than a spread hand.
The leaves are eaten by the occasional caterpillar, but there are no

Above: *Abutilon vitifolium*

Above: *Abutilon hybridum* 'Strawberry Crush'

devastating pests, and so the dark green foliage looks good all year. These evergreen leaves are slightly hairy, dark green above and pale beneath. Having hairy leaves allows them to grow in breezy sites, but strong winds will break the stems. The bushes are prone to breaking at the joints where the branches grow from the main stem. If this should happen, the bush is easily pruned and quickly regenerates. You can prune them lightly or drastically, depending on your mood and the climate. The bush will cope with either method of pruning and quickly recover. Height 10 ft (3 m) x width 6–15 ft (2–5 m). ZONE 8.

Abutilon megapotamicum
TRAILING ABUTILON

Dark, evergreen, arrowhead leaves and thin brittle stems hold the pendulous flowers like floats from a fishing rod. The bell-shaped flowers up to 1½ in (4 cm) are intriguing, the showiest part being the bright red, waxy calyx (the part that protects the flower and is usually green). The calyx looks a bit like a bishop's miter, and the dainty lemon-yellow petals emerge at the bottom to form a thin tube. The contrast of the bright red top and yellow tube beneath is stunning and the brush of purple stamens emerging from the yellow tube only enhances this bizarre flower. It is as if the plant has been designed by a committee. The flowers appear from summer through to fall.

Left: *Abutilon megapotamicum* 'Variegatum'

It is a rangy, open-growing shrub, best used as a climber, or else it needs frequent pruning to keep it tidy. Height x width 6 ft (2 m). This species originates from Brazil. ZONE 8.

There is a variegated form where the leaves are splashed with yellow, as if a painter has run amok. My recommendation is to avoid it at all costs—it's horrible.

Megapotamicum = big river.

Abutilon vitifolium

Most abutilons are very easy to grow but this one is another matter altogether. While it has one of the most beautiful blue flowers—a kind of smoky lavender-blue—it is also one of the trickiest plants to grow. If you are lucky enough to have one, regard this as a brief love affair because it is invariably short-lived. The saucer-shaped flowers appear in early summer and are 3 in (8 cm) across with long stamens.

This species is frost-tender and hates wet feet; poor drainage will lead to root rot. Wind rock (where the wind sways the bush backward and forward) is another problem, damaging the roots and allowing soil-borne fungi to invade the plant.

This bush forms a large, upright shrub and is the tallest of the genus, hence the increased risk of wind rock. The gray-green, furry leaves are a little like a maple or grapevine. The leaves and

Above: *Abutilon vitifolium*

stems are covered in soft white down or hairs, giving a dull, downy green quite different from the rich dark green of most abutilons. The highlight, however, are those beautiful blue flowers all summer long.

If I had to choose a climate for this wonderful plant I'd go for a region with mild frosts. Too warm a climate and it gets root rot and borer grubs in the stems, too severe a frost and it simply dies. Unlike the hybrid abutilons, this plant needs full sun and will be leggy and sparse if grown in the shade. It is easy to grow from seed, so save a few for future use. Some seedlings will have white flowers or occasionally a rich dark-purple color. Height 15 ft (5 m) x width 8 ft (2.5 m). A native of Chile. ZONE 8.

Abutilon ochsenii is a similar plant with violet- to light purple flowers. Height 10 ft (3 m) x width 8 ft (2.5 m). ZONE 8. There are several named hybrids between *A. ochsenii* and *A. vitifolium* known as **A. x suntense**. They are named after Sunte House in England. Height 12 ft (4 m) x width 8 ft (2.5 m). ZONE 8.

Vitifolium = from "vitis," meaning grape.

Aesculus

BUCKEYE, HORSE CHESTNUT
Hippocastanaceae

*A*esculus include some of the showiest flowering trees in the world. Flamboyant panicles of flowers in white, pink or red decorate these trees in late spring or early summer. All species are deciduous, and while some are tidy, rounded trees ideal for smaller city gardens, others are huge, and so only suitable for very large gardens or park-like grounds.

Aesculus prefer a deep, moist soil, but some will cope with a dry summer when they are established. It is one of the few trees that seems as happy in alkaline, or limey, ground as it is in acidic soil. A place in the sun is the next requirement. It always looks more stately in isolation and doesn't blend easily with other trees.

Easily transplanted in fall, they form round, dome-shaped trees with a bold canopy of leaves. All have large palmate or hand-like leaves with five large leaflets. When the buds expand before the leaves emerge, they are covered in a glossy, shiny wax. As well as being late to come into leaf, they are often one

of the first trees to lose their leaves in fall and, usually, without any great fanfare or color. They are not generally affected by pests or diseases.

Aesculus = mast-bearing tree, from "esca," meaning nourishment, because a flour was ground from the kernels. The chestnuts are not edible in the same way as castanea or "Spanish chestnut."

Aesculus californica
CALIFORNIA BUCKEYE
The scented white flowers appear in long cones 8 in (20 cm) tall in early summer and have distinctive whiskery stamens. This small tree is able to grow in hotter, drier climates than most of the family. As the name suggests, it is a native of California, thus the drought- and heat-tolerance. The leaves often have a blue-gray surface, as do many plants from dry climates. Height 25 ft (8 m) x width 30 ft (10 m). ZONE 7.

Aesculus x *carnea*
RED HORSE CHESTNUT
This is a hybrid between the huge *Aesculus hippocastanum* and the smaller, red-flowered *A. pavia*. It forms a tidy, rounded tree with showy pink flowers. The hooded flowers appear in late spring and early summer in panicles 8–12 in (20–30 cm) tall. They open as pale pink with a hint of yellow, fading to a warm pink color. Although it is a hybrid, it comes true from seed. Because of the *A. pavia* influence, it is able to grow in warmer, drier climates than *A. hippocastanum* and it can be grown in small gardens. Height x width 30 ft (10 m). ZONE 6.

There is a good form called **'Briotii'** which needs to be grafted, but it repays the effort with richer, darker reddish-colored flowers.

Carnea = flesh-colored.

A related hybrid called **Aesculus x plantierensis** is sterile, which is an advantage, as the big seeds of most chestnuts can be dangerous to walk over, causing sprained ankles and other injuries. The flowers are pale pink. Height x width 30 ft (10 m). ZONE 3.

Aesculus hippocastanum
COMMON HORSE CHESTNUT
This massive, wide-spreading tree has swooping branches that dip down toward the ground and back up to the light. It is certainly one of the most showy flowering trees for cool climates, with masses of flowers in huge white spikes 12 in (30 cm) tall appearing in late spring. The yellow blotch within each flower deepens to red as it ages. It needs rich, deep, moist soil to prosper and will not flourish on poor, thin soils. It is native to Greece but is now well-established throughout western Europe. Height 80 ft (25 m) x width 70 ft (20 m). ZONE 3.

A form called **'Baumannii'** (syn 'Flore Pleno') has beautiful, double, white flowers and is sterile. Therefore it has no seeds and so no spiny fruit. Height 80 ft (25 m) x width 70 ft (20 m). ZONE 3.

Hippo = horse, as in hippodrome, and *castanea* = chestnut.

Aesculus indica
INDIAN HORSE CHESTNUT
If you have a hot or dry climate then this tall, upright chestnut is for you. It thrives in heat, and is lethargic in cool or moist climates. Lovely pink new growth is followed by huge candles of

Above: *Aesculus* x *carnea*

flowers 12–16 in (30–40 cm) long. The flowers appear in summer and are white tinged with pink, becoming red with time. *A. indica* comes from the northwest Himalayas. Height x width 50 ft (15 m). ZONE 7.

The clone **'Sydney Pearce'**, raised at Kew Gardens in London, England, is grown for its consistently good deep pink, yellow-centered flowers, whereas seedlings can give variable results. Height x width 50 ft (15 m). ZONE 7.

Indica = from India.

Aesculus neglecta

A "confused" species from the southern states of the U.S.A. that is thought by some to be a hybrid. The flowers are yellow with a hint of red and appear in cones 6 in (15 cm) tall in midsummer. The fall color of this conical tree is yellow. The species is rightly famous for the clone **'Erythroblastos'**. Apart from having an extraordinary name, it has fabulous shrimp-pink new growth in the spring, and then a dramatic foliage change from pink to green. Unfortunately, this brilliant spring color is only a feature in certain cool climates. In warmer regions there is no show of color to speak of and the leaves just open to green. Height 30 ft (10 m) x width 25 ft (8 m). ZONE 5.

Aesculus parviflora
BOTTLEBRUSH BUCKEYE

This plant is a little out of the ordinary because it is a creeping, spreading shrub that sends suckers underground to form a thicket. In a garden setting, it is difficult to blend with other shrubs and looks best in isolation. Even though the individual

Right: *Aesculus parviflora*

flowers are small, the flower heads are large and very pretty. These 12 in (30 cm) tall cones of spidery white flowers have red anthers. They are especially treasured as they appear in high summer when few shrubs are flowering. An unusual, creeping shrub, it grows naturally from North Carolina down to Florida. Height 10 ft (3 m) x width 15 ft (5 m). ZONE 5.

Parviflora = small flowers.

Aesculus pavia, syn *A. splendens*
RED BUCKEYE

A small, upright, tidy tree, ideal for small town gardens. Some versions are magnificent, depending on the clone, and it is worth selecting a good flowering form. It has a much neater leaf than the usual blowzy chestnuts. A strong red petiole or leaf stalk extends into red leaf veins and perfect symmetrical veining. Even the flower panicles are neater, forming short, dense 6 in (15 cm) tall cones of long, red, tubular flowers in early summer. The best specimen I have ever seen was at the Biltmore Estate in North Carolina. It grows wild from North Carolina down to the Mississippi delta. Height 15 ft (5 m) x width 10 ft (3 m). ZONE 5.

The form **'Atrosanguinea'** (from *atro* = dark and *sanguin* = blood) is appropriately named, with its dark red flowers. Height 15 ft (5 m) x width 10 ft (3 m). ZONE 5.

Pavia = named for Peter Paaw (d. 1617),
Professor of Botany at Leydon University, Holland.

Below: *Aesculus pavia*

Amelanchier

JUNEBERRY, SHADBUSH, SNOWY MESPILUS
Rosaceae

Amelanchiers have, at times, been cataloged as mespilus, aronia, pyrus or crataegus, and then when we look at the species, it seems only the botanists can tell one from another. From the point of view of humble gardeners, all I can say is that they are beautiful plants and we should select named forms so we get the bush we want.

Although the individual flowers are small, *en masse* the overall effect is stunning. To see vast areas of the mountaintops smothered in a white haze of amelanchier flowers is, for me, one of the highlights of an Appalachian spring. The simple, white, apple blossom-like flowers appear from early to mid-spring and are followed by small, black or purple fruits. Amelanchiers are desirable not for the outright showiness of the flowers, but for their abundance and bravery at flowering in cold and storms. The flowers must be very tough to survive frost, snow and biting cold winds. Then, at the end of summer, these wonderful plants oblige us with stupendous fall colors in shades of orange and red.

Amelanchiers grow right across the cooler regions of the Northern Hemisphere. They are all hardy, deciduous shrubs or small trees with clean, oval leaves and are easy to grow in any soil that is not too dry or poor. Most of them need an acidic or neutral soil. They are supremely cold- and wind-hardy. Full sun

Above: *Amelanchier asiatica*

is ideal as they become thin in shade. With an upright, brush habit, they are an ideal plant for the back of a perennial or shrub border. Some form small trees and can be used as lawn specimens. I have moved very big specimens quite successfully, and they can be transplanted at any time during the dormant winter period. They don't mind being pruned, either for outline shape or, more drastically, if your plant becomes too big for its allotted space. Amelanchiers are prone to cankers and fireblight.

Amelanchier = an adaptation of an old European name.

Amelanchier alnifolia

ALDER-LEAVED SERVICEBERRY, SASKATOON

A big, bushy plant from northwestern U.S.A., with clusters of white flowers in racemes 3 in (8 cm) long borne in late spring. It does not spread wildly, in fact a lot of the amelanchiers tend to sucker a little, gradually forming a thicket from the base but not enough to concern most gardeners. This species will grow in alkaline or acidic soil. Height x width 12 ft (4 m). There is a compact form called **'Regent'**, growing as a small, suckering plant, to around waist height. Height x width 4–6 ft (1.2–2 m). Both ZONES 4 TO 9.

Alnifolia = leaves like an *Alnus*, or alder.

Amelanchier arborea

DOWNY SERVICEBERRY

The 2–3 in (5–8 cm) long arching racemes of white flowers are sweetly scented and often appear in mid-spring. They are followed by red berries. This species is bigger than *Amelanchier alnifolia* and may need pruning in a garden situation to form it into a tidy, rounded, small tree. The oval leaves are slightly hairy or downy and have colorful fall tints. It comes from northeastern U.S.A. Height 20 ft (6 m) x width 15 ft (5 m). ZONES 4 TO 9.

Arborea = tree.

Amelanchier asiatica

ASIAN SERVICEBERRY

A large, upright shrub with bronzy new growth and smooth stems. In spring it has racemes of large, white, scented flowers. This species will cope with limey soil. From China, Korea and Japan. Height 25 ft (8 m) x width 30 ft (10 m). ZONES 5 TO 9.

Asiatica = from Asia.

Amelanchier canadensis

SHADBUSH, SHADBLOW

This species has the typical white flowers on erect racemes borne in spring, followed by black berries. It is a handsome, upright shrub with a tendency to sucker. The smooth green leaves turn fiery reds and oranges in the fall. Native to northeastern U.S.A. and Canada. Height 10 ft (3 m) x width 6 ft (2 m). ZONES 3 TO 9.

Canadensis = from Canada.

Amelanchier x grandiflora (*A. arborea* x *A. laevis*)

APPLE SERVICEBERRY

This plant is appropriately named as it has the best flowers of all the amelanchiers. The big clusters of large, white flowers borne on racemes 2½–3 in (6–8 cm) long are dazzling in the spring. The new spring leaf growth that follows is initially bronze, changing to green for the summer and on to a stunning mix of scarlet, orange and yellow in the fall. Most forms have a tidy, upright shape and they can be trained as a single-leader bush (that is with one stem or trunk), thus making them more amenable to planting as a lawn specimen, as the single trunk is easier to mow around. Height 25 ft (8 m) x width 30 ft (10 m). ZONES 4 TO 9.

'Autumn Brilliance' has particularly good red fall color, and **'Ballerina'** is a Dutch selection renowned for its terrific flower display and fine fall colors (and it has the added attraction

Above: *Amelanchier lamarckii*

Above: *Amelanchier lamarckii*

of being resistant to fireblight). The cultivars **'Robin Hill'** and **'Rubescens'** have pink-tinged flowers. For all, height 25 ft (8 m) x width 30 ft (10 m).

Grandiflora = big flowers.

Amelanchier laevis
ALLEGHENY SERVICEBERRY
A large shrub or small tree, covered in fragrant white flowers in spring. New leaves are often bronzy red, changing to green for the summer and to rich fall colors. This is one of the best forms for both flowers and leaf color. *A. laevis* comes from North America. Height 10–12 ft (3–4 m) x width 6–10 ft (2–3 m). ZONES 5 TO 9.

The cultivar **'Cumulus'** is bigger and more disease-resistant. Height 12 ft (4 m) x width 10 ft (3 m).

Laevis = smooth.

Amelanchier lamarckii
This lovely plant has confused gardeners and botanists alike for many years. First it was called *Crataegus racemosa* by Lamarck, as long ago as 1783. At times, it has been thought of as a European species, then a hybrid and then, perhaps, an obscure American species. It has also been lumped in with *Amelanchier canadensis* and *A. laevis*. Now it is thought to be a minor North American species. Whatever the complexities of its origin, it is a fabulous plant with all the positives of an amelanchier: neat foliage, great fall color and nice flowers. The new growth in spring is bronzy and quickly followed by a mass of dainty white flowers. During summer, the leaves always look clean and presentable and turn fiery oranges and reds in fall. It is a bush with a very tidy habit and it can be trained into a small tree or standard shape. Height 10–12 ft (3–4 m) x width 6–10 ft (2–3 m). ZONES 4 TO 9.

Lamarckii = named for Jean Baptiste Lamarck (1744–1829).

Aronia

CHOKEBERRY
Rosaceae

An easily overlooked group of plants from the Appalachian Mountains in eastern U.S.A. Initially, you may think they do not have much to commend them, but slowly they reveal their qualities. These deciduous shrubs are grown for both their spring flowers and wonderful fall colors. They are related to *Sorbus* and have similar heads of off-white flowers that appear in late spring on the tops of the stems in dainty clusters.

Throughout summer, aronias fade into the background, simply providing greenery, but you will notice them again come fall when the leaves turn scintillating shades of orange, red and scarlet.

These North American natives grow in full sun or part-shade. They cope with wet or dry soil, and are often found growing in swamps in the wild. Preferably the soil should be acidic or neutral, as they do not like lime. Aronias are easy-care shrubs, ideal for borders or in woodland gardens. They have a reasonably tidy, upright shape and can be pruned to keep them neat. Easy to transplant in winter. The plants are not bothered by any pests and diseases.

Aronia = an old name for one of the *Sorbus*.

Below: *Aronia arbutifolia*

Right: *Berberidopsis corallina*

Aronia arbutifolia
RED CHOKEBERRY

Clusters of white flowers appear in late spring and are followed by attractive red berries. This upright, hardy shrub has simple, dark green leaves that turn to dazzling reds and orange in the fall. The leaves are hairy on the lower surface. Native to northeastern U.S.A. Height 10 ft (3 m) x width 5 ft (1.5 m). ZONE 5.

'Brilliantissima' is a selected form with more flowers, glossier, larger fruit and stunning fall colors. Height x width 6–8 ft (2–2.5 m). ZONE 5.

Arbutifolia = leaf like an *Arbutus*.

Aronia melanocarpa
BLACK CHOKEBERRY

The clusters of off-white flowers appear in late spring and are followed by shiny, black berries. This shoulder-high shrub with glossy leaves also has fabulous fall color. Sometimes the bush suckers and becomes a thicket. The clone **'Autumn Magic'** has consistently good fall color and bigger berries. It is native to eastern North America. Height 6 ft (2 m) x width 10 ft (3 m). ZONE 4.

Melanocarpa = black fruits.

Berberidopsis

Flacourtiaceae

This genus is sometimes described as monotypic (i.e. it contains only one species), but I have seen other species. *Berberidopsis corallina*, described below, was introduced from Chile in 1862 by Richard Pearce, one of the many plant hunters sent out by the Veitch Nursery in England. It is grown for its racemes of beautiful, crimson, bell-shaped flowers.

Only those with a cool, moist climate should try to grow this Chilean evergreen climber. If you have a nice shady dell with a climate free of harsh droughts or too much heat, then the plant will be fine. Alternatively, you might choose to grow it in a cool conservatory or fern-house. *Berberidopsis* will grow in very cool climates, but it does need to be free from severe frosts, and any overhead shade and shelter you can give it may be just enough to keep off the worst of them. If you manage to get it growing well and flowering, your garden visitors will be most impressed, because a vine laden with racemes of crimson bells is a lovely sight.

Caterpillars and root rot are the biggest threat to *Berberidopsis*, other than unsuitable climate and soil. Good, free-draining soil that is acidic or neutral is essential. If your plant ever becomes untidy, you can judiciously prune it in spring, but it is never likely to run rampant.

Berberidopsis = you might think it is related to berberis because of the name, but the only connection is the shape of the flower; *opsis* = like, and so it translates as like a berberis flower.

Berberidopsis corallina
CORAL VINE

Red, teardrop buds open out to waxy, red bells about the size of a large fingernail. They appear in summer and the plant can flower for months if it is happy with its location. Simple, arrowhead, evergreen leaves are dark, glossy green above and almost silvery below. The leaves never look as good as they might. It is not a plant to put on a trellis or in a highly visible position because the leaves often look tatty and bedraggled. Instead, plant it up through an open shrub where the stems can weave to and fro, allowing the bright red flowers to dangle at head-height or just above. Height x width 15 ft (5 m). Native of Chile. ZONE 8 OR 9.

Corallina = as in sea coral, refers to the red color of the flowers.

Bignonia

CROSS VINE
Bignoniaceae

*B*ignonia used to be a huge genus, but the botanists have chipped away at it, removing *Tecoma* and *Campsis* and many others, and now it is down to just one species. A combination of a long flowering period, lush evergreen leaves and a healthy, robust nature makes for an easy-care climber for a prominent position. A lovely evergreen, or at least semi-evergreen, climber, it uses tendrils to get where it wants to go. The deep green leaves are set opposite each other on the stem, and are usually made up of two leaflets, with the addition of tendrils to help it climb. It is quite a vigorous climber, too, so take care that it will have enough room to grow where you decide to plant it.

Bignonia = Abbé Bignon, librarian to Louis XIV.

Bignonia capreolata, syn *Doxantha capreolata*
CROSS VINE

The flowers appear in late spring in terminal clusters and each flower is reddy brown on the outside of the tube, opening to five yellow petals at the mouth of the trumpet. It flowers over several months and if it should need pruning to tidy or reduce the size of the vine, then immediately after flowering is the ideal time. If you want something dramatic to plant through your trellis or over a pergola, this vine could be just the thing. Like most climbers it likes its top in sunlight and the roots in shade, and it is not too fussy about soil. Height x width 30 ft (10 m). Native to the woods of southeastern U.S.A. ZONE 6.

While the wild plants vary in flower color, there are some choice cultivars available. **'Atrosanguinea'** have richer red, thin tubular flowers with an orange throat, and **'Tangerine Beauty'** is a beautiful orange-colored form, consistently laden with flowers every year.

Capreolata = with tendrils.

Bougainvillea

Nyctaginaceae

*B*ougainvilleas are some of the most flamboyant flowers on the planet, so it comes as some surprise to discover that they have no petals at all. All the showy bits are bracts. (On most flowers the bracts are the green covering that protects the flowers buds. However, on some plants they are very colorful, and overshadow the true flowers completely.) This is possibly why they are so tough and last so long, as they "flower" for months on end. All you need is sufficient heat and sunshine hours and your vine will be draped with flowers from midsummer onward. Certainly these conditions are prerequisites to success, as bougainvilleas love warmth and lots of sun. Choose a frost-free location or as close to frost-free as possible. If your climate is marginal, consider having one as a container plant until it is woody (when it will be hardier than a young, soft plant) and then plant it.

Although they are stringent about heat and cold, they are willing to grow in any soil, except very wet ground. Good drainage is essential to keep the soil temperatures high. Wet soils are always colder than free-draining sites.

These wonderful evergreen climbers will also grow vigorously in warm, wet climates but tend not to flower as well. What they need in this situation is some stress, either through a restricted root run or periods of drought. Two possibilities come to mind: one is to plant in a tub or in a confined, narrow border next to the house with limited room for the roots to roam. The second is to plant them under the eaves of the house or in the lee of a wall or fence where they receive less rain. In fact, given enough stress, like drought or cold, they are deciduous.

Plant in isolation on a wall or strong trellis as the strident colors will clash with anything else. The vines are incredibly

Above: *Bougainvillea* 'Scarlett O'Hara'

heavy and any flimsy structure will collapse under the weight. They climb using vicious thorns as support, eventually using their own stems to support the new growth.

You can prune them to any shape you wish and they can be overly vigorous, with vast amounts of new growth every summer, so a good spring clean and cutback is a good idea. Flower heads appear on new wood so any spring pruning will not reduce the number of flowers.

They transplant easily from pots when young. No one would attempt to shift an established plant as it is easier to buy another one.

Bougainvillea commemorates French explorer Louis Antoine de Bougainville (1729–1811), commander of the first French circumnavigation of the globe (1766–1769) and after whom a large island nation near Papua New Guinea is named.

There are three species of bougainvillea in cultivation, from Brazil and Peru, and they are confusing to identify. It makes no difference to gardeners, as most of the ones we see are hybrids.

'**Magnifica**' has brilliant magenta flowers and is one of the hardier types. '**Scarlett O'Hara**' has fantastic scarlet-red flowers. Height for all approximately 30 ft (10 m). ZONE 9.

Brachyglottis, syn Senecio

Asteraceae

These genus of evergreen daisy-like bushes from New Zealand and Tasmania is quite remarkable for containing woody members of the groundsel family. Like daisies they have showy flower heads in summer or fall, and the combination of the flowers, the attractive, evergreen foliage and their ability to grow almost anywhere makes them great landscape plants. Put them in and forget about them. Grown in full sun, these

Above: *Brachyglottis greyi*

Above: *Brachyglottis perdicioides*

Left: *Brachyglottis repanda*

tough plants cope with wind and even salt-wind, as well as drought and hot sun. Any old soil will do as long as it is free-draining—cold, wet soil or very heavy frosts will kill them. They do not like shade, overhanging branches or crowding from neighboring plants, and prefer a breezy or open site. Apart from the odd rogue caterpillar they are unharmed by bugs and other problems.

Left to their own devices *Brachyglottis* naturally form neat, rounded bushes but can become straggly with age. It is a good idea to give them a light trim with the shears after flowering. With older plants you can prune more drastically; they usually regenerate and repay you with strong, bushy growth.

Brachy = short; *glottis* = throat.

Brachyglottis greyi, syn *Senecio greyi*

A terrific, small, dense, evergreen shrub (or rather, "evergray," as it has felty, gray, finger-length leaves), the whole bush is smothered in large yellow daisies during summer. A light trim after flowering will keep it dense and bushy. Native of New Zealand. Height 6 ft (2 m) x width 10 ft (3 m). ZONE 7.

Brachyglottis compactus and the hybrid **'Sunshine'** are very similar. Height 3 ft (1 m) x width 6 ft (2 m).

Greyi = Governor Grey (1812–1898), Governor of South Africa and later New Zealand.

Brachyglottis perdicioides, syn *Senecio perdicioides*

This robust, upright shrub has bright yellow daisy flowers in mid-summer. It also has very unusual bright green, wavy-edged leaves. It is good as a screen plant or at the back of a mixed border. Originates from New Zealand. Height 6–10 ft (2–3 m) x width 6 ft (2 m). ZONE 8.

A hybrid between this plant and *Brachyglottis hectori*, called **'Alfred Atkinson'**, has bigger leaves, large heads of white flowers and tolerates shade. Height 10 ft (3 m) x width 6 ft (2 m). ZONE 8.

Brachyglottis repanda

The froth of creamy off-white flowers that sit on top of the stems in spring are slightly scented. This intriguing plant also has big, paddle-like leaves—bigger than your hand—that are felted underneath. They have a wavy edge and the top surface is usually pale green, but different forms come in darker greens and even purple. A useful shrub for dry or shady places, as well sunny spots. Native of New Zealand. Height x width 10 ft (3 m). ZONE 9.

Repanda = wavy.

Buddleja, syn *Buddleia*

Loganiaceae

This genus is grown mainly for its panicles of small, tubular flowers, many of which are also fragrant. They come in a range of blues, purples and pinks, and also white, and appear from early to late summer depending on the species. If, like me, you've grown up knowing this plant since childhood as buddleia, it is hard to accept that the "ja" spelling is technically correct now. Named after the Reverend Adam Buddle (1660–1715), an English vicar and botanist who wrote a volume on plants using Dr Houston's new classification system. Dr Houston repaid the compliment, naming buddleja after him.

Prior to cultivation, buddlejas managed to colonize large parts of the globe, including large portions of Asia, Africa, and South America and now, with our help, they are colonizing even more land, especially as *Buddleja davidii* is naturalized in many countries. They are a mix of evergreen and deciduous shrubs, usually with long, lance-like leaves, often covered in hair or down.

These plants are almost too easy to grow and handle virtually any soil—heavy clays, sand, chalk, etc. are all fine. I have seen them growing out of brick walls and gutters, so there is nowhere they can't thrive. They are best in full sun but they will grow in the shade of buildings. Most are wind-hardy, some extremely so. They do vary in their cold-tolerance, some being supremely cold-hardy while others are tender. Left to their own devices they spread and sprawl, taking up more ground every year and can even root down where stems touch the ground. To keep the more robust ones tidy, select one stem to be the main structure and cut all the branches back to this trunk every winter. This works especially well for *B. davidii*.

Buddleja alternifolia

The whorls of soft lilac flowers have a lovely fragrance and it is worth planting it in a prime position near a path or junction. This species is not instantly recognizable as a buddleja, with its small, narrow leaves that are dark green and alternate, rather than the usual opposite leaves we associate with these plants. Its habit is slightly unusual too, being an arching, airy shrub. Turn this into an advantage by making it into a standard or a weeping bush. It flow-

ers on last year's growth in early summer, so don't prune it until after flowering, if at all. Originates from China. Height x width 12 ft (4 m). ZONE 6.

Alternifolia = referring to the alternate leaves.

Buddleja colvilei

A bulky, robust shrub, too big for most gardens, but certainly worthy of a place in larger spaces. In midsummer the tips of the stems are decorated with huge panicles of pinky red, almost wine-colored, bell-shaped flowers. Certainly this plant has the largest individual flowers in the genus. It has no discernible scent, which is unusual for a buddleja. Large, dagger-like leaves are felted with gray or sometimes brown hairs. There is a named clone called **'Kewensis'**, with darker flowers and more handsome, thicker leaves. It is evergreen in warm zones, but otherwise deciduous. Discovered in 1849 by Sir Joseph Hooker, who went on to become Director of Kew Gardens in London, England. He named it after a Calcutta judge, Sir James Colvile, who provided him with supplies for his expeditions in the Himalayas. Height x width 20 ft (6 m). ZONE 8.

Buddleja davidii

BUTTERFLY BUSH, SUMMER LILAC

Aptly named the butterfly bush, as the scent of its purple or lavender, orange-throated flowers has a hypnotic effect on butterflies and gardeners alike. There are many superb clones with rich red, purple, blue, pink or white flowers. Look for **'Black Knight'**, with its deep violet flowers, **'Royal Red'**, **'Royal Purple'**,

Right: *Buddleja colvilei*

'Pink Pearl' and 'White Cloud'. A big, sometimes sprawly, bush that can be kept tidy by drastic pruning in winter as the long racemes of flowers are produced from summer to fall on the tips of the new summer's growth, so it doesn't matter how ruthlessly you prune in winter. Left to its own devices, it becomes a very large shrub with a thin veneer of grayish, lance-like leaves. The wild species was collected in western China and named after Père David (1826–1900), a French missionary. Grow it for the flowers, for the scent, or as a wind- or coast-hardy plant. Height 10 ft (3 m) x width 15 ft (5 m). ZONE 6.

Buddleja globosa
ORANGE BALL TREE

This is quite different from a typical buddleja, with its round balls of bright orange flowers. Each flower is the size of the circle made with your thumb and forefinger, and appears in clusters at the ends of the stems in early summer. They are fragrant and quite showy but not in the same league as *B. davidii*. The plant becomes a huge, dense bush with grayish green, felty leaves, and is really most useful as a backdrop or in a large garden as a screen. It comes from Chile and Argentina. Height x width 15 ft (5 m). ZONE 8.

Globosa = globe-like flowers.

Buddleja lindleyana

In late summer, the tips of the stems of this species have long, narrow, intense purple flowers. The flowers are small but very pretty. Also, the dark green, narrow leaves set it apart from most plants. A useful shrub in cool climates, it is a little too vigorous in mild areas. My only reservation about this plant is that it sometimes suckers and pops up among other shrubs. If this suckering does not occur, however, it is a tidy shrub. Named after John Lindley (1799–1865), a botanist who began the famous English *Gardener's Chronicle* magazine. It is from China. Height x width 6 ft (2 m). ZONE 7.

Above: *Buddleja davidii* cultivar

Above: *Calluna vulgaris* 'Elsie Purnell'

Calluna

HEATHER, LING
Ericaceae

This is a genus of one species of evergreen shrub. You could be forgiven for thinking there are lots of wild species, as there are countless forms and cultivars available for gardeners, ranging from tiny, ground-hugging varieties to some nearly waist-high. The tiny, almost minuscule, leaves hang onto the stems like scales on a fish. The tiny, bell-shaped flowers are arranged in racemes at the tops of the stems. Colors include purple, pink and white, and they are a surprisingly good cut flower, and very effective as dried flowers, too. By planting different cultivars the flowering season can be extended from midsummer until early winter.

Callunas are neat and tidy plants and placed in groups or drifts, they are a perfect ground cover. They bring unity and stability to any scene with their even height and spread and a carpet of callunas is an ideal way to highlight a choice plant. Imagine a drift of bushy callunas around a bold red rhododendron, setting off the rich green leaves and bright red flowers to perfection. Mostly they are seen in conifer and heather gardens, where all the plants look very similar and so their abiltity to make other plants shine is lost. They do have a very conifer-like look about them and could easily be mistaken for a conifer on first glance.

Callunas are so robust you can walk across the top of them to do any trimming or weeding. To achieve a dense, weed-free ground cover you must get the ground free of perennial weeds before you plant, or the weeds will grow up through the calluna and you'll always have a problem. Ideally, eliminate all the

perennial weeds, then plant the callunas. Then, to prevent any new weeds, use a mulch of bark or wood peelings about 2 in (5 cm) thick, spread all over the ground. This looks attractive, keeps the soil moist and suppresses or prevents any weed seeds from germinating. Eventually the calluna will form such a thick mat, the weeds won't stand a chance. Some landscapers recommend planting them through weedmat or polyethylene to prevent new weeds. The weedmat or polyethylene is laid flat over the ground, pinned down in some way and crosses are cut in the surface where you want to plant a shrub. After planting, these flaps where you cut the crosses are pinned back down so in effect you have an artificial surface over the soil with just the tops of your shrubs above it. Weedmat works well because it allows water to penetrate and air to circulate, so the only complaint is that it is not natural-looking. Polyethylene, by comparison, is not good for the soil or the plant as it prevents rainwater from seeping through to the ground and it creates a steamy atmosphere underneath because air cannot circulate. After a year or so, the soil turns dank and smelly from the anaerobic conditions and the shrubs start to suffer.

Callunas thrive in acidic soil and hate lime. They will grow well in poor soils and even slightly boggy ground. In rich soil or fertilized ground they tend to grow thin and leggy. They form a dense mat of roots just below the surface and will put out new roots where a sprawling stem touches the ground. It is possible to move a plant to another part of the garden by lifting these mats in winter. You can even separate old plants to make new ones, a technique known as "Irishman's cuttings" (when the cuttings already have roots).

Sleet, snow, cold and wind hold no threat to these plants and they actually seem to prefer a dose of revolting weather every now and then. In a warm, mild climate they look sparse and bedraggled. If they become straggly, it pays to give them a regular trim with the shears to keep them neat and tidy.

Immediately after flowering is the best time for this, giving the shrub a whole year to make new growth for next season's flowers.

Calluna = to cleanse, referring to the way the brush-like stems were used for brooms.

Calluna vulgaris, syn *Erica vulgaris*
LING, SCOTCH HEATHER

This plant bears dense racemes of small, bell-shaped flowers enclosed by colored sepals in shades of red, purple, pink or white. These appear from midsummer to late fall. There is a huge variety of cultivars available and far too many to list; suffice to say you can get most colors and flowering times to suit your requirements. These plants are also sought-after for their colorful foliage, especially when grown in combination with conifers. As well as the obvious green, there is a range of bronzy reds and orange to choose from, as well as many golden varieties that are always useful as color contrast. Most are just chance seedlings selected by keen-eyed nurserymen. Callunas are native to the heaths of the U.K. and northern Europe. Height 4–24 in (10–60 cm) x width 30 in (75 cm). ZONE 5.

Vulgaris = common.

Camellia

Theaceae

Camellias are one of our best-loved evergreen shrubs, especially when smothered in their showy flowers. The sheer flower-power of this genus is surpassed only by that of roses and hydrangeas. The name camellia is puzzling at first, named as it is after George Joseph Kamel, a Jesuit missionary

Right: *Camellia japonica* 'Bob Hope'

Above: *Camellia* 'Volunteer'

branches and opening them up. You can even prune them drastically to bare stumps if you wish and they will quickly regenerate.

Strong winds are no problem to most of them, though the flowers may be battered by storms and the white-colored forms are particularly susceptible in this regard. They seem affected by cold in some mild climates, while in other colder regions they seem to thrive. Perhaps the hot summers ripen the wood to cope with the winter frosts.

They act as host to the occasional caterpillar or cluster of aphids, but never in such numbers that you need to venture out with a remedy.

All the known species come from Asia, notably China and Japan.

Camellia japonica
COMMON CAMELLIA

This is the ultimate easy-care, free-flowering shrub. A big, dense, upright bush covered with hundreds of equally spaced pink, red or white flowers. The big, bold, rounded flowers—the size of the palm of your hand—appear in winter and early spring. There are hundreds of cultivars of C. *japonica*, with a variety of flower shapes and color. They are very popular as flowering plants and can be clipped or shaped. In Portugal they are used for topiary, including

who traveled widely in Asia and wrote an account of the plants he found in the Philippines. He latinized his name as *camellus*, and later Linnaeus chose to name this group of Asian shrubs after him. Linnaeus was the man who simplified the Latin naming of plants and animals and also latinized his own name from Carl von Linné.

Camellias are the ultimate easy-care shrub. If ever I need an upright evergreen to make a garden more secluded, or to shield one's eyes before emerging into a new garden area, then camellia is always the first plant to come to mind. They take full sun or quite dense shade. In some regions, gardeners insist they be grown in shade, possibly it is to protect the plants from heavy frosts, or perhaps to prevent the soil drying out to such an extent that the leaves get "crisped," to prevent the leaves getting sunburnt.

They seem oblivious to soil type, other than that it must be acidic or neutral. Sometimes you see them looking anaemic and yellowing in the leaf: this is easily cured with a dose of Epsom Salts (magnesium sulfate), containing the wonderful greening magnesium fertilizer. All camellias cherish a mulch of leaves or bark chips to keep the soil cool and moist. They need good drainage, and like regular rainfall, though this is not essential. Likewise, they prefer constant humidity but will cope with hot, dry summers.

Camellias are easy to transplant from containers and even large, aged specimens can be moved in early winter. I find it pays to move them before midwinter, as the success rate declines as spring beckons. It is also a good idea to reduce the amount of foliage on the bush when transplanting large specimens. Camellias have a good, natural shape and rarely need pruning, but should you have to, they can be trimmed lightly with shears, or you can make them into interesting shapes by removing

Right: 'Jury's Pearl', a *Camellia pitardii* x *C. japonica* cross.

Right: 'Nicky Crisp', a *Camellia pitardii* x *C. japonica* cross.

Right: *Camellia reticulata* 'Robert Fortune'

Camellia oleifera

The single white flowers of this small, erect tree are scented and appear in midwinter. This seems to be the hardiest of the camellias, and for this reason it is cherished by gardeners in cooler parts of North America. Native of China. Height 20 ft (6 m) x width 10 ft (3 m). ZONE 6.

Oleifera = oil bearing, as the fruits were squeezed for camellia oil, used for cooking and cosmetics.

Camellia reticulata

Considered by many to be tender, but if your climate is warm enough to grow them, *Camellia reticulata* has the best flowers of the genus. The single red flowers tend to be more subtle as there are fewer flowers on the shrubs, but each is larger and more exquisite than other species. They appear in late winter to early spring. This species has a distinctive leaf shape and pattern, different from the usual glossy surface. The leaves are usually pointed and have a duller mat finish. First introduced to the West in 1820 by Captain Rawes of the East India Company, it flowered for the first time in 1826. They have caused much excitement since, and many books have been written about them. The Chinese have cultivated them in Yunnan province for 3000 years. Height 20 ft (6 m) x 15 ft (5 m). ZONE 8 OR 9.

There are many cultivars available, but a few choice ones include **'Robert Fortune'** (also known as **'Pagoda'**). This is the original *Camellia reticulata* in the West. A large, formal flower 5 in (13 cm) across in cerise-pink. Height 15 ft (5 m) x width 10 ft (3 m).

elaborate outdoor summerhouses clipped from a dozen large plants. If ever you need a dense evergreen shrub to block out a view, this plant is hard to beat. As the name suggests, its home is Japan and it is also found in Korea and northern China. Height 10–20 ft (3–6 m) x width 3–10 ft (1–3 m). ZONE 8.

Nowadays, there are numerous hybrids available as breeders cross *Camellia japonica* with other species.

Left: *Camellia reticulata* 'S. P. Dunn'

'S. P. Dunn' has a lovely, cabbage-like flower head in rich red. The bush has a wider, more spreading habit. Height 15 ft (5 m) x width 10 ft (3 m).

'William Hertrich' has beautiful, cherry-red flowers 7 in (18 cm) across that appear in early spring. The thick, luscious petals have a "good enough to eat" quality about them. The leaves are edged in fine saw-toothed fashion. Height x width 20 ft (6 m). For all, ZONE 8 OR 9.

> *Reticulata* = finely netted or net-veined, referring to the dark, dull surface of the leaves with an obvious network of veins.

Camellia saluenensis

George Forrest collected this plant in western Yunnan, China, in 1924, naming it after the Salween River that flows through Yunnan on its way to the Indian Ocean. It is a large shrub with single, soft pink flowers up to 2 in (5 cm) across that appear in late winter to early spring. Some forms are white or pink and white. Height x width varies between 3–15 ft (1–5 m). ZONE 7.

J.C. Williams of Caerhays Castle in Cornwall crossed this species with *C. japonica* to give us **C. x williamsii**, a group of free-flowering, easy-to-grow hybrids. The most famous of these is the indispensible camellia **'Donation'**. It has showy, colorful semi-double pink flowers that appear in late winter and never seem to be tatty, as some camellia flowers are. It is an ideal screen plant and useful as a hedge with its tidy, upright shape. Height 15 ft (5 m) x width 8 ft (2.5 m). ZONE 7.

Camellia sasanqua

One of the joys of fall for me is the flowering of the sasanqua camellias, coinciding as it does with the colorful leaves of this season. Strangely enough, even though the camellias tend to be in pink and cerise (and white), they still blend well with the reds and golds of fall, which is not what you would expect. Another reason I like the sasanquas is the smaller blooms and the more informal

Above: *Camellia saluenensis* hybrid 'Water Lily'

shape of the shrub. The flowers are usually single and small, about the size of a small coffee cup. They vary from a single row of petals to semi- and fully double. Most have a central cluster of stamens, beneath which is a source of nectar highly prized by bees and nectar-feeding birds. It is a breath of fresh air compared with the more blowzy flowers and rounded shape of *C. japonica*.

Leaves are small compared to most other camellias, being slightly longer than a finger joint, with a toothed or serrated edge. They have the usual glossy surface and, being evergreen, look good all year round. Sasanquas initially are fairly tidy and upright and then take on a wider, arching habit with age. It is at this stage that you can trim the basal trunks and turn them into a more interesting, open shrub, showing off the smooth gray trunks.

Above: *Camellia sasanqua* 'Moonlight'

Sasanquas are more tender than most and do not thrive in colder climates, but if your climate suits, then you must find room for at least one of these gorgeous plants. In cooler regions they can be trained espalier-style against a wall to give them extra heat and protection from the cold. When close to a path you can enjoy the wonderful fragrance of the flowers, that smell like sweet tea. Height 20 ft (6 m) x width 10 ft (3 m). ZONE 8.

'**Hiryu**' has an unusual and rather strident cerise-colored flower. This plant looks good against a building and against the color of reddy brick walls.

'**Mine-no-yuki**' is also known as '**Moonlight**' and this is my favorite. If you see the small, double, white blooms covered in dew or rain drops in the fall sun you will be hooked.

'**Plantation Pink**' is a lovely single pink that is a great favorite with nectar-feeding birds.

For all, height 20 ft (6 m) x width 10 ft (3 m).

Sasanqua = based on the Japanese name for these plants.

Campsis

TRUMPET VINE, TRUMPET CREEPER
Bignoniaceae

The first time I set eyes on a *Campsis* was on a farmhouse wall in France and I just knew I had to have one. The vine was covered with stunning orangy red trumpet-shaped flowers. Initially I wasn't sure what I needed to grow it well and I've since discovered the key—maximum sunlight and summer heat and, *voila*, you have a thriving *Campsis*.

They have self-clinging, tenacious roots like ivy, capable of climbing fences, walls and trees and it is not a good idea to plant them against house walls, as the clinging roots are difficult to remove. One of the best ways of displaying a *Campsis* is to erect a thick pole, such as a piece of an old telegraph pole, and plant it at the base. In no time the vine will smother the pole and you

will have a column of flowers in the summer. However, they are never vigorous enough to cause concern, as some climbers do.

These plants not fussy about soil as long as the drainage is good. Ideally you should shade the roots as, like most climbers, it naturally has its roots in shade and top in sun. They are quite drought-tolerant once established. *Campsis* also cope well with strong winds and even coastal gales, though a really severe storm can pull the stems away from their support. The opposite leaves are pinnate and ash-like, and each leaflet tapers to a point.

Being deciduous, *Campsis* look rather sparse in winter and they can be pruned at this time because they flower on new wood formed in the spring. You can prune them quite drastically back to the main stems, as you would a grapevine. They are hardy to cold, being deciduous, and thrive in a continental climate or in a constantly mild climate.

Campsis are easy to transplant in winter and even older plants could be shifted then if it were not for the problem of detaching them from their host. Sometimes they have a tendency to sucker and the suckers can be removed to create new plants. If the suckers become a nuisance, rip or pull them off, as cutting back with secateurs will only create even more of them. This genus seems immune to pests and diseases.

Campsis = bent, relating to the curved stamens.

Campsis grandiflora, syn *Bignonia grandiflora*, *Campsis chinensis*, *Tecoma grandiflora*
CHINESE TRUMPET CREEPER, CHINESE TRUMPET VINE
This deciduous Chinese *Campsis* is the prettier of the two species, but not as hardy. As always seems to happen, the more we cherish something, the more tender it is likely to be. The terminal flowers are big, wide-mouthed trumpets in soft, orangy red and appear in high summer. When grown in shade or in cool, wet summers the

Above: *Campsis grandiflora*

flowers may never develop or open. It has fewer aerial or gripping roots and may need tying for support. Height up to 30 ft (10 m) when given a tall enough host. ZONE 7.

Grandiflora = big flowers.

Campsis radicans, syn *Bignonia radicans*, *Tecoma radicans*

TRUMPET VINE, TRUMPET CREEPER

A vigorous, deciduous vine, flowering on new wood like its Chinese cousin. The flowers are smaller and arranged in panicles at the ends of the new stems in summer. Each flower is a long, thin tube flared to a trumpet at the end. They are a rich, reddy orange, but there is a yellow-flowered form called **'Flava'** (syn 'Yellow Trumpet'). *Campsis radican*'s native home is the southeastern states of the U.S.A., though it has been cultivated in Europe since the 1640s. Height to 30 ft (10 m) or more. ZONE 5.

Radicans = rooting, referring to the aerial roots.

Campsis x tagliabuana (*C.grandiflora* x *C. radicans*)

No one is exactly sure where the first of these hybrids originated. They are named after two Italian brothers called Tagliabue, who had a nursery near Milan. One assumes they bred the first plants, but there have been subsequent attempts to cross the two wild species, and the hybrid group name applies to all of them. The orange-red flowers appear from midsummer onward and are as big as *C. grandiflora*, but this form seems to incorporate the hardiness of *C. radicans*—in other words, the best of both worlds. Height 30 ft (10 m) or more. ZONE 5.

'Guilfoylei' is an Australian hybrid with rich, orangy red trumpets. **'Madame Galen'** is an older hybrid with softer, salmony red flowers. Both height 30 ft (10 m) or more. ZONE 5.

wafting, pendulous habit. Sometimes strong new growths, known as watershoots, grow up through the bush from near the base. These watershoots help fill the structure of the bush and have a different style of growth to the more flat-plane stems. I would never be confident enough to shift an established plant, but I'm told by braver gardeners that they do survive the move.

Above: *Campsis* x *tagliabuana* 'Guilfoylei'

Cantua

SACRED FLOWER OF THE INCAS
Polemoniacae

*C*antua have some of the most exciting blooms known to gardeners. The way the tubular flowers glisten and shimmer in the sunlight is unique. Most people dismiss this plant as unexciting, but if I were to show you one in full flower you would demand to know where you could buy one. It is not a plant you often see for sale, partly because it looks undesirable when grown in a pot and so it is rarely bought by a casual buyer. You will have to search it out from specialist or mail order nurseries—but it is worth it.

Not too fussy about soil, they seem to grow equally well in wet or dry regions, but do need reasonable drainage. Ideally, I would choose a spot in full sun, but they cope with a little shade. Cantuas will grow near the sea, but need shelter from strong winds as they strip the leaves off them. The bush itself is supremely wind-hardy. I have seen them bowed and blasted by gales without any damage to the stems or the structure. Cantuas have a naturally arching habit (some would say scruffy), growing about head height. The tidy gardeners among you will be pleased to hear they tolerate severe pruning, but I rather like the

Right: *Cantua buxifolia*

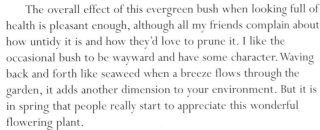

Right: *Cantua pyrifolia*

The overall effect of this evergreen bush when looking full of health is pleasant enough, although all my friends complain about how untidy it is and how they'd love to prune it. I like the occasional bush to be wayward and have some character. Waving back and forth like seaweed when a breeze flows through the garden, it adds another dimension to your environment. But it is in spring that people really start to appreciate this wonderful flowering plant.

At the end of nearly every stem is a cluster of flowers, each one the size of your little finger. The overall effect is one of a plant dripping with flowers. Flowering lasts for three or four weeks in spring or late spring, depending on your climate. Sometimes they delay their flowers until the summer in cold regions. For the most part cantuas are easy-care plants. They are reasonably cold-hardy, but more likely to be damaged by frost when grown in a cold, wet soil. Evergreen in mild climates and semi-evergreen if the location is cool. ZONE 8 OR 9.

Cantua = a Peruvian name for these plants.

Cantua buxifolia, syn *C. dependens*
SACRED FLOWER OF THE INCAS
In summer, this species bears clusters of long, shimmering, tubular flowers in cerise-pink. You have never seen anything like this before. In their native lands of Peru, Bolivia and Chile they are pollinated by hummingbirds. Some forms have a hint of yellow in the flower or they can be two-tone, but they are not as exciting as the pure pink forms. Compared to the scintillating flowers the foliage can only be described as boring. Height 6–15 ft (2–5 m) x width 5–8 ft (1.5–2.5 m). ZONE 8 OR 9.

Buxifolia = like a *Buxus* or boxwood.

Cantua pyrifolia
An ungainly bush identical to *C. buxifolia* until it flowers. In fact, it is hard to see how the separate species are distinguished in cultivation when the only difference is the flower color. This species has long, tubular flowers that are a rich butter-yellow in the tube and white or very pale yellow at the end. The overall effect is all yellow, but early morning or late evening sun highlights the two contrasting colors. Even the flower buds are exciting; the green-and-yellow-striped buds are spiraled like a barber's pole, terminating with an arrowhead point. This spiral gradually unfurls to display the full trumpet with five flared petals in cool lemon-ice. The plant is from Ecuador, Peru and Bolivia. Height 6–15 ft (2–5 m) x width 6–8 ft (2–2.5 m). ZONE 8 OR 9.

Pyrifolia = pear leaf.

Cassia, syn *Senna*

BUTTERCUP TREE
Fabaceae

I raved over *Cassia corymbosa* when I lived in England, where it is coveted and grown in special sites to protect it from frosts and cold. Then I moved to a warmer clime where *Cassia* grow easily and gardeners regard it with disdain. It fell into further disrepute because the flowers are yellow or gold—a color that was somewhat out of favor at the time. Regardless of popular opinion, I still love them and they lift my spirits when the fall flowers appear.

Left: *Cassia corymbosa* 'John Ball'

To grow *Cassia* easily you need a warm, sunny climate, good drainage and preferably not too much wind. They will tolerate wind, even coastal winds, but it often defoliates them and if they've grown too quickly (which believe it or not can be a fault) they can be blown out of the ground because of the leverage effect of the top-heavy growth. Pruning back half of last year's growth immediately after flowering keeps them in proportion and stops them becoming top-heavy and leggy. As they flower on new growth tips, it is all right to prune them and you then get a dense, rounded bush.

Any soil is acceptable regardless of acidity, the only prerequisite is that it is free-draining. They seem untouched by pests, with the only risk being storm winds. Occasionally a plant will die from root rot, but this is usually as a result of strong winds breaking some roots. The plant will cope with hot, dry summers once established. Transplanting from pots is easy, but take care to unravel any twining roots. Do not attempt to shift older specimens.

Cassia are originally from Argentina and Uruguay, and selected or hybrid forms are often seen. Botanists are now suggesting some cassias should be in the genus *Senna*. There are numerous species growing in the tropics and sub-tropics, if you have a warm enough climate to try them. All of them have the distinct gold or orange flowers.

Cassia didymobotrya is an African shrub with fabulous foliage and unusual spikes of golden-yellow, crinkle-petaled flowers on the tip of each stem in late summer to fall. Height 8 ft (2.5 m) x width 6–10 ft (2–3 m). ZONE 9.

Cassia = "kasian," the name of a related plant found in the Mediterranean.

Left: *Cassia didymobotrya*

Cassia corymbosa

Shimmering gold-yellow flowers are just like buttercups on fist-sized heads of flowers. It can be a show-stopper at a time when few shrubs are inclined to flower—in late summer and fall. Granted, it is hard to blend with other plants, but the bush usually

Right: *Ceanothus* 'Dark Star'

flowers in splendid isolation so this doesn't really matter. If you want an "instant" flowering bush for a sunny border then this cassia is a good choice. The plant is evergreen, though it can be semi-deciduous in cooler climates. The cultivar **'John Ball'** is worth seeking out as a consistently good plant and the hybrid **C. x *floribunda*** is similar but slightly more hardy. Height x width 6–10 ft (2–3 m). ZONE 9.

Corymbosa = clustered in corymbs.

Ceanothus

CALIFORNIAN LILAC
Rhamnaceae

Ceanothus capture the two things gardeners desire most—fragance and blue flowers. Not any wishy-washy blue or pathetic scent either; both are as good as it gets. There are a few ceanothus with pink or white flowers, but they are unexciting compared to the blues. Each flower is tiny, but the crowded panicles are so jam-packed with flowers they always make a show. Most are evergreen but there are a few ornamental, deciduous forms, too. In California they thrive in poor soil, hot sun and free-draining sites. On such sites they stay more compact and tidy and tend to live longer. Free-draining soil is the one essential ingredient for success. Ceanothus grow in acidic or alkaline soil. While they prefer full sun, they will grow in the shade of a wall or building—they just don't like overhead tree shade. One of the things I like about them is that they are dependable, flowering properly every year, and they don't need tidying or removing of spent flowers. Certainly you can prune them after flowering (and the plant will last longer if you do this), but they'll forgive you if you forget.

These plants have many positive uses around the garden. You can use them as a ground cover or a border shrub, or they look sublime when trained against a wall. It is almost as if they were bred to be planted against a wall, they look so good. Some of them are terrific foliage plants with rich, dark green, corrugated leaves. Being drought-hardy and willing to grow in full, hot, baking sun or windy places is a boon for seaside gardeners. They are extremely tough and, being evergreen, they look good all year round.

Ceanothus grow quickly and become pot-bound, so buy small, young, healthy plants, put them in their final position and never be tempted to move them. Often a grow fast/die fast shrub, living only about 10 or 12 years.

Ceanothus = from the Greek word for spiny.

Ceanothus arboreus
CATALINA CEANOTHUS
As the name suggests this is a tree-like version of this genus (*arbor* = tree). The flowers vary from rich blue to anaemic blue when grown from seed, so choose forms such as **'Trewithen Blue'** to be sure of the color. It bears fragrant, mid-blue flowers in spring and early summer. This is an excellent shrub to plant against a wall, but it can become rangy and leggy. Native to western U.S.A. Height 12 ft (4 m) x width 10 ft (3 m). ZONE 8.

Ceanothus **'Burkwoodii'** is a complex hybrid, mixing spring-flowering evergreens and the late-flowering, deciduous types. Valued for its lovely blue flowers in late summer, its hardiness and being an evergreen. Height x width 6 ft (2 m). ZONE 7.

The purple buds of *Ceanothus* **'Concha'** open to rich blue, sweetly scented flowers in late spring. This big, handsome bush also has very pleasing, shiny foliage and a lovely arching habit. It looks great planted *en masse* on a bank. Height x width 6 ft (2 m). ZONE 8.

Ceanothus **'Dark Star'** has tiny leaves and possibly the darkest blue flower of any form. Borne in late spring, they are delightfully scented. Height x width 6 ft (2 m). ZONE 8.

Arboreus = tree-like.

Ceanothus impressus
SANTA BARBARA CEANOTHUS
A wonderful garden shrub, forming a low, dense bush smothered in deep blue flowers in the spring. The small, dark green leaves have deeply impressed veins, hence the name. Hardier than most to both cold and wind. Native to western U.S.A. Height x width 6–10 ft (2–3 m). ZONE 7 OR 8.

'Puget Blue' is a good selection, with profuse dark blue flowers. Height x width 6–10 ft (2–3 m).

Impressus = referring to the deep veining on the leaves.

Ceanothus papillosus
A big, dense, evergreen shrub with beautiful cobalt-blue flowers in little, tight heads that appear in mid- to late spring. Discovered in 1833 by David Douglas and introduced to the Veitch Nursery in England by William Lobb in 1850. Native to California. Height x width 12 ft (4 m). ZONE 8.

Ceanothus papillosus **var** *roweanus* is a more compact, spready version, ideal as a dense, high ground cover. Height 5 ft (1.5 m) x width 10 ft (3 m). ZONE 8.

Papillosus = refers to the pimpled, rough leaves.

Above: *Ceanothus papillosus*

Above: *Ceratostigma plumbaginoides*

Ceratostigma

Plumbaginaceae

A small group of shrubs and sub-shrubs from the Himalayas and China. There are really only two reasons for growing them, but they are good reasons: beautiful, blue, starry flowers all through summer and the low, dense habit, making them ideal ground-cover plants. They are mostly deciduous, though some can be evergreen in mild regions. Full sun is ideal but part-shade is acceptable, too. Long, hot summers improve their performance. Any soil seems to suit as long as the drainage is free, and these plants can even cope with drought. They are easy enough to transplant when young and easy to grow. Ideal low plants for those difficult narrow borders around the house, or as a drift of ground cover in a larger border.

Ceratostigma = refers to the little horns on the stigma.

Ceratostigma griffithii
It is a small, dense, evergreen shrub, more tender than the other species but with beautiful, blue, coin-sized flowers. First discovered in Bhutan by Roland Cooper of the East India Company. Height 1½ ft (45 cm) x width 3 ft (1 m). ZONE 8 OR 9.

Griffithii = named for William Griffith (1810–1845), who worked for the East India Company.

Ceratostigma plumbaginoides, syn Plumbago larpentiiae
This is halfway between a perennial and a shrub as it forms a woody rootstock but the tops tend to die back in cold winters. The leaves turn a nice shade of red in the fall and late summer brings scintillating blue flowers and bright green, pointed leaves. China is its home and it is named after the plumbago shrub. Height to 1½ ft (45 cm) x width 1 ft (30 cm). ZONE 6.

Plumbaginoides = like a *Plumbago*.

Ceratostigma willmottianum

This plant is a bigger version of *Ceratostigma plumbaginoides*, growing up to waist-high, but with the same brilliant blue blooms all summer. The terminal clusters of flowers are like a spiky ball and on any one day, three or four flowers open, giving a succession of blooms for weeks or even months. The leaves are bright green with a bronzy edge and quite pointed. It is deciduous and has good red fall color. This Chinese species was first grown by Ellen Willmott from seed sent to her by E. H. Wilson, and so was named after her. Height 3 ft (1 m) x width 5 ft (1.5 m). ZONE 6.

Cercis

Fabaceae

Cercis are one of the best spring-flowering trees for gardens, but they don't always receive the credit they deserve. These showy flowering trees can rival cherry blossom and yet they are rarely given that status. They are easy to grow in any warm summer climate and they are native to the Mediterranean region, the hot northern parts of China and the Appalachian Mountains in eastern U.S.A.

The trees tend to have a spreading habit and, even if they grow tall, the tops still seem to have a rounded, arching look. Sometimes they are ungainly and multi-branched when young and may need some pruning and training to give the desired shape. The stems of the younger branches are smooth and often dark in color, and in spring they are teeming with flowers before the handsome heart-shaped leaves appear. Happy in acidic or alkaline soil, cercis prefer moist, well-drained sites but they are quite tolerant of heavy clays and dry soils. They resent transplanting and so care should be taken at this stage. Being genuine sun-lovers, they are quite at home in any warm summer climate. They are tolerant of cold winters, provided they have enough summer heat to ripen the wood and will even cope with hot inland climates with periods of drought. They are generally thought of as being happy from zone 4 to zone 10, provided they have adequate summer heat. Coral spot fungus may attack them in cool climates.

Cercis is a good choice for your garden for the sheer mass display of flowers in the spring, and because it is one of the earliest trees or shrubs to flower. Last but not least, their bold, heart-shaped leaves are undamaged by wind and weather and look as good near fall as they did in the spring.

Cercis = from the Greek "kerkis," meaning shuttlecock.

Cercis canadensis
EASTERN REDBUD

Eastern redbud sets the hills and gardens alight in spring with masses of rose-pink, pea-like flowers. It grows all through the eastern U.S.A. and Canada. It occasionally grows in some shade but flowers best in full sun. Like most cercis it needs summer heat to ripen the wood to survive cold winters, and this is why it does not thrive in cool summer regions. Fall color is usually pale yellow and not spectacular, though some years it seems a stronger canary yellow. **'Appalachian Red'** is the best red-flowered form available. For both, height x width 30 ft (10 m). ZONE 5.

Canadensis = from Canada.

Cercis chinensis
CHINESE REDBUD

This species forms a small, wide-spreading tree. The clusters of pink to lavender-pink flowers appear earlier than most other

Right: *Cercis chinensis*

Above and top: *Cercis siliquastrum*

Chaenomeles

FLOWERING QUINCE
Rosaceae

Flowering quince, although rather ungainly bushes, are popular with some gardeners for the early appearance of their apple- and peach-like flowers. Along with forsythia, they usher in the spring. Flower colors range from white, cream, or pale apricot, moving into orange, pink, red and rich crimson, and bravely appear in early spring before the leaves emerge. With the blossoms appearing only on older wood, it is just as well they appear on bare stems or they would be hidden by the leaves. These early blooms seem surprisingly tolerant of spring winds and cold snaps. Even if some flowers are damaged, there always seem to be more coming as they emerge over a period of several weeks. In fact, in some years they flower for months. *Chaenomeles* are also treasured for indoor decoration as cut flowers in an otherwise spartan season.

These plants are, however, not a good choice for "tidy" gardeners or for formal gardens. The only time they suit a tidy garden is when they are trained in a fan-like fashion on a wall. While the thorns and the ungainly habit may put off some gardeners, the *Chaenomeles* certainly have their virtues. They are easy-care shrubs, growing well in any climate and virtually any soil. Even heavy clay on limestone ground or extremes of acidity hold no terrors for them. They thrive in continental climates with very hot summers and yet seem just as happy in mild

Below: *Chaenomeles x superba* 'Rowallane'

species and so are vulnerable to late spring frosts. It has a very dense, twiggy nature and so does not have the simple clean structure of some other *Cercis*. The bold, heart-shaped leaves are glossy above and have a distinct point, and the gray stems have prominent black buds.

It is sometimes thought that this plant does not like cold winters, but as it comes from the Beijing region of China this does not make sense. I am more inclined to think that like most cercis it thrives in climates with warm to hot summers and, given this, it will tolerate winter cold. Height 15–20 ft (5–6 m) x width 15–30 ft (5–10 m). ZONE 6, keeping warm summers in mind.

'Avondale' is a selected prolific flower form with particularly vivid purple blooms. Height x width 10 ft (3 m).

Chinensis = from China.

Cercis siliquastrum

JUDAS TREE

The pretty rosy purple flowers appear on the bare stems in spring, followed by smooth, heart-shaped leaves. It is usually a small, deciduous tree with an arching habit, and is often much wider than it is high.

It is a southern European tree, flourishing in hot, dry conditions and given a hot summer climate they seem to grow much higher than they are wide, reaching 30 ft (10 m) or more. Height x width 30 ft (10 m). ZONE 8.

Siliquastrum = from "siliqua," the botanical term for pod.

Right: *Chaenomeles speciosa* 'Falconnet Charlet'

climates. They grow in full sun, but don't mind shade; they tolerate drought and yet don't resent high rainfall. Of course, being deciduous makes them all the more resilient and hardy.

As the plants tend to become overly dense and rather cluttered, they do need some pruning. Prune immediately after flowering before the new spring growth emerges. There is no set pattern for pruning them other than to be aware of them flowering on older wood, so the more you remove, the less they will flower next year. These plants are armed with fierce thorns, so only the bravest of gardeners wants to tackle them. It is not as if they are laden with thorns, it just seems as if they are when you try and prune them.

The leaves are fairly plain, about thumb-size, and there is no fall color worth mentioning. Large, golden-yellow fruits are popular for making "quince" jelly, although they taste extremely tart when eaten raw.

Chaenomeles have virtually no pests or diseases, which is unusual for any plant in the rose and apple family. Even if they are attacked, it is unlikely to be devastating or to require you to find a remedy.

It is easy to transplant them and even aged specimens can be shifted to another part of the garden during the winter months. I would suggest covering the ground with a layer of mulch to keep the weeds down. This reduces the need to get near the plant and those nasty thorns.

Chaenomeles can be grown as a rounded shrub in a border, or trained on walls as an espalier. As a shrub, they are typically wider than they are high, say 10–12 ft (3–4 m) wide and 6 ft (2 m) high, though they can be kept much smaller. Plant them where they are likely to be seen in that early spring period when gardeners and visitors are reluctant to make forays into the garden.

While most gardeners are only likely to encounter hybrids and cultivars, there are several different species from East Asia.

Chaenomeles = from the Greek "chaino," to gape and "meles," an apple.

Chaenomeles cathayensis

An upright, head-high shrub with white flowers in early to mid-spring, except in the form *Chaenomeles cathayensis* var *wilsonii*, which has salmon-pink flowers. *Chaenomeles cathayensis* has big, hard, heavy, dull green fruits that are excellent for making jellies. Native to Central China. Height x width 10 ft (3 m). ZONE 6.

Cathayensis = from Cathay, an archaic name for China.

Chaenomeles japonica, syn *C. maulei*

JAPONICA, JAPANESE FLOWERING QUINCE
This low, dense bush is the basis of most hybrids, and the hybrid *Chaenomeles* are often referred to as "japonicas." It has brick-red flowers in spring followed by yellow-green, fragrant fruits. Sometimes the flowers appear with the leaves rather than on bare stems. It was introduced from Japan by a nurseryman called Maule in Bristol, England, and used to be known as *Cydonia maulei*. The species name refers to its homeland. It is also a native of Korea. Height 3 ft (1 m) x width 6 ft (2 m). ZONE 5.

Japonica = from Japan.

Chaenomeles speciosa, syn *C. lagenaria*, *Cydonia speciosa*, *Pyrus japonica*

This is usually an upright, dense, bushy plant, but it can be sprawly and open too. The flowers appear on bare wood in early spring and are followed by shiny leaves. The flowers are usually scarlet-red and the yellowy fruits often have a blush of red, like some apples. Introduced from China by Sir Joseph Banks, the man responsible for initiating Kew Gardens in London. There are numerous garden cultivars with predominantly red colors available. Height 8 ft (2.5 m) x width 15 ft (5 m). ZONE 5.

Speciosa = showy and handsome.

Chaenomeles x *superba* (*C. japonica* x *C. speciosa*)

A group of hybrids, similar to *C. speciosa* but usually with a more erect habit. New, young growth is hairy, and from spring to

Above: *Chionanthus virginicus*

summer white, pink, orange-scarlet or crimson to orange flowers appear depending on the cultivar. Good cultivars include **'Crimson and Gold'** and the blood-red **'Rowallane'**. Height 5 ft (1.5 m) x width 6 ft (2 m). ZONE 5.

Superba = superb or splendid.

Chionanthus

FRINGE TREE
Oleaceae

The two hardy, deciduous species of this genus are unusual in that they have snowy white flowers that look like someone has draped shredded paper over the bush. A large group of plants of which only these two seem to have made it into cultivation. (They were once thought to be the only chionanthus, but now a large group of tropical evergreens has been lumped in with them.) The two deciduous types form small, tidy trees with a naturally good habit and there is no need for pruning. Both species have large, opposite leaves the size of a cherry tree leaf and the texture of the related ash tree. The fall color can be yellow, but is rarely stunning.

Chionanthus is another of those genera linking North America with China and Asia, as one species is from China and Korea and the other from eastern U.S.A. They are easy to grow in any climate, but really need continental conditions (hot summers and cold winters) to create the profusion of flower for which they are famous. In mild climates they are healthy enough, but they don't perform as well. Full sun is best, although they cope with shade from tall trees. Like most of the olive family they are indifferent to soil and are quite happy on clays and limestone soil. Ideally, plant them on a lower slope so that you can look down on the crown of flowers, or give the plant a dark backdrop to show off the white flowers.

The plants are easily transplanted at any age, having a mass of fibrous roots. Sometimes they are grafted onto seedling *Chionanthus*, which is fine, or onto related ash seedlings, giving mixed results. They are tricky to propagate and thus the need for grafting. Most of the plants seen in gardens are seedlings that vary in leaf size and floral display.

Chion or *khion* = snow and *anthus* = flower, as the flowers are snowy white.

Chionanthus retusus
CHINESE FRINGE TREE

The fragrant white flowers are produced on the new summer's growth and are held in dense panicles. Big, bold leaves are usually a dark black-green on a stiff, upright tree. The stems and trunks sometimes peel like birchs and are also seen with the outer layer splitting in small diamonds to reveal new shiny bark beneath. The fringe tree was introduced from China by Robert Fortune in 1845, but remained rare until reintroduced into cultivation by Charles Maries. It is also native to Korea and Japan. Height x width 10 ft (3 m). ZONE 6.

Retusus = blunt, referring to the blunt ends of the leaves.

Chionanthus virginicus
FRINGE TREE, OLD MAN'S BEARD

Given the right climate, this small tree is smothered in white, pendant, slightly fragrant flowers in late spring and summer. This form is called *virginicus* because it comes from the state of Virginia and the eastern seaboard of the U.S.A. It is usually found on the tops of ridges and drier areas, and this gives us a clue as to how drought-tolerant this plant can be. It has larger leaves than *C. retusus* and they are glossy on the surface. Seedlings vary considerably in size and color. Height x width 10 ft (3 m). ZONE 3.

Below: *Cistus laurifolius*

Right: *Cistus ladanifer*

Cistus

ROCK ROSE, SUN ROSE
Cistaceae

Cistus are indispensable, or at least they ought to be, as they are smothered in large, saucer-shaped flowers all summer long. They come in white, pink, cerise and purple, with the added joy of fragrance. Only roses and hydrangeas can compete for sheer numbers of flowers and length of flowering season. It is a mystery to me why more gardeners don't plant drifts of these wonderful plants. It is true that they are short-lived and they will not tolerate horrendous frosts, and they must have sunny, well-drained sites. In their favor, however, they cope with hot, dry places and droughts, and any free-draining soils including limestone. They are a "must" for seaside gardeners coping with everyday sea breezes and occasional storms.

Being dense, bushy evergreens makes them great weed suppressors. Use a mulch around them and in no time you will have a thick, dense cover that gives the weeds no chance at all. They do not like being transplanted, so find young, healthy, container-grown plants and secure them in some way to prevent wind-wobble when young. Some people put a rock at the base of the plant just to hold it in place until it is established.

Cistus make a great display *en masse* on banks, and they are an excellent "nurse" plant. A nurse plant is fast-growing and often short lived. The idea is to plant a fast-growing *Cistus* in between your slow-growing choice shrubs. The *Cistus* makes the immediate impact and gives good value for a few years. Gradually your slower, more choice shrubs get going and then you can chop out the nurse plant. *Cistus* are usually short-lived and so by the time they are getting tatty the choice shrub is established.

Some people give *Cistus* a light shearing to keep them bushy and compact and this has the added advantage of extending their life. Just a light trim after flowering or in the spring before they start flowering is all that is needed. Heavy pruning usually kills them.

Cistus = an old Greek name for the plants, some of which are native to Greece.

Cistus x *corbariensis*, syn *C. hybridus*

This is a natural hybrid between *Cistus populifolius* and *C. salviifolius*. Its red buds open to white flowers with yellow centers and stamens in late spring to summer. It is similar to, but hardier than, most other species. Native to southern Europe. Height 3 ft (1 m) x width 5 ft (1.5 m). ZONE 7.

Corbariensis = from Corbière, a place in southern France.

Cistus ladanifer
COMMON GUM CISTUS

This classic cistus has big, white flowers with a chocolate blotch at the center of each one. In a classic case of garden snobbery, the *Paeonia* 'Joseph Rock' has exactly the same colors, sending gardeners into ecstasies over the short-lived flowers. Meanwhile, this cistus produces hundreds of identical flowers all summer long and gardeners think it is ordinary. I am enthusiastic about both: the cistus is not diminished in my eyes because it is so fecund. A native of Portugal and Spain. Height 6 ft (2 m) x width 5 ft (1.5 m). ZONE 8.

Ladanifer = the plant has a resinous gum called labdanum, used for incense and perfume.

Cistus laurifolius

This is one of the bigger cistus and there is a mass of large, white flowers 3 in (8 cm) across in summer, each with a gleaming boss of golden stamens in the center. You will notice that the plant is

Above: *Cistus* x *purpureus*

strongly scented on hot, sunny days. A native of southern Europe and much of the Mediterranean, this plant is one of the hardiest of the genus. Height x width 9 ft (3 m). ZONE 7.

Laurifolius = leaf like a laurel.

Cistus x purpureus (*C. creticus* x *C. ladanifer*)

This is a very old hybrid and still deserving of a place in our gardens. In summer, it has rich pinky red flowers 3 in (8 cm) across, with the typical *Cistus ladanifer* blotch at the base of each petal. It has long, narrow, sticky, dark green leaves. Two named clones are **'Brilliancy'** and **'Betty Taudevin'**, the latter with brighter pink flowers. Native of southern Europe. Height 6 ft (2 m) x width 3 ft (1 m). ZONE 7.

Purpureus = purple.

Cistus 'Anne Palmer' (*C. crispus* x *C. palhinhae*)

Large, soft-pink flowers adorn this plant all summer. It is a small, tidy shrub with long, wavy-edged leaves and a hint of red in the stems. Raised by Collingwood Ingram and named after Lady Anne Palmer (now Lady Anne Berry), who gifted her Rosemoor garden in Devon, England, to the Royal Horticultural Society. Height x width 3 ft (1 m). ZONE 8.

The Hillier hybrid, **C. 'Silver Pink'**, is similar, but it is a smaller bush with smaller, silvery pink flowers with prominent gold stamens. Height 30 in (75 cm) x width 36 in (90 cm). ZONE 7.

Clematis

OLD MAN'S BEARD, TRAVELER'S JOY, VIRGIN'S BOWER
Ranunculaceae

The flower shape and color of the various species in this extensive group of plants varies tremendously, but in the garden, the right clematis can be a show-stopper. Although we think they have big, showy flowers, in truth they have no petals at all but rather four, or sometimes eight, colorful sepals.

We usually think of clematis as climbers, but there are a few herbaceous species, too. The 200-plus species of *Clematis* cover most of the globe and sometimes when they naturalize it seems

they may in truth cover it. It is a shame that a few rampant species have given the genus a bad name, when in fact most are moderate growers and never likely to take over.

Some clematis are evergreen, though most are deciduous. The leaves are in opposite pairs, sometimes simple, single leaves but more often divided into multiple leaflets. They climb by twirling leaf stalks around the stems of shrubs and trees or simply by twining their way up through any support. The deciduous types have no fall color and often look scruffy and bedraggled as the limp leaves hang despondently. Grown over trellis fences and up and over pergolas and buildings, these plants cover themselves in flowers. Like most climbers, the plants begin in shade, seeking the sunlight with the tops draped over trees and the flowering part in sun.

A good, deep, moist soil is ideal; they are more of a struggle to grow on heavy soils or in light, dry sand. Many of the hybrids prefer a limestone soil or a regular feed of lime. Transplant when young from container-grown specimens and don't be tempted to shift them. Most are cold-hardy and a few cope with wind, but it is safer to say that they need shelter.

Pruning of clematis is a bit complicated but they generally fall into one of three categories:

1. Early flowering forms like *C. montana* and *C. macropetala* should be pruned immediately after flowering to give a summer of growth to provide next year's flowers.
2. Early summer hybrids with large flowers where the flowers appear on short side shoots from last year's wood. These are easy as they need little or no pruning, maybe just a bit of thinning after flowering.
3. Late summer flowering forms. These die back and look drab in the winter, so give them a good hard prune and tidy in late winter just before the spring growth.

There is a disease called clematis wilt that attacks the hybrids more than the species. The stems or vines are often killed to ground level, and that may be the end of the plant. Sometimes, however, it shrugs off the disease and makes healthy new growth the following spring.

Clematis = from the Greek "klema," meaning vine.

Below: *Clematis armandii*

Above: *Clematis* x 'Jackmanii'

Right: *Clematis* 'Henryi'

Clematis armandii

This is an early flowering species and the good forms have 2 in (5 cm) creamy white flowers in spring like small saucers, with the added bonus of scent. There are poor versions in cultivation, too, so it is worth finding a named cultivar. A pink-tinged form called **'Apple Blossom'** is a worthy selection. The glossy, evergreen leaves in threes look a little like cinnamon leaves with three prominent veins. Plant where the tops will grow in the sun and only prune for shape. It is not as fussy as some regarding soil and is happy in acidic or alkaline conditions. Named after Armand David of *Davidia* fame, this Chinese vine was introduced to the Veitch Nursery in England by E. H. Wilson in 1900. Height 10–15 ft (3–5 m) x width 6–10 ft (2–3 m). Although it is cold-hardy to ZONE 7, it does like summer heat and warmth.

Clematis x 'Jackmanii' (*C. lanuginosa* x *C. viticella* 'Atrorubens')

Way back in the 1860s a batch of hybrid seedlings was raised at the Jackman Nursery in Woking, England. The flowers were large (3–4 in/8–10 cm) across and purple-red to deep purple. These hybrids went on to form the basis of many of the modern hybrids. As well as large flowers they have the added virtue of flowering on this season's growth after midsummer. Prune drastically in winter as they flower on new growth each summer. They enjoy a feed of lime and protection from slugs and snails. Today there are a myriad hybrids and cultivars including the excellent **'Horn of Plenty'**, **'Henryi'** and **'Marie Boisselot'**. Height x width 10 ft (3 m). ZONE 4.

Clematis montana

This early-flowering, hardy, deciduous clematis is a blanket of white flowers in the spring. It can be quite rampant and is certainly easy to grow compared to some of the more temperamental species. Ideal for clambering up and over old trees and for covering unattractive buildings. This plant was introduced from the Himalayas by Lady Amherst in 1831. Wife of the Governor of India, Lady Amherst was a keen botanist and ornithologist who used her husband's travels to seek new plants. She was honored for her endeavors by the naming of the beautiful Lady Amherst pheasant. Height up to 40 ft (12 m). ZONE 6.

Montana = of mountains.

Clematis montana var rubens is supposedly hardier than the white form and has rosy-colored flowers. Native to China. Height 30 ft (10 m). ZONE 5.

Rubens = refers to the rosy red flowers.

Clematis paniculata

An evergreen climber with a froth of white flowers in spring. In the wild, splashes of white appear across the valleys where plants grew unseen before. It creates a similar display to *Cornus florida*. The male plants have larger flowers than the females and both are fragrant. It needs a mild climate in the Northern Hemisphere. Native of New Zealand. Height 30 ft (10 m). ZONE 8.

There is a Japanese species, **Clematis terniflora**, that is sometimes referred to as *C. paniculata*. It is a vigorous deciduous climber with hawthorn-scented, white flowers in the fall. Height 30 ft (10 m). ZONE 6.

Paniculata = in panicles.

Clematis tangutica

RUSSIAN VIRGIN'S BOWER, LEMON PEEL CLEMATIS
Green, ball-like buds open to cute little, yellow, cap-like flowers with pointy petals. Appearing in late summer and fall, they will add spice to your garden. It is as if someone has taken an orange and split it in four from the base; hence, it is sometimes known as the lemon peel clematis. It is a rambly, scrambly sort of deciduous

vine, ideal for growing on fences and tree stumps. The fluffy seed heads are pretty, too. From Kashmir and western China. Height 15–20 ft (5–6 m) x width 6–10 ft (2–3 m). ZONE 6.

Tangutica = region of China.

Above: *Clematis montana* var *rubens*

Clematis texensis

LEATHER FLOWER, SCARLET CLEMATIS, TEXAS CLEMATIS
Clematis texensis is a Texas native with red, bell-shaped flowers that are white on the inside. The pinnate leaves are a glaucous blue. It is often cut back by winter cold, and as the plant tends to get rather scruffy it is a good idea to prune it back anyway. Like so many plants, it seems to be more winter-hardy if it gets plenty of summer heat. It is summer flowering and the parent of many large-flowered red hybrids. Height 6–15 ft (2–5 m). ZONE 5.

Texensis = from Texas.

Above: *Clematis montana*

Clianthus

Fabaceae

A genus of two species of evergreen shrubs both with showy flowers that look like parrots' beaks. Being a legume flower it has two wings, a standard and a keel, the finger-length prominent keel being the parrot's beak. The arching shrub's lush, pinnate leaves are typical of a legume.

To grow *Clianthus* choose full sun, but a well-lit site against a wall where it gets half-day sun is fine. When grown as a fan splayed against a wall, the flowers are better displayed. Too much

Top right: *Clianthus puniceus*

Right: *Clianthus puniceus* f. *albus*

shade, especially from trees, makes them thin, weak and sparse. Do not attempt to transplant this plant to another site because it won't survive the shift. Young plants and seedlings should be container-grown and planted before the roots circle the bottom of the pot. Free-draining situations are best, but the plants will grow in slow-draining clays.

Although the plant looks soft and delicate with seemingly fragile, soft green, pinnate leaves, it thrives in windy places. I have grown *C. puniceus* on the sheltered side of a lattice fence and the stems all zoomed through into the wind where it blossomed, both literally and figuratively. It is tempting to give the plant a

support or stakes, but it will be more wind-hardy if left to its own devices. You may need a small cane just until it is established.

I am not a great fan of any shrub I have to mollycoddle. It is probably the reason I only enjoy roses in other people's gardens. So for me, any shrub that needs lots of attention to keep it healthy and free of bugs doesn't usually get a space in the garden. However, in the case of clianthus, it is such a beautiful flower I'm prepared to make an exception. And if you grow roses, then it is probably no bother to give the *Clianthus* a burst of spray when you're passing.

The caterpillars and aphids are the easy pests to kill, but the leaf miners living within the leaf will need something more lethal to keep them in check. But by far the worst pests are slugs and snails. Even your neighbor's snails are going to make the effort to dine on your plant. They devour the leaves and strip the green bark off the stems. They even climb the bush to get at the more delectable new growth. The plant is often short-lived, even without the snail attacks. They seem to be grow fast/die fast plants. If you prune them lightly after flowering they should live longer.

Kleios = glory, *anthus* = flower.

Clianthus puniceus

GLORY PEA, LOBSTER CLAW, PARROT'S BILL, KAKA BEAK
Clusters of shimmering scarlet flowers appear near the tips of the stems in late winter or early spring and each curved flower is like a parrot's beak. The bush is a soft green color and looks like an opened umbrella, growing to around waist-high. There are white and pink forms (**f. *albus*** and **f. *roseus***) but neither are as exciting

as the red. The only merit I can see in the white is that at night, the flowers glow in reflected light. Native of the North Island of New Zealand. Height 12 ft (4 m) x width 10 ft (3 m). ZONE 8.

Puniceus = scarlet.

Cornus

DOGWOOD, CORNEL
Cornaceae

*C*ornus are fabulous flowering plants—or are they? In truth, what we think of as large, showy petals are really bracts surrounding the flower. But they are showy, nonetheless. However, while their flowering virtues are many, often *Cornus* species are grown for different reasons: their colorful winter stems, as in *C. alba* and *C. stolonifera*, or perhaps for their wonderful leaves, as in *C. controversa*. *Cornus* are mostly deciduous trees and shrubs from Asia and North America, with just a few evergreen types to add spice to the range.

With such a diversity of form it is not surprising that they have been grown for flower, foliage, fruit and ornamental stems. *Cornus* is a happy group of plants, and while preferring deep, rich, well-drained soil, they are found growing in most types. They are generally drought-tolerant and some, like *C. stolonifera*, will cope with wet and boggy ground. In a garden situation, keep the roots cool with a mulch of bark or woodchips.

Full sun and shelter from cold winds are the requirements for the ornamental flowering *Cornus*. It grows best in a continental climate, with hot summers, cold winters and a long, hot, dry fall to ripen the wood and encourage flowering.

There is a devastating new disease affecting dogwoods called anthracnose. First noticed as spots or blotches on the new leaves, the next stage is severe die back of the branches. *Cornus florida*
and *C. nuttallii* are particularly susceptible, while *C. sanguinea* and *C. alba* are also affected.

Cornus = refers to the hard wood used for spears; *dogwood* = from an old custom of bathing mangy dogs using the bark of *C. sanguinea*.

Cornus florida
FLOWERING DOGWOOD

In its Appalachian homeland, *Cornus florida* is the flower of spring. Beacons of white flowers beam out across the hillsides—the showiest flower of the forests. The flowers are perched along the branches like butterflies, and though the wild forms are pure white, many pink and red cultivars are available. You will need a large or woodland-type garden for them to look the part. Ideally cornus should be planted with a dark leaf backdrop to show off the white bracts in spring.

The trees have a pleasing tiered habit and clean, gray-brown stems. Leaves are a smooth gray-green and, given the right conditions (hot summers), the fall color is a scintillating palette of reds, gold and orange. In a mild climate or fluctuating winter temperatures, this *Cornus* doesn't perform well and is susceptible to late spring frost damage. Also the fall color does not "sing." It thrives on the hot summers, allowing it to survive the cold winters. This plant likes a neutral or acidic soil, and it needs to be free-draining to keep root rot at bay. Shelter from wind is essential, too. Given the right conditions, this is the ultimate woodland shrub: wonderful flowers, good structure and great fall color. Native of eastern North America. Height 20 ft (6 m) x width 25 ft (8 m). ZONE 5.

Some cultivars to watch out for are **'Apple Blossom'**, which has soft pink and white flowers, as you would imagine with this name. Height x width 15 ft (5 m).

'Cherokee Chief', with its deep rose-red bracts. Height x width 15 ft (5 m).

'Rainbow' is a rich tri-colored yellow, and a green leaf with a hint of red turning to rich scarlet. It is definitely one of the better variegated plants. Height 10 ft (3 m) x width 8 ft (2.5 m).

'Ormonde' is a hybrid between *Cornus floribunda* and *C. nuttallii*. It has big, shiny, white flowers with reflexed sepals. It requires the same conditions as *C. floribunda* cultivars. Height x width 25 ft (8 m).

> *Florida* = rich in flowers (not Florida the state, as we may imagine).
> Plants from Florida are called *floridana*, as in *Leitneria floridana*.

Cornus kousa var chinensis
KOUSA DOGWOOD

Cornus kousa is the Asian equivalent of *C. florida*. Each of the bracts or flowers is pointed rather than rounded, but in other ways they are similar, including the magnificent fall colors. *Kousa* is the Japanese name for their native tree, but the variety we see in our gardens is the Chinese form, introduced by E. H. Wilson from central China in 1907. A bush with a tiered habit that is covered in large, white flowers in summer turning red-pink. Height x width 25 ft (8 m). ZONE 5.

> *Kousa* – Japanese name for this dogwood.

Cornus mas
CORNELIAN CHERRY

A big, wide, spreading bush or small tree with finger-length, dark green leaves and stems. The fall color is purply red but the real highlight is in early spring when the bare branches are dotted with starry clusters of saffron-yellow flowers. These are followed by red, cherry-like fruits, thus the common name. *Cornus mas* comes from the hotter parts of southern and central Europe. Height x width 15 ft (5 m). ZONE 5.

> *Mas* = male, as in *mascula*. In ancient times it was thought *C. mas* was the male and *C. sanguinea* the female of the same species.

Below: *Cornus* 'Ormonde'

Above: *Corylopsis himalayana*

Corylopsis

WINTER HAZEL
Hamamelidaceae

This easy-care group of deciduous shrubs are generally grown for their early spring chains of delicately-scented yellow flowers. The foliage is a little like hazelnut bushes, thus the common name. They are happy in a sheltered garden setting in sun or part-shade, with good, free-draining, acidic soil and adequate light. They are not as demanding as that may sound, but they perform better with kindness than without. Most of the plants need neutral or acidic soil and only *Corylopsis pauciflora* will cope with alkaline conditions. Clay soil is acceptable if the drainage is all right. They transplant fairly easily at any stage, as long as you move them in the dormant winter period.

Generally *Corylopsis* are very cold-hardy but a few, such as *C. himalayana*, are more tender. Most have arching branches, creating a dome or open umbrella shape. Choose a species that grows to the height you want, as the flowers are fairly similar on all the species except for *C. himalayana* and *C. pauciflora*. I have seen them trained against a wall to give the impression of a climber. The wall of foliage looks very effective and the mass of pendulous flowers in spring is simply stunning. None of these plants is known for their fall color; usually the leaves fade to yellow before falling, but not enough to get you excited. They are ideally suited to a woodland garden away from strong winds. In other ways they are easy-care plants with no pests or diseases.

They all come from the Asian region, from the Himalayas, through China to Japan and Taiwan.

> *Korylos* = hazel and *opsis* = like, so "like a hazel."

Corylopsis himalayana

This is the gem of the genus as regards the leaf cover, and is possibly the best for flowering, too. This outstanding plant is new to

Above: *Corylopsis himalayana*

Left: *Corylopsis pauciflora*

cultivation and likely to become a firm favorite. Prominent, bright yellow, pointy buds are full of promise in late winter and the flowers emerge very early in spring and may be frosted, so it is worth picking a prime site for such a beauty. The flowers are more than twice as wide as most other species and a pale primrose-yellow. Glaucous blue foliage forms a dense canopy, whereas most *Corylopsis* tend to be arching shrubs with a rather thin facade of leaves. A wall of foliage weeps down, creating a full and lush appearance. *C. himalayana* looks good all summer, whereas most forms are great for two to three weeks and then average for the rest of the season. A sheltered woodland setting is perhaps the ideal position for this lovely specimen. Native to the Himalayas. Height 10–15 ft (3–5 m) x width 6–10 ft (2–3 m). ZONE 8 OR 9.

Himalayana = from the Himalayas.

Corylopsis pauciflora
BUTTERCUP WINTER HAZEL

This is the perfect shrub for small gardens, forming a low, dense mound with more primrose-yellow flowers in early spring packed into a tiny bush than any of the bigger versions. Ironically, *pauciflora* generally means not much or not many flowers, from "paucity," meaning few. When you see this little bush absolutely laden with flowers you'll wonder how on earth it got that name. Typically it forms a bush about knee-high, sometimes growing up to waist-high, and it tends to be wider than it is tall. The leaves are like small, rough hazel leaves and are possibly the least interesting of the genus, but the plant more than makes up for this with the twin attributes of compact size and profusion of flowers. It comes from Japan. Height 5 ft (1.5 m) x width 8 ft (2.5 m). ZONE 6.

Pauciflora = few or not many flowers, rather a misnomer considering the profusion of flowers this small bush produces.

Corylopsis spicata

In spring, this big, sometimes open, spreading shrub bears bright yellow flowers with red to purple anthers. Usually the outer face of the bush has a thin veneer of leaves, but as the plant ages, it becomes more sparse and open. You can prune it back if you want to make it more dense, but allow enough time for the bush to grow new stems for next year's flowers. If the wide-spreading, arching habit is going to take up too much room in your garden, then try training it against a wall. Native to Japan. Height 6 ft (2 m) x width 10 ft (3 m). ZONE 5.

Spicata = spikes like ears of corn.

Corylopsis willmottiae 'Spring Purple'

This cultivar has wonderful bursts of pale yellow racemes of flowers in spring, as do the rest of *Corylopsis willmottiae*, but it is also a contender for the best foliage on a corylopsis—so why not have the best of both worlds? This cultivar has emerging leaves in soft purple, although the effect is soon lost as the leaves age and turn to green. It was raised by Hilliers Nursery in England. Height x width 12 ft (4 m). ZONE 6.

Crinodendron

Elaeocarpaceae

This genus has two species of evergreen shrubs, with pendent bell-shaped or lantern-shaped flowers in either red or white. Coming from the moist forests of southern Chile, these plants will not grow in hot or dry climates, and they seem to be difficult to grow in warm, moist climates, too. Cool, coastal areas are ideal, but even then they need protection from drying winds. Too warm a climate makes it prone to root rot, and conditions that are too cold will kill it outright. I plant a couple of them every year and they gradually fade away on me, but I don't stop trying. One day I imagine I'm going to find the perfect spot—away from the hot sun, on a well-drained bank, no frosts, etc. I've even been blessed with a flower once or twice, but nothing to brag about.

These plants need acidic, free-draining soil and grow best in rhododendron country. They do not like to be too wet or too dry around the roots, and are prone to wilt in hot sun or if given

Above left and right:
Crinodendron patagua

Below: *Crinodendron hookerianum*

fertilizers. They need year-round moisture and are not accustomed to droughts. To say that they are fussy is an understatement. Disease seems to be limited to those dreaded root rots that sometimes kill plants overnight, but they can also lead to a slow, lingering death. There is a black leafspot disease, too, but it is seemingly pest-free. On the positive side, they transplant easily from pots or from open ground.

The narrow, upright habit lends itself to confined spaces and the dark, blacky, evergreen foliage is superb. They can be pruned, should your plant ever get out of bounds.

Krinon = lily and *dendron* = tree.

Crinodendron hookerianum, syn *Tricuspidaria lanceolata*
LANTERN TREE

Now here is a challenge. You see, this plant is prized by gardeners the world over, but just to be contrary it is a swine to grow. I'm never quite sure if these things are treasured because they are beautiful, or because they are rare. For me, it is truly beautiful and I would have a dozen if they were easy to grow. If ever you see a good specimen you will be mesmerized. The large, red, bell-shaped flowers will have you entranced and determined to waste your money ever after on new attempts to please it. Hanging like chinese lanterns, these smooth bells seem to glow and look like decorations. The thin flower buds, like droplets of blood, appear in fall but don't open until the spring. The tidy, upright habit makes this an attractive shrub in any season.

Crinodendron hookerianum was first introduced by William Lobb in 1848 for the Veitch Nursery in England. It is ironic that the plant should grow so well in Lobb's native county of Cornwall. William Lobb was the first of the twenty or so collectors the Veitch Nursery sent out to scour the world for plant treasures. He also spent time plant-hunting in California, arriving during the height of the gold rush, in 1849. Native to Chile. Height 4–10 ft (1.2–3 m) x width 3–6 ft (1–2 m), though I have seen them grow taller than this. ZONE 8.

Hookerianum = named for William Hooker, the great plantsman and curator of Kew Gardens, London.

The other species, ***Crinodendron patagua***, is less exciting, and so is naturally easier to grow. It forms a small tree with small, dark leaves of no great merit and white, bell-shaped flowers. It is the sort of plant you can walk right past when it is in full flower and not even notice. Native of Chile. Height x width 10–15 ft (3–5 m). ZONE 8.

Patagua = Chilean name.

Cyrilla

LEATHERWOOD
Cyrillaceae

You can always tell the botanists are having trouble with a plant when you see the family name is the same as the genus. It means they don't know where to put it, so they make up a new family name to fit the genus. Some suggest this genus is vaguely related to *Ilex* or hollies. It is a genus of one species, *Cyrilla racemiflora*, which is found growing from Virginia and North Carolina down to Florida and across to Texas. It even grows in the West Indies and into South America. Its hardiness depends on the origins of the plant, so select stock from the north if you need the hardiness.

Found growing naturally in swampy, wet places, yet, like so many of these plants, it is not so readily established if you try to grow them in wet places in your garden. I shouldn't give the impression they are fussy, because they are not. Although a moist, free-draining, acidic soil would be ideal, I have seen them growing in heavy clays. It transplants easily and is readily propagated from cuttings. Full sun is fine and they will grow in part-shade, though the fall color will be diminished. It is named after Dominico Cirillo (1739–99), an Italian physician and professor of botany.

Cyrilla racemiflora

Numerous small, white flowers appear in long racemes from early summer onward, often flowering for a long time. The plant looks like a shuttlecock of spreading fingers—up and out as well as down. Being slightly scented, the flowers are popular with bees. Leaves are small, thin and shiny and about 2 in (5 cm) long.

We really need to describe this plant as if it were two species, though the two forms obviously merge. The northern forms are usually small, shrubby, deciduous and inevitably hardier, whereas the southern types are more tree-like and evergreen. As a northern, cool region plant it forms a bush around waist-high, with stupendous fall color in a mixture of scarlets, orange and lemons. The southern, evergreen forms clearly miss out here.

It is an excellent and unusual shade tree in mild regions, where the growth is fast, and as a shrub in woodland gardens, blending well with the likes of rhododendrons, enkianthus and clethras. Alternatively, it looks good kept as a mounded shrub in suburban gardens and can even be trained as an unusual wall shrub, showing off the showers of flowers to great effect. It does not mind being pruned and so shaping is a matter of taste.

Perhaps this is another contender for selection of different clones, some to remain small and bushy and others more vigorous to use as specimen trees. Likewise, the evergreen and good coloring, deciduous forms could be chosen to suit gardeners from different climates.

I sometimes wonder how plants like this arrive in various countries around the world. This plant was first sent to England in 1765 and was subsequently "lost" until it was reintroduced about 1900. Then one keen plantsman in Australia, New Zealand or Europe made an effort to get plants either from England or America. While we acknowledge the person who first brought a plant from the wild to cultivation, there is a small army of people who perform the next stage of introductions into their country, for the benefit of gardeners everywhere. Most of the dates given for introductions of plants refer to England or France, as these were the countries that sent collectors in the early days.

Height 4 ft (1.2 m) x width 30 ft (10 m). Native to southeastern United States, ZONES 5 TO 9.

Racemiflora = the flowers are in long racemes.

Cytisus

BROOM
Fabaceae

The pea-like flowers of these hardy, colonizing plants have all the shapes of a typical legume, with wings and a keel. *En masse* in spring they can be a spectacular sight and have the added bonus of scent.

Brooms thrive in heat and sun and as a colonizer they take over newly turned ground, but tend to grow fast and die fast. You can delay their demise by pruning immediately after flowering. If you trim the plant back by around a third of its height after flowering, the plant will take longer to reach mature height and be less prone to wind rock, where the top-heavy plant is blown over at ground level (because of the leverage effect of wind pushing on top-heavy growth). To be more precise about the pruning, you should look at the growth the plant made last season and cut off nearly all of it, leaving just a finger's length of last summer's stems. The plant will then make vigorous new stems to bear the next crop of flowers. They become lanky and woody if left unpruned.

Brooms are good for covering dry, inhospitable banks and other difficult sites. Heavy clay is all right for these plants, and poor, rocky or sandy soils are fine, too. One of the reasons this is a great colonizing plant is its ability to grow in these poor sites, and in very hot, dry places with not much soil or water. Most colonizing plants need full sun to thrive and this is true for all brooms.

Right: *Cyrilla racemiflora*

46

Above: *Cytisus* x *beanii*

to grow in hot, dry, inhospitable places. Brooms are more willing to grow in alkaline soils than most shrubs. Cultivars grown from cuttings have a more sprawly root system and can handle most ground conditions. They do not enjoy having their roots disturbed at all. When you plant a potted broom, take care to spread the roots, as plants that have roots circling the bottom of the container will not live long.

Kytisos = from a related medicinal plant.

Cytisus x beanii (C. ardoinii x C. purgans)

This is a small, semi-prostrate shrub with rich yellow flowers in spring. It looks wonderful tumbling over a wall or bank and is an ideal plant for large rockeries. Grows happily in limestone or scidic soils. Height 2 ft (60 cm) x width 3 ft (1 m). ZONE 7 OR 8.

Beanii = after Mr Bean, Director of Kew Gardens, London, England, in the 1940s, and author of an excellent manual for trees and shrubs.

Cytisus x kewensis (C. ardoinii x C. multiflorus)

This is very similar to the above species, but with creamy yellow flowers in late spring. It is also happy in limestone or acidic soils. If your soil is acidic, try both species in combination with small, blue-flowered rhododendrons—the effect is stunning. This form is named for Kew Gardens, London. Height 1 ft (30 cm) x width 5 ft (1.5 m). ZONE 6.

Being in the legume or Fabaceae family, it is also capable of acquiring nitrogen from the air in the soil and using it as plant food, that in turn is returned to the soil and used by succeeding plants. Nitrogen is essential to all plants as the element that makes them green and grow faster. Very few plants other than legumes have the ability to make use of the nitrogen in the atmosphere.

Grown from seed, brooms send down a long tap root and are tolerant of a wide range of soils. These tap roots allow them

Cytisus multiflorus, syn C. albus, C. leucanthus

PORTUGESE BROOM, WHITE SPANISH BROOM

Known as both the Portugese and Spanish broom, this glorious white broom is covered in flowers from late spring to early summer. It starts as an upright plant, gradually spreading and demanding more space. It grows around 10 ft (3m) high and the lower branches can be pruned off to make an arching, high shrub to allow perennial plants, such as pulmonaria, some space in the foreground. Native of Spain and Portugal. Height 10 ft (3 m) x width 8 ft (2.5 m). ZONE 7.

Multiflorus = lots of flowers.

Cytisus x praecox (C. purgans x C. multiflorus)

This is a fairly tidy, compact broom, ideal for small gardens. The pale primrose-yellow flowers appear in late spring or early summer. Unfortunately, they have a rather heady, nasty smell, so don't plant near the house or use as a cut flower. It may need a trim after flowering to keep it dense and bushy, as the bush some-times gets top-heavy with the weight of blooms. There are several cultivars available, including a rich yellow called **'Allgold'**. The original hybrid with creamy yellow flowers is now known as **'Warminster'**, from the town in England of the same name. Height 4 ft (1.2 m) x width 5 ft (1.5 m). ZONE 6.

Praecox = early.

Right: *Cytisus scoparius*

Cytisus scoparius

SCOTCH BROOM

Scotch broom is despised by many because it has colonized farm-land in temperate regions around the world. While I can sympa-thize with the farmers, I can also see a place for the garden cultivars of this fine plant. For those of you unfamiliar with species as a difficult-to-eradicate naturalized weed, you'll wonder what all the fuss is about as these easy-care plants are a beacon in early spring in every shade from yellow to gold, orange to red.

One of the great things about brooms is that they flower for months and months, but that's only part of their appeal. Most are delightfully scented and they are good for cut flowers.

The bush itself is an upright, multi-stemmed plant, arching out at the top as gravity takes over. Thin, string-like stems are rich green and capable of photosynthesizing when and if the leaves fall off, as they usually do. So they appear to be evergreen when in fact the tiny, clover-like leaves often only last a matter of weeks before they fall.

This species was called "broom" because the flexible stems were bound together to make brooms, like witches' brooms. The name was then applied to other plants in the genus. Native of western Europe. Height x width 6–10 ft (2–3 m). ZONE 6.

There are many named cultivars including **'Cornish Cream'**, **'Golden Sunlight'**, with their creamy to yellow flowers. For bi-colored flowers in reds and yellows look for **'Burkwoodii'**, **'Lord Lambourne'** and **'Andreanus'**.

Desfontainia

Potaliaceae

A peculiar genus of one South American shrub that at first sight looks like a holly with flowers. The key difference is that the leaves are opposite each other on the stem, whereas on a holly they are alternate. Like the hollies, this plant does have spines and a shiny surface and, like most typical hollies, it is evergreen.

Desfontainia = named for French botanist Rene Desfontaines (1750–1833), director of the Botanic Gardens in Paris.

Desfontainia spinosa

If you see this species in flower, you will know that it is something rather special. The orangy red, waxy blooms hang down beneath the stems and each tubular flower has five yellow petals flared out at the bottom end. A long flowering season from midsummer into fall makes this plant a valuable addition to any garden.

Desfontainia spinosa grows naturally almost the entire length of the Andes, although the plants in cultivation come from Chile and are therefore presumed to be hardier. William Lobb first introduced it into cultivation in 1843. It reportedly varies considerably according to the climate (perhaps it would be valuable to gardeners if forms were collected from different regions).

The cultivated forms like a cool, moist climate as you might imagine given their homeland, and the plant seems to perform best in regions with rain all year round, for example the Pacific Northwest. Give it some shade to protect it from severe frosts and strong sun (though perversely the more sun it gets the better it flowers). A rich, well-drained, acidic soil is essential and a mulch will help keep the roots cool and moist.

Try not to disturb the roots of the plants once it is established. Normally it becomes a small shrub and it is unlikely that you will ever need to prune it, as it naturally makes a dense thicket. Plant one on a bank in a shady dell so that the flowers will be at eye

Left: *Desfontainia spinosa*

Above: *Deutzia gracilis* with *Azalea* 'Goyet'.

level. The flowers are often hidden among the foliage when viewed from above. Remember to set these plants back from paths because of the spines. Native of South America. Height 3 ft (1 m) x width 4 ft (1.2 m), but can reach 10 ft (3 m). ZONE 8.

Spinosa = spiny.

Deutzia

Philadelphaceae

These are without a doubt one of my favorite shrubs, although I often having difficulty convincing others of their true beauty. Perhaps I can convince you to grow one or two in your garden. The pretty bunches of pink, white and mauve flowers appear in late spring, after the main flush of spring color in the garden. They sometimes appear in clusters just above a new pair of leaves, and at other times they are on long, thin, upright panicles. Usually the blooms are on little side growths appearing from the buds on last year's stems. If you were to prune in winter, you would be cutting off all these flower buds.

Deutzias are ideal plants to start your gardening career because they are so easy to propagate and transplant from open ground or pots, and bigger plants can be moved during the winter months. Deutzias grow in any soil, even in akaline clay or acidic peat.

Some forms are arching, some are ground covers, while others are stiff, upright shrubs over head high. If they have a fault, it is their somewhat ungainly habit. In time they become crowded and rather tatty-looking, but this is easily remedied with an annual prune after flowering. If you are a lazy gardener like me, you can prune them more severely every four or five years.

The leaves are simple, usually pointed and serrated, and they are functional rather than beautiful. Deutzias are useful because they are pretty and excellent fillers between the more stunning plants in your garden. Gardeners often want every plant to be a feature, but a space full of highlights looks like a hotchpotch. You need some subtle flowers like deutzias to soften the effect of the dazzlers. Link plants are those that you use in drifts or throughout the garden to give continuity. Some plants do whatever job they are given without any fuss and rarely get any credit.

The cultivated species come from Japan, Korea, Taiwan, China and the Himalayas.

Deutzia = Johann van der Deutz (1743–1784), an Amsterdam lawyer who was a friend and patron of Carl Peter Thunberg, a botanist employed by the Dutch East Indies Company and based in Japan.

Deutzia gracilis
SLENDER DEUTZIA

A perfect example of a hardworking plant, this deutzia grows to waist-high and in spring is laden with sprays of five to twenty white, starry flowers. Gradually the weight of stems and flowers cause them to bow and they form a small, arching shrub. Plant a group of them in front of small-leaved Japanese maples, such as *Acer palmatum* 'Crimson Queen', and you'll never dismiss deutzias again. This plant is from Japan. Height x width 3 ft (1 m). ZONE 5.

Gracilis = slender, referring to the thin, upright panicles.

Deutzia x hybrida (*D. discolor* x *D. longifolia*)

A beautiful group of plants that are smothered in flowers in the spring. This group of hybrids includes **'Joconde'**, with large, rosy, two-toned flowers, and **'Mont Rose'**, with its big, rounded clusters of mauve-pink flowers and rough textured, almost corrugated, leaves. 'Mont Rose' is tidier than most, forming an upright bush.

My favorite is **'Magicien'**, with purple buds opening to

Above: *Deutzia x hybrida* 'Joconde'

49

Above and below: *Deutzia scabra* 'Candidissima'

starry, soft purple- and white-striped bells. As they age, the flowers fade and so each cluster seems to have a color mix of rich mauve through to almost white. For all, height x width 5 ft (1.5 m). ZONE 6.

Deutzia ningpoensis, syn D. chunii

One of my favorite deutzias, this form has long, terminal panicles of around fifty flowers in late spring. The long, satin-white petals are slightly upturned, forming a Turk's cap-style flower. A mass of bright eggyolk-colored stamens emerge from the bottom of the flower.

This is an upright bush, renewing itself by sending long, vigorous suckers up through the bush from near ground level. These strong shoots eventually become the new structural stems and the older woody growths can be removed after flowering. This is slightly oversimplifying the pruning, but it is quite easy to tell the new from the old wood. The older stems look twiggy, crowded and slightly tatty. From eastern China. Height 6–10 ft (2–3 m) x width 6 ft (2 m). ZONE 6.

Ningpoensis = Ningpo is a region of China, the plant's homeland.

Deutzia scabra 'Candidissima'

A big, upright shrub with opposite leaves, shaped like arrowheads. Each flower or floret on the finger-length racemes hangs down and, when turned upside down, you will see a double, almost treble, flower looking like a sea anemone, with three rows of pure white petals. In other forms, for example, **'Pride of Rochester'** and **'Flore Pleno'**, the backs of the flowers take on a rosy-pink sheen as a reaction to sunlight, so the shaded parts of the flower remain pure white. Unlike *Deutzia ningpoensis*, the stamens are white and almost invisible. The species is from China and Japan. For all the above, height 10 ft (3 m) x width 6 ft (2 m). ZONE 5.

Scabra = rough, referring to the leaves.

Above: *Deutzia* x *hybrida* 'Magicien'

Dichroa

Hydrangeaceae

Dichroas are quite new to cultivation and, while a series of them is emerging from the forests of China, there is one outstanding species from North Burma and Yunnan Province called *Dichroa versicolor*. Dichroas are equally happy in sunny sites or in the shade of buildings or deciduous trees—and they will cope with the dryness of these situations. It is happy in any soil, including acidic or mildly alkaline, and seems quite at ease in wettish soil. Even soil dried out by competing roots causes no obvious stress. It is supremely happy in a wet climate and even grows with its roots close to water. Initially, everyone treats it as frost-tender because it looks so tropical, but it tolerates moderate frosts. I have managed to kill some off by excessive pruning. I foolishly thought they would take drastic pruning like the related hydrangea, but instead they went into a

sulk. They can get a bit thin and leggy after a number of years, so a light pruning is possible but rarely required. The difficulty is finding a season when there are no flowers on the bush. If you are like me, it seems a travesty to prune a plant when it is in flower. Unfortunately, the flowers don't last in a vase, so you can't pick them and then prune the bush. Transplanting is easy from pots but I'm inclined to think mature plants will not shift as easily as the related hydrangeas. There are no obvious pests or diseases so far.

Dichroa = two colors.

Dichroa versicolor

Althought *versicolor* means variable color, unlike the related variable hydrangeas, this plant is consistently blue in flower color. It flowers most of the year in a mild climate, often with just one or two flower heads, and then in a burst of flower in spring and another in late summer. The flowers are a true blue, that rare quality gardeners crave. Made up of small, blue, starry flowers, the heads are about the size of a large fist. The overall effect is vaguely like a hydrangea, which is not surprising as it is in the same family. As a bonus, the plant is evergreen and has fabulous dark green, glossy leaves with a distinctly tropical air. Each leaf is the size of a large hand and has a purple leaf stalk or petiole.

One of my missions in life is to bring new plants to people. Dichroa is a first-class shrub that one day will take the world by storm. Remember, you read it here first. I have seen this plant growing in conservatories in England. I think it would cope with garden climates there in the south, especially if a shaded site was chosen to reduce frost damage. It would be ideally suited to Cali-

fornian and Pacific Northwest climates, as well as those of many of the coastal cities of eastern U.S.A. *Dichroa* would make an excellent patio plant and looks equally good in formal or woodland gardens. Native to Burma. Height 6–8 ft (2–2.5 m) x width 4–6 ft (1.2–2 m). ZONE 8 OR 9.

Versicolor = variable color.

Another species in the genus is ***Dichroa febrifuga***, with soft blue flowers (occasionally smoky pink) appearing in small terminal heads the size of a cookie. The leaves are about finger-size. It is a smaller, more compact bush that *D. versicolor* and the best blue-flowered forms are ideal town garden plants. Native to China and Nepal. Height 6 ft (2 m) x width 4–6 ft (1.2–2 m). ZONE 8 OR 9.

Embothrium

CHILEAN FIRE BUSH
Proteaceae

These Chilean shrubs can look scruffy and unkempt, but somehow when these plants flower you forgive them all their foibles. Embothriums are not easy plants to blend into a garden as the floral display is so dramatic and can last for two months. Many of the less highly colored plants we grow would be overwhelmed by the hot-scarlet, firecracker flowers. Yellow and white forms have been introduced but are rarely for

Right: *Dichroa versicolor*

sale and, frankly, are not a patch on the more common red version.

Embothriums are narrow, upright trees; the stems are shiny and brown and the trunks clean and smooth. The plants have a tendency to sucker and sometimes form a whole thicket of stems. This can be helpful if you have the room to accommodate them, as normally the trees are liable to damage by wind rock. The rocking motion can lead to root rot, or even blow the trees out of the ground. If they have suckered, it gives the plants stability, as our plant proved when it survived a storm with hurricane-strength winds.

If you do decide you want to plant one, buy a small plant or get a sucker from a friend's plant around 1 ft (30 cm) high. Big plants dislike transplanting: never try to move an embothrium once planted as it will certainly die. Embothriums hate being in pots for any length of time, which is why we rarely see them in garden centers. This drawback severely affects their popularity. Poor, acidic soil and a moist climate are perfect, so choose a sheltered bank with free-draining conditions. Conversely, they don't like drought. Choose a sunny site where there is a breeze to reduce frost and humidity. They are often short-lived in humid climates, where they are prone to root diseases. They are more cold-hardy than is usually realized and will tolerate some frosts, especially if grown in a warm summer climate. Never weed around the plants, but use a mulch or some dense ground cover to suppress the weeds.

Like most protea family members, they hate fertilizer in virtually any form, especially phosphates, lime or animal manure. The plants have virtually no pests, and root rot is the only disease to worry them (choosing that sheltered slope is the best way to prevent this problem).

Embothrium = refers to the position of the anthers down in the flower.

Above and left:
*Embothrium
coccineum*

Embothrium coccineum

A fireball of bright orangy red shooting spears decorates the tops of the stems in late spring. Each head is made up of thin flower tubes with a round ball of petals at the tip. This opens and the petals reflex right back, leaving the stigma sitting proudly at the end. Pollination is by nectar-eating birds, as is the case with most red-flowered Southern Hemisphere plants. The flowers can last for two to three months, depending on the season and the climate. Sometimes the flowering is sporadic and at other times so profuse it is breathtaking.

The finger-sized leaves are a lovely smooth, dark green on top and pale underneath. They are very handsome and tend to be in whorls at the tips of each season's growth. This means lots of bare stem beneath the leaves and so the plant often looks half-dressed. Embothriums are evergreen, more-or-less so, depending on the form grown and your local climate. In cool climates they do tend to lose most of their leaves.

The plant was discovered on Captain Cook's second voyage to the Southern Hemisphere and was later introduced by William Lobb for the Veitch Nursery in England in 1846. Native of Chile. Height 15–20 ft (5–6 m) x width 15 ft (5 m) or more. ZONE 8.

There is a clone called **'Inca Flame'** that seems indistinguishable from the species.

Coccineum = red or scarlet.

Embothrium coccineum var lanceolatum

This plant was collected high up in the Argentinian Andes by Harold Comber around 1927. Comber was a professional plant collector sent out from England who came across this hardier

form of embothrium. Long, narrow leaves and a real "fox-brush" of orange flowers make this the most spectacular of the subspecies. A form called **'Norquinco'**, from the valley of the same name, is the best selection. It will withstand frosts and tends to be more or less deciduous in a cooler climate. Height 15–20 ft (5–6 m) x width 15 ft (5 m). ZONE 7 OR 8.

Lanceolatum = referring to the lance-shaped leaves.

Embothrium coccineum var longifolium

This is a faster-growing type that is prone to sucker, keeping the plant stable in the most severe gales, so do not remove the suckers as they are the guy ropes holding the plant securely in place.

Right: Ericas in a garden setting.

This form has the added bonus of producing hot-orange flowers all along the stems, rather than just at the terminals. It will flower for a longer period, but unfortunately is not as cold-hardy as the straight species. As the name suggests the leaves are longer than those of the species. Height 15–20 ft (5–6 m) x width 15 ft (5 m). ZONE 8.

Longifolium = long leaves.

Erica

HEATH, HEATHER
Ericaceae

Most gardeners think of ericas as low, hardy, creeping shrubs, similar to low conifers. In reality, most of the ericas are from the Cape Province in South Africa and are upright, very pretty shrubs in myriad colors, shapes and forms. Some are even trees, growing to 20 ft (6 m). All are evergreen and have spikey-looking foliage, although some are soft to touch. The flowers are made up of heads of pretty little bells in white, pink or red, and some are surprisingly good cut flowers.

Most ericas need acidic or at least neutral soil, and they generally hate lime. All of them benefit from a light trim after flowering with hedge shears to keep them bushy and neat. The hardy types put up with cold winters, including snow, and wet,

boggy ground. They are rarely attacked by pests or diseases and have many uses as ground covers, winter foliage, and spring and summer flowers. The taller varieties are useful at path junctions where you need a tidy, upright shrub. Although portions of the creeping types can be separated and transplanted with ease, the bushy types should not be moved once they are established.

Erica = from the Greek "eriko," meaning "I break,"
because the stems are brittle.

Erica arborea
TREE HEATH
A shrubby, upright bush with deliciously fragrant flowers emerging in early spring to clothe the tops of the bush with long brushes of white bells. The flowers last for weeks and are scented like honey. It grows naturally from southern Europe down into Africa. Height 20 ft (6 m) x width 10 ft (3 m). ZONE 9.

There is an alpine version, **E. a. var** *alpina*, from the mountains of Spain, that is much hardier. The rich, green foliage is possibly its best feature, though the pure white flowers are fragrant and long-lasting. Height 6 ft (2 m) x width 2½ ft (75 cm). ZONE 8.

Arborea = tree-like; alpina = from the alps.

Erica australis
SPANISH HEATH
Left to its own devices, this plant is an open, rather gawky shrub, but it does have pretty, soft purple flowers with black stamens appearing in late spring. It is not as hardy as some species, as it prefers a warm climate similar to its native home in southern

Above: *Erica carnea*   Below: *Erica vagans* 'Lyonesse'

Europe. There is a white form called **'Mr Robert'**. Native of Spain and Portugal. For both, height x width 6 ft (2 m). ZONE 8.

Australis = southern, and is used to describe a species growing to the south of most other European species.

Erica carnea, syn *E. herbacea*
WINTER HEATH, SPRING HEATH

This is a deservedly popular plant in cold-climate gardens, as it is such a wonderful ground cover. The hardy ones are usually seen in drifts and masses of cute little bell-like flowers appear in late winter and on into spring. Nowadays, there are dozens of differently-colored flower and foliage forms available. You can have flowers in pink, white, reds and purple, and foliage ranging from yellow to bronze, pale lime-green to dark green.

In mild climates or rich soils, these spready types of erica grow too well, too fast and become thin and sparse. A cold, hard climate seems to suit them best and they are very tough. They need full sun to remain dense and bushy and will cope with all the elements like strong winds, snow and cold. A light trim with the shears is needed after flowering to keep them neat. The wild forms grow in the European Alps through central Europe, northwest Italy, northwest Balkans and eastern Europe, so they are lime-tolerant. Height 8–10 in (20–25 cm) x width 22 in (55 cm). ZONE 5.

Carnea = flesh, referring to the rosy-colored flowers.

Erica tetralix
CROSS-LEAVED HEATH

Known as the cross-leaved heath, because if you nip the top out of a stem the leaves are in fours in a cross fashion. Clusters of rosy-colored flowers appear from midsummer onward and there are numerous pink and white cultivars available, including the white **'Alba Mollis'** and pinks **'Pink Glow'** and **'Pink Star'**. This very hardy, low-growing shrub is native to northern Europe, the U.K. and Ireland and found in peat bogs, thus the need for acidic soil. Height 12 in (30 cm) x width 20 in (50 cm). ZONE 3.

Tetralix = four times, referring to the leaves in fours around the stem.

Erica vagans
CORNISH HEATH

Opening from the base in mid- to late summer, the red, pink or white flowers put on a terrific show. The sprays of flowers are long-lasting. **'Lyonesse'** is an excellent white cultivar and **'Lilacina'** a good pink. This European and British native is initially a dense bush but tends to become open and straggly if not maintained. Like most of the ericas it looks good in drifts, and some people peg down the stems to make it a denser bush. It needs a constantly moist climate and hates drought. Height 16–32 in (40–80 cm) x width 32 in (80 cm). ZONE 7 OR 8.

Vagans = rambling or spreading.

Erythrina

CORAL TREE
Fabaceae

This group of trees and shrubs from the tropics has scintillating brilliant red and scarlet flowers that are attractive to nectar-feeding birds. Most of the species are evergreen, with a few deciduous ones to tempt cold-region gardeners. Thankfully, some are hardy enough to withstand light frosts and they are definitely worthy of a place in your garden if

Below: *Erythrina* x *sykesii*

Above: *Erythrina crista-galli*

current season's growth dies back after flowering (and during the winter) to leave a central trunk. It is often easier to prune them (carefully avoiding the spines) to a central trunk, as you would a buddleja. In cooler climates (zone 7 and below) they will die back to rootstock, like a herbaceous plant. Find a really hot spot and plant one for a hint of the tropics, but plant it away from any paths as the spikes on the leaves and stems will catch anyone passing by. Some gardeners plant them in big tubs and put them under cover in winter and back out in the sun in the summer. These plants are from Brazil and Argentina. Height 25 ft (8 m) x width 12 ft (4 m) in warmer climates. ZONE 9/Height 5–8 ft (1.5–2.5 m) x width 5 ft (1.5 m) as a woody perennial. ZONE 8.

Crista-galli = cockscomb.

Erythrina caffra, from South Africa, and the hybrid **E. x sykesii** become large, fleshy trees to 50 x 50 ft (15 x 15 m), with brilliant heads of scarlet flowers in late winter and spring. The smaller, shrubby **E. blakei** and **E. humeana** are worth seeking out, too. Height x width 10 ft (3 m). All ZONE 9.

Escallonia

Escalloniaceae

Scorned by many gardeners, easy-care shrubs such as this are essential for every garden. One needs strong evergreens to provide the backbone of a garden, thus highlighting the real "dazzlers." With one exception, escallonias are evergreen and the shiny handsome leaves always look healthy and glossy. Most species have leaves that are small, rounded or oval with a serrated edge, and they are often thick and rather fleshy. As well as providing the evergreen backdrop, most escallonias flower in summer, though spring and fall blooms are seen, too. And they tend to flower for weeks, if not months. The little waxy flowers are produced in such numbers that they are quite showy. Being waxy means they are as tough as the leaves and not easily damaged by the elements. Every part of the flowers, including the leaves and even the stems, are waxy. Newly emerging stems are sticky and waxy before they harden up and turn woody and brown.

Escallonia is happy to be in any position—be it windy, hot, dry, sunny, or heavy, wet clay. In turn we denigrate it or else ignore it altogether. It is fun to turn these attitudes on their heads occasionally. I planted an *Escallonia* 'Alice' in a prime position in our garden and I'm glad I did. It looks wonderful with its new bronze foliage in the spring and is smothered with showy pink flowers for weeks and weeks in summer. It never looks drab or dull, and it draws many favorable comments.

Escallonia thrives in windy places, even growing beside the sea. Any soil, be it acidic or alkaline, sand or heavy clay, will do fine. Even periods of drought or waterlogging are not usually the death of it. It is easy to transplant from open ground or pots, and is free of pests and diseases, too. Let's just call it indestructible. If someone were to design or breed a new plant with such wonderful qualities it would be heralded in all the gardening magazines and proudly displayed at horticultural shows.

Escallonias form a tidy plant, around shoulder height, and it is this tidy nature, plus their ability to regenerate from any pruning, that makes them such good hedge plants. The main

you can grow them. Erythrina are best grown in full sun or somewhere with plenty of light and heat. Soft, sappy stems are brittle and easily broken in storms, but they do recover quickly. The trunks are often green and smooth, though they become attractively furrowed with age. Look out for the viscious thorns hidden away among the lush foliage. Even though the leaves can be quite large, usually divided into three or more leaflets, they seem to have little visual impact. Mostly they are a pale green and somehow seem to fade into the background. There are no pests. These plants are not fussy about soil and seem to thrive in heavy, poorly-drained conditions. Some of the larger tree species will grow in waterways, like willows, with every fallen branch bedding down somewhere to become a new tree. Hot, dry, sandy soils and droughts are tolerated.

Coral trees have big, fleshy roots and often a deep tap root, so plant out when young, and if the roots are twined around each other, unravel them. You can transplant them from open ground when young, but it is not a good idea to shift them later, and it is extremely hard work. The wood is very heavy and even a small plant is very weighty.

Erythrina = from the Greek "erythros," meaning red.

Erythrina crista-galli
COCK'S COMB, COMMON CORAL TREE
Big spikes of rich scarlet-red, parrot-beak flowers appear on the tips of the new growth from summer to fall. The hotter the climate, the sooner they appear. Each flower is 2–2½ in (5–6 cm) long and the spikes are 12–24 in (30–60 cm), so in flower this plant is a very impressive sight.

Cock's comb is usually seen as a deciduous shrub or sub-shrub, but it can grow into a small tree in warm regions. Often the

Above: *Escallonia bifida*

Escallonia rubra **var** *macrantha* is a popular form with bright rose-red flowers and is much used for hedges. Height x width 10 ft (3 m). ZONE 8.

Above: *Escallonia rubra* var *macrantha*

Macrantha = long-flowering.

criteria for a hedge is the ability to take regular pruning and not to die out, because if one plant dies, the hedge is ruined.

The genus is named for Señor Escallon, a Spanish traveler in South America, the home of escallonias.

There is a series of hybrids bred from *Escallonia rubra*. They include the robust **'Alice'**, with strong pinky red flowers. Height x width 10 ft (3 m). **'Apple Blossom'**, with soft pink and white flowers. Height x width 6 ft (2 m). Some hybrids were raised in Ireland with names like **'Donard Beauty'**, rosy-red flowers, **'Donard Brilliance'**, a red-flowered hybrid with an arching habit, **'Donard Gem'**, with large, pink, scented flowers, and **'Donard Seedling'**, with soft pink, almost white flowers. Height x width 6 ft (2 m). All ZONE 8.

Below: *Escallonia* 'Alice'

Escallonia bifida, syn E. montevidensis

This shrub is slightly tender and is the parent of many garden hybrids. Large 6 in (15 cm) long panicles of pure white flowers appear in the later part of summer. Unfortunately they have a slightly offputting smell. It is a tall, evergreen bush with dullish leaves and is a great backdrop plant where you need a tough, hardy bush. Native to Brazil and Uruguay. Height 10 ft (3 m) x width 8 ft (2.5 m). ZONE 8 OR 9.

Bi = two and *fidus* = cleft, while *montevidensis* = of Montevideo.

Escallonia 'Iveyi' (E. bifida x E. x exoniensis)

This form is quite different from most in that it tends to form a small, upright tree, eventually becoming quite open, rather than looking like the usual dense bush we associate with escallonias. It is a reliable flowering plant for fall, which is a rare beast as nearly all shrubs flower in spring or early summer to allow them several months of warm weather to produce their seeds. Large panicles of showy, pure white flowers will attract attention from some considerable distance, and they are also fragrant. The plant is named after Mr Ivey, a gardener at Caerhays Castle, Cornwall, England, where it occurred as a natural hybrid. Height x width 10 ft (3 m). ZONE 8.

Escallonia rubra

This dense bush is as tough as can be and makes an ideal hedge in seaside gardens. Sprays of red flowers are casually draped at the tips of the stems in loose posies from late summer through to fall. In its native Chile and Argentina it grows to 12 ft (4 m) high and wide, but is usually only half that in cultivation. ZONE 8 OR 9.

Rubra = red flowers, though the new stems are often red as well.

Above: *Euryops pectinatus*

Euryops

Asteraceae

Daisies are the top-selling plants for gardeners. Not surprising when you consider the daisy family, Asteraceae (that was Compositeae) is the largest plant family on the planet with literally thousands of species. They are familiar to us as garden perennials, indoor plants and even as weeds and wayside flowers, and when we go to the garden center we tend to buy something we already know. We don't usually think of daisies as shrubs, but there are some notable exceptions including *Euryops*, *Brachyglottis* and *Olearia*.

Like most of the daisy family, *Euryops* are sun-lovers. It is a big genus, including annuals, perennials and shrubs, with most native to the southern parts of Africa. There are two woody shrubs from the genus presented here. First, because of their mass of long-lasting flowers and second because they are useful for dry or windy places. If you are looking for a mass of flowers on a neat bush then these plants could be for you. Use them to fill a spot while some other slower-growing plant matures or for narrow borders by the house.

Ideally, *Euryops* like good drainage and seem to thrive in hot, dry places, even surviving regular drought; but they will also grow in heavy soils as long as the drainage is reasonable. They are not worried by acidic soil or by any bugs or mildews. They are truly easy-care plants. Prune them lightly after flowering to keep them bushy. Easy to transplant when young, they don't like to be moved or have their roots interfered with when mature.

Euryops = wide eyes, refering to the flowers.

Euryops pectinatus

A super plant, this is an evergreen, or "ever-gray," shrub covered in big, showy, yellow daisies for months during summer. The gray, ferny foliage is worth the price of the plant alone. It seems the hotter and drier the climate, the more silvery gray it becomes. Big, bright yellow daisies 2 in (5 cm) across sit way above the bush on long thin stems. The plant forms a bushy shrub, usually with a wide, almost top-heavy, look. Narrow-angled branches will be broken by extreme winds, but in general it is happy in breezy situations and is an ideal seaside plant. Native of South Africa. Height x width 3 ft (1 m). ZONE 8 OR 9.

Pectinatus = comb-like or scalloped, describing the leaves.

Euryops virgineus

In late winter and early spring clusters of tiny yellow flowers appear, and, like their cousins above, the flowers seem to last for months and are immune to wind and weather. A spiky-looking shrub with tiny, bristly leaves clustered around the shooting-star

Left: *Exochorda korolkowii*

branches. Each stem is covered in rich green leaves with five points like a "Yeti" footprint in miniature. The overall effect is neat, bristly foliage clinging all the way up the stems. Native of South Africa. Height just over 4 ft (1.2 m) x width 4 ft (1.2 m). ZONE 8 OR 9.

Virgineus = chaste or pure.

Exochorda

PEARLBUSH
Rosaceae

Plants, like everything else, go through fashions and *Exochorda* are currently "out of fashion." I think they are beautiful and our grandmothers grew them for their abundant showy, white flowers that appear in spring and summer. If they could see the beauty and value of these plants, why can't we? The common name pearlbush, coined because the unopened flowers look like pearls, gives a clue to when they were popular, as pearls were once more fashionable than they are now.

Exochorda species are very similar in their leaf and flower, with their clean green leaves and pure white flowers, so you would probably only want one in your garden. It's just a matter of deciding which one to have. *E. racemosa* is the most common species despite its wayward, sprawling habit. It arches out and takes up more space every year, thus making it difficult to fit in small gardens. My own personal favorite, *E. korolkowii*, has a tidy, upright habit, and if I were to plant another one, I would try to use a dark conifer backdrop to set off the white flowers.

Exochordas are tough, hardy plants. Full sun is best, but I've seen good ones in semi-shade at the back of a border. Found naturally in the drier parts of east Asia and China, drought poses no great threat to these plants once they are established and yet they thrive in high rainfall areas too. Typical of most members of the rose family, any old soil will do, be it alkaline or acidic, sand or clay, as long as the drainage is reasonable.

Transplant from pots or as bare-root open-ground plants when young. They are too cumbersome to try and move at a later date (and they probably won't like it anyway). No pests and diseases trouble *Exochorda*, so they are the ultimate easy-care shrub. You could prune if you felt inclined to tidy some of the more unruly species, and if you prune them hard they will regenerate quite readily. Flowers appear on last year's wood, or on tiny new growths from last year's wood, so any pruning in the winter will reduce the crop of flowers in the spring. To avoid this, prune immediately after flowering.

Exochorda = "exo," means external and "chorde" or cord , refers to the structure of the fruits.

Exochorda giraldii
REDBUD PEARLBUSH

A large free-flowering shrub and the form ***Exochorda giraldii var wilsonii*** has the largest flowers of the whole genus. They are like big white buttercups 2 in (5 cm) across, and like the white species flowers appear in late spring. The species is named after an Italian missionary, Guiseppe Giraldi, who lived in China from 1888 until his death in 1901. Like many Chinese missionaries he spent much of his time collecting and collating new plants. He sent seeds of this fine plant to the botanic gardens in Florence. Both native to northwest China. Height x width 3 ft (1 m). ZONE 4.

Exochorda korolkowii

This plant seems to get the worst press of all the species and yet it is my favorite. If I moved to a smaller garden it would be near the top of my list of "must have" plants. During my life I've grown literally thousands of different plants and this one is in my top ten. The key word for this species is erect, as most *Exochorda* are loose, arching shrubs, so already it has more appeal to the tidy gardener. And the flowering display of a good form of this species puts any other to shame. The upright racemes of white flowers in late spring simply festoon the bush.

Discovered and named by Professor Albert Regel of St Petersburg, it was introduced by him in 1886 as *Exochorda albertii*. However, by the time it was distributed, the Frenchman Lavallée had already named it as *E. korolkowii*. Plant naming rules say the first name in print is the correct one. Native of the colder regions around Turkestan in central Asia. Height 15 ft (5 m) x width 10 ft (3 m). ZONE 4.

Korolkowii = named for General Nikolai Iwanowitsch Korolkow (born 1837), who was Govenor of Sirdarja in Turkestan, the home of this plant.

Exochorda x macrantha

This is a hybrid between *Exochorda korolkowii* and *E. racemosa* raised by Messrs Lemoine of Nancy in France. It favors the latter parent, having an arching habit and lax racemes of large white flowers. A popular hybrid, **E. x macrantha 'The Bride'**, has white flowers in late spring and early summer and being tidier in habit than most *Exochorda* is better suited to suburban gardens. It has the advantage, too, of being a known quantity—you know what you are getting, whereas seedlings of the species vary. Height 6 ft (2 m) x width 10 ft (3 m). ZONE 5.

Macrantha = large flowers; from *macro* = big and *antha* = flowers.

Below: *Exochorda racemosa*

Exochorda racemosa
COMMON PEARLBUSH

A large, ungainly shrub that wins its way back into favor in spring when covered in a mass of white flowers. Branches laden with long racemes account for the species name. It tends to come into flower and leaf at the same time in warmer climates, thus losing some of the impact of flowering. It forms a big, rounded bush with a habit of producing new stems from the base in the same way as *Forsythia*. It needs lots of room or regular pruning to keep it within bounds and seems to prefer acidic or neutral soil to grow well. Native to northern China. Height x width 10–12 ft (3–4 m). ZONE 4.

Racemosa = racemes of flowers

Exochorda serratifolia

This species has the typical mass of white flowers in spring, but it also has possibly the best foliage of the genus, with its larger, serrated-edge leaves. Also, the bush tends to remain more compact than other species. It is very variable from seed, so poor clones are often seen. From northern China and Korea. Height x width 10 ft (3 m). ZONE 5.

Serratifolia = serrated-edge leaves.

Forsythia

GOLDEN BELLS
Oleaceae

This is one of the most popular shrubs in Northern Hemisphere gardens, growing happily from the cold north, down to the hot, dry regions in the south. In fact, many gardeners are put off these plants because they are so common. Yes, they are too easy to grow and yes, forsythias do look rather ordinary during the summer (and even worse in the winter), but to me that flash of bright yellow in spring is worth the eleven months of looking average. In fairness they do provide good fall colors in areas with hot summers and a dry fall.

Forsythias also earn their keep by filling spaces and roles other plants would not accept. Any soil is suitable, including the very alkaline, which can be an asset. It seems many of the plants in the olive family will accept limestone-based soil. They are not fussy about sun or semi-shade and are surprisingly easy to grow at the base of large trees, as long as there is adequate light. Drought and drafts are all taken in stride, and add to that the ability to survive transplanting at any age or size during the winter months.

Forsythias look great in flower, even when growing at the back of a border. In fact it's a good idea to tuck them in out-of-the-way sites as they will brighten up a dull spot for two or three weeks and then fade back into anonymity. It is just as well they flower early, because their strong color doesn't blend with other shrubs. Whorls of vibrant yellow flowers appear before the leaves in very early spring. They can be used for cut flowers—cut them as soon as the buds begin to open. The flowers are a series of bright yellow bells, the only color variant being a richer golden yellow.

No pruning is necessary, other than an occasional trim for shape, although they will cope with severe pruning if required. Some people recommend removing a third of the number of stems down near the base of the bush to rejuvenate it. They often

Above and below: *Forsythia* x *intermedia* 'Spectabilis'

grow new plants from layers where the arching branches have touched the ground. This is an easy way to grow more plants to give to friends and is possibly one of the reasons they are so common.

Because we use them in tough sites in our gardens, city planners have taken this to extremes, planting them on dry, inhospitable banks alongside the highway. It's no wonder we think of them as bland and not worthy of any position in our gardens. That's what you get for being a no-fuss, tough customer.

The genus was named in honor of William Forsyth (1737–1804), one of the founders of the Royal Horticultural Society and Curator of the Chelsea Physic Garden in London, England.

Forsythia giraldiana

This species can be relied upon to come into flower in late winter or very early in the spring with lovely light yellow bells. The new leaves sometimes have a bronzy tinge. It has a fairly sturdy habit

and a better shape than most. Named after the Italian missionary Guiseppe Giraldi who collected plants in Shaanxi Province in China. Height x width 12 ft (4 m). ZONE 5.

Forsythia x *intermedia* (*F. suspensa* x *F. viridissima*)

A wonderful group of hybrids with much larger flowers than most. The deep yellow blooms are 1 to 1½ in (2.5–4 cm) across and appear in early and midspring. Height x width 5 ft (1.5 m). ZONE 6.

There are some beautiful named forms, all bearing rich deep yellow flowers. Look for **'Beatrix Farrand'**, **'Karl Sax'**, **'Lynwood'** (sometimes known as **'Lynwood Gold'**) and **'Spectabilis'**. They all have large showy flowers. Typically, height for these forms is 7 ft (2.2 m) x width 5 ft (1.5 m). All ZONE 6.

Intermedia = intermediate between two forms, often used to describe a hybrid plant.

Forsythia ovata
EARLY FORSYTHIA, KOREAN FORSYTHIA
Usually just a small bush with pale yellow blossoms in early spring, this is probably the best forsythia for tidy gardeners. It is super-hardy, as you would expect coming from Korea, but like so many plants from there, it doesn't perform well in warmer climates (zone 8 and up). **Forsythia ovata var koreana** is a superior form with larger yellow flowers. **'Tetragold'** is a tetraploid form with even bigger flowers. The ¼–1¼ in (2–3 cm) blooms appear in early spring on a neat, compact bush. For all, height x width 5 ft (1.5 m). ZONE 5 TO 8.

Ovata = oval leaves.

Forsythia suspensa
WEEPING FORSYTHIA
Although it has lovely golden-yellow flowers in early to midspring, this is not a plant for tidy gardeners because of its arching, floppy habit. The name *suspensa* means hanging or lax and is usually used to refer to flowers, but in this case it is the trailing shoots. However, this can be used to advantage and this species is ideal for planting on banks or draped over retaining walls. Native of China.

Forsythia suspensa var fortunei has a more vigorous and tidier habit, growing up and then out. The flowers are dark yellow and wide-mouthed. Because of its strong, healthy growth you can cut the bush back hard each year after flowering and the new growth will be laden with flowers the following spring.

Forsythia suspensa var sieboldii is historically interesting as it was one of the first forsythias brought into cultivation from Japan. But like so many plants, it was later found to be of Chinese origin. It has been superseded by other varieties for flower-power and has the annoying habit of gaining more ground by rooting wherever the lax stems touch the ground.

For all, height x width 10 ft (3 m). ZONE 6.

Suspensa = hanging or lax.

Forsythia viridissima
GREEN-STEM FORSYTHIA
This shrub has a fairly tidy, upright habit and bright yellow flowers with a greenish cast. It is nearly always the last forsythia to come into bloom and is therefore poorly rated. Gardeners always seem to treasure the first of the season and by the end we are ho-hum. It often flowers just as the new leaves are emerging, adding

to the green haze effect. It is from China. Height 6 ft (2 m) x width 5 ft (1.5 m). ZONE 5 OR 6.

'Bronxensis' is a small bushy form ideal for city gardens. It is very floriferous, with a mass of pale yellow flowers. Height x width 3 ft (1 m).

Viridissima = green.

Fremontodendron, syn *Fremontia*

FLANNEL BUSH
Sterculiaceae

This is a genus of only two species, both from the U.S.A. and north Mexico. Both are grown for their large, showy, yellow flowers. They will not cope with shade from trees, though they can be grown or trained against a wall where it is well lit but not necessarily sunny all day. In hot, dry climates or in poor soil they put on modest annual growth and remain reasonably tidy. The stress of the situation also seems to make them flower more profusely, but they get thin and rangy in a lush climate where it is hard to keep a good shape to the bush. Poor sandy or rocky soils are just perfect. They need very good drainage and seem indifferent to acidity or alkalinity. Choose a breezy, open site with low humidity. They like plenty of space, so don't crowd them with other shrubs. The tops are tolerant of wind, with the fine hairs protecting them from damage and water loss. However, the branches are brittle and the bush is often blown clean out of the ground as they become top heavy.

Fremontodendron californicum
CALIFORNIA FLANNEL BUSH

They say all good things can be found in California, well this is surely one of them. This absolutely splendid plant grows in the dry hills of southern California, Arizona and Mexico, and, as you would imagine, thrives in hot, dry conditions and resents humidity. The glossy golden flowers are a treasure and the plant doesn't stint on numbers, producing hundreds of flowers, each one lasting for weeks at a time. The bush is literally smothered in flowers all through summer and beyond. So if it is a dazzling display of color you want, this plant is hard to beat. Each flower is the size of a small coffee cup (2 in/5 cm across), but better described as a golden chalice. (The showy bit is actually a calyx and not petals, but let's not quibble when it looks this good.)

The pointed seed capsules contain hard, jet-black seeds for starting a new generation. They need soaking overnight to germinate. Sometimes the plants flower and seed so profusely they go into a decline.

The leaves and stems are covered in a coating of fine brown hairs that help protect the plant from the hot sun, wind and water loss. In high humidity areas these hairs trap moisture and cause the plant to decline. They are reasonably cold-tolerant if it's a hot summer/cold winter climate, though they can lose a portion of their leaves in winter. The leaves are shaped like the ace of clubs, usually with three lobes and occasionally up to seven.

Fremontodendron can be trained against a wall, almost espalier-like, thereby showing off the flowers to perfection. The wall gives them extra heat, shelter and stability. Pruning may be necessary to keep the plant orderly and compact. Have a care when pruning because the rusty wool covering on the stems and the seed pods can be a real skin irritant. Children use it as itching powder. It's not poisonous, just irritating. Occasionally caterpillars take a liking to the young leaves, but the dreaded root rot is the biggest threat.

The plant has one or two other drawbacks. They are not usually long-lived and sometimes die overnight for no apparent reason. Because they hate being shifted, they are sold as small potted plants. Don't ever try to move one; it will be the death of it for sure. Even when planted out from pots, they sometimes keel over.

Another problem is they look rather scruffy as potted plants and are not very appealing when seen for sale in garden centers. This accounts for the scarcity of fremontodendrons in most parts of the world. It's a plant you have to seek out, but I assure you it's well worth the hunt. If you want a sublime combination, plant it next to a fellow Californian, a blue ceanothus. The rich blue and golden yellow combination is simply stupendous.

It was discovered by John Charles Frémont (1813–1890), a surveyor and pioneer of the West, who made several hazardous journeys in this region and was the first person to see and describe the Joshua tree. Height 20 ft (6 m) x width 12 ft (4 m). ZONE 8.

Right:
Fremontodendron californicum 'California Glory'

There is another species, **Fremontodendron mexicanum**, with shinier, five-lobed leaves. The flowers are more starry shaped and sometimes more orange than yellow. It was discovered as recently as 1926 by Miss K.O. Sessions near Encenado, Mexico. Height 20 ft (6 m) x width 12 ft (4 m). ZONE 9.

A hybrid, **'California Glory'**, has bigger, brighter flowers up to 2½ in (6 cm) across. It also has more of them and so is worth seeking out. The other bonus is that it produces few seeds and therefore lives longer. Height 20 ft (6 m) x width 12 ft (4 m). ZONE 8.

'Pacific Sunset' and **'San Gabriel'** are two other prolific-flowering hybrids with similar-sized yellow flowers to 'California Glory'. For both, height 20 ft (6 m) x width 12 ft (4 m). ZONE 8.

Fuchsia

Onagraceae

Fuchsias are mainly South and Central American shrubs with just a few siblings in far away Tahiti and New Zealand. A mixture of evergreen and semi-deciduous species, they have become a fixture in gardens and conservatories all over the world. They are treasured for their profuse flowers in unique and showy colors. Their popularity is helped by being easy to grow and they are also easily propagated, making them a regular gift between friends.

For the most part, fuchsias don't like the cold and need to be in near frost-free conditions. They prefer a climate which is moist year-round and will benefit from a little shade and shelter. Some even grow in seaside localities given enough protection. Having said that, I've seen fuchsias broken and defoliated by storms and just a week or two later they were fully clothed and laden with flowers, so they have remarkable powers of recovery. The fact they flower on new growth is useful, and so any damage is soon mended.

Their preference is for moist, well-drained soil in a sheltered location with morning sun. Yet they will grow in clay soils in full sun if that is what they are given. Alkaline soils are acceptable too, though they do sometimes look pale and anaemic and would benefit from a little acidic fertilizer. Dry soil or drought is the biggest threat to their well-being. Mulching helps keep the roots moist and deters frosts, or you could plant low shrubs, such as ericas, at the base of the plant for frost protection. The tops of the bush may be frosted in winter, but providing the base of the bush survives they will quickly regenerate in the spring. In fact, they need pruning in spring to encourage new growth and thus more flowers.

Aphids can be a pest in spring, as well as whitefly and mildews, but for the most part they are easy-care shrubs. They transplant easily from pots and even quite large specimens can be moved if the top growth is cut back. Named after Leonard Fuchs (1501–1566), a German botanist who first proposed the idea that plants and animals have just two Latin names. Linneaus was later to get the credit for this concept.

Above: *Fuchsia hybrida* 'Bicentennial'

Fuchsia arborescens, syn *F. arborea*
LILAC FUCHSIA

A bold, head-high bush with handsome dark leaves and unusual flowers. They are in clusters at the tips of the stems and the little, starry, lilac-pink blooms are not immediately recognizable as a fuchsia, and it tends to have one burst of flowers in spring rather than all summer as most fuchsias do. Native of Mexico and Central America. Height x width 10 ft (3 m). ZONE 8 OR 9.

Arborescens = tree like.

Left: *Fuchsia arborescens*

Above: *Fuchsia magellanica* 'Variegata'

Fuchsia hybrida

The lovely common garden fuchsias are a complex group of hybrids grown simply for their stunning flowers in combinations of white, pink, red, plum and purple. Most of them have hanging flowers with a big, waxy calyx and a circle of showy petals beneath with big, whiskery stamens. Most prefer a cool, moist, shady spot and many are grown in containers on patios or in conservatories. Height x width 3–6 ft (1–2 m). ZONE 8 OR 9.

Above: *Fuchsia* 'Thalia'

Fuchsia magellanica

This species has dense, dark foliage and lots of small, red, bell-shaped flowers in typical fuchsia fashion. Each flower has shiny red sepals and an inner corolla of purple petals. It is a great little flowering shrub for borders around the house and is in flower for months in the summer. It was named after Ferdinand Magellan, the Portugese explorer who sailed around the bottom of South America and named the Pacific Ocean. It is probably the hardiest species and is sometimes grown as a hedge. Native of Chile and Argentina. Height x width 10 ft (3 m). ZONE 7 or 8 (with protection).

Fuchsia riccartonii (syn *F.* **'Riccartonii'**), named after the Riccarton Garden in Edinburgh, Scotland, is similar in flower to *F. magellanica*, and possibly even hardier. Height 10 ft (3 m) x width 6 ft (2 m). ZONE 7 OR 8 (with protection).

Fuchsia 'Thalia'

One of the hardier hybrids with *F. triphylla* blood, this fuchsia has long, striking, tubular flowers in hot orangy red. A small, dense bush, it is ideal for narrow borders, providing flowers over several months during summer. It will grow in sun or part-shade. Height x width 1½ to 3 ft (45–90 cm). ZONE 9.

'Gartenmeister Bonstedt' is similar with darker bronzy leaves and brick-red flowers. It is a very free-flowering, upright bush. Height 2–3 ft (60–90 cm) x width 1½–2 ft (45–60 cm). ZONE 9.

Left: *Fuchsia hybrida* 'Glenby'

Left: *Garrya elliptica*

Garrya

Garryaceae

Who was Mr. Garry after which this genus was named? Nicholas Garry was a director for the Hudson Bay Company from 1822 to 1835. He had two forts named after him as well—inspiringly called Upper Fort Garry and Lower Fort Garry. Some plants are named after daring explorers who risked life and limb, but just as often they are named after some local dignitary. In this case Mr. Garry helped the intrepid botanist David Douglas (1799–1834), who for all his courage only ended up with a little herbaceous plant named after him, *Douglasia laevigata*. All of the *Garrya* species come from the western U.S.A. down into Mexico and most have failed to make an impact with gardeners even though they are quite attractive. They all have long catkin-like flowers reminiscent of hazelnuts or *Corylus*.

Garrya elliptica
SILKTASSEL BUSH

Garrya is a fine plant to have named after you, even though only one of the species seems to be seen in gardens, and even then it is only the one sex. The *Garrya elliptica* seen in gardens is inevitably the male form of the shrub. The familiar long tassels are the male flowers, while the shorter female flowers are found on a separate plant, which is hardly ever seen. The strange-looking tassel flowers show up well against the bold green background of the leaves.

They are as long as a hand (6–8 in/15–20 cm) and look like strange prehistoric caterpillars. The overlapping, yellowy-gray scales open up to become a loose-fitting collection over a central strand with the flowers attached in under the scales. If you have a female bush you'll have the bonus of small, grape-like, purply fruits.

Garrya elliptica is a big, bold, rounded evergreen with thick, leathery leaves, smooth dark green above and wooly beneath, with slightly wavy margins. Some say the plant is tender, but in my experience I've seen better specimens in cold regions than any milder climates I've visited. It also seems quite resistant to strong winds, that is, at least the leaves are tough enough, but sometimes the whole plant can be blown over. (Plants are often described as wind-hardy when the leaves cope with strong or constant winds, but so often these same plants get blown clean out of the ground in a real storm, mainly because they get top-heavy.)

In theory this species should thrive in a Mediterannean-like climate, but they seem more prone to stem borer and root rot in these milder regions. It will grow near the sea and handles city pollution, too. Best grown in full sun, it will cope with part-shade when grown against a wall, but it doesn't like shade from overhead trees. It is a particularly splendid sight trained against a wall, especially when the cascade of flowers smothers the fan of foliage. Flowering begins in midwinter to late spring depending on the climate. Perversely it seems to flower later in warm climates.

They cope with drought, but are happy in wet climates, too. Drought-hardiness is an asset, especially when planted in the lee of a wall, which receives little rain. It'll be quite happy on a dry, sunny bank and is not fussy about soil, growing in clays or sand, as long as the drainage is reasonable. It hates being transplanted from

Right: *Gordonia axillaris*

open ground and is grown in pots for safety, so take care when you plant it out and tie it to a cane until established. Don't be tempted to move it to another site. Native to western U.S.A. Height x width 12 ft (4 m). ZONE 7 OR 8.

'James Roof' is a selected male clone with extremely long 8 in (20 cm) catkins. Height x width 6 ft (2 m).

Elliptica = refers to its elliptical leaves, they are twice as long as they are wide.

Gordonia

Theaceae

Imagine a camellia on steroids and you have some idea of what their large and robust relatives, the gordonias, look like. When you see the flowers they look like a single camellia flower, but tend to be thin-petalled, single and very delicate-looking. Thankfully looks deceive, and the flowers are robust enough to provide a show for gardeners. It is tempting to compare them to fried eggs because the white papery outer petals surround a central boss of golden yellow stamens. These glossy-leafed big cousins of camellias grow very fast and in less than five years you will have a large shrub. Although the growth slows, they do become trees, some with very appealing bark.

If you have room, they are definitely worth growing for their luxuriant foliage and masses of white flowers. Like camellias, they are easy to grow given plenty of sun, acidic to neutral soil and reasonable drainage. They prefer a moist soil, but can handle drought conditions. Gordonias are easy to transplant, and apart from an occasional caterpillar chewing the leaves, pest free and easy-care.

Gordonias thrive in warm climates and flower best in regions with hot summers. They are quite happy in scorching sunlight, but will put up with some shade. It seems most of them will cope with cool winters if they have had enough summer heat to ripen the wood. It is in moist, mild climates that they are more likely to be damaged by frost and cold.

These evergreen shrubs provide another link between the plants of eastern North America and China, with species of this genus being found in both continents. They are named for Alexander James Gordon (c. 1770), a nurseryman at Mile End, London, England.

Gordonia axillaris

This dense evergreen has been in cultivation a long time without ever setting the horticultural world alight. However, given a hot summer climate it will thrill you with a series of white flowers over a long period from fall through to spring. In mild climates it is often in flower in midwinter, but more sensibly is a spring-flowering bush in colder regions. The bush is rarely laden with flowers at any one time, but they tend to appear in succession. Crinkled papery-white petals surround a big boss of golden yellow stamens almost the exact size of fried egg (3–5 in/8–13 cm across).

Neat, finger-length, dark green leaves are glossy and almost laurel-like. They spiral up around the green stems and the flowers are tucked in the axils, hence the species name *axillaris*. The plants often appear ungainly as the weight of the stems distorts what would otherwise be a neat habit. It tends to be slower-growing and tidier if grown in a drier climate, and eventually forms a small tree. It is then that you can make a feature of the smooth, peeling, brown trunks. It will grow and flower in shade if you have a hot summer/cold winter climate. It is also more wind-hardy than the other species, as the leaves are tough and leathery and the structure of the plant is solid and stable. Native to south China and Taiwan. Height x width 22–30 ft (7–10 m). ZONE 8 OR 9, but I have seen it in zone 7 with hot summers.

Axillaris = refers to the flowers appearing in the axils.

Gordonia lasianthus
LOBLOLLY BAY

Gordonia lasianthus grows naturally in the warmer southeastern states of the U.S.A., from Virginia to Louisiana and down to Florida, often growing in wet places. Creamy white blossoms with a delicate fragrance appear in high summer. It becomes a large, upright shrub or small tree and can be ungainly when young, but it usually improves with age. The rich green, long, glossy leaves sometimes have a reddish-bronze tinge. The plant seems to handle a variety of climates and soils and is generally quite easy to grow. Height 30 ft (10 m) x width 15–20 ft (5–6 m). ZONE 8.

Lasianthus = hairy flowered (*lasi* = hairy).

Gordonia yunnanensis
This species is a fairly new introduction to our gardens and without a doubt it is one of the best shrubs to be found. The mass of white, camellia-like flowers, each with a yellow center of stamens, appear in late winter and spring and are a real show-stopper. The leaves are shiny, pointed and serrated, but it is their color and glossiness that makes this the best of the gordonias. The color is hard to describe: it is reddish-bronze at first, maturing to bronze with a sheen of gray.

This plant has an upright habit when young and is very fast-growing. The outer stems are quite lax, which is typical of gordonias, especially when grown in a mild, moist climate. It has a tidier habit and flowers more prolifically in the winter months as long as it is given hot summers. The narrow-angled branchs are prone to split in strong winds, but it copes well with drought and shade.

Native to Yunnan Province, China. Height 30 ft (10 m) x width 15–20 ft (5–6 m). ZONE 9 (7 with hot summers).

Gordonia chrysandra and *G. szechuanica* are similar species, both height 30 ft (10 m) x width 15–20 ft (5–6 m). ZONE 9 (7 with hot summers).

Yunnanensis = from Yunnan Province, China.

Halesia

SILVERBELL, SNOWDROP TREE
Styracaceae

Until recently *Halesia* was thought of as an exclusively North American genus, growing only in the eastern U.S.A., but with new discoveries it seems that, like *Liquidambar* and *Liriodendron*, it also has Chinese relatives—namely *H. macgregori*. It is a somewhat confused genus, even in North America, where some botanists classify it as three or more species, others say they are all variants of just one. But be it one, two, three or four species, they are all wonderful. The little, white, snowdrop-like flowers dripping off the branches in spring are delectable. They usually appear before the leaves, though in some regions they appear simultaneously. There is a lot of variation in flower size and even in color, as some have pink flowers.

Growing naturally on the slopes of mountains, they need good drainage and as young plants they are prone to root rot if the soil stays wet for too long. Otherwise they seem free of pests and diseases. Their mountain home means they like a cool, moist climate but they will cope with drought once established. Ideally give them a good, deep, acidic or neutral soil and a spot in full sun or just dappled shade. *Halesia* sparkle in a clearing within a woodland setting, sheltered from the worst of winds. It is hard to imagine them as stand-alone suburban garden trees because they are so prone to wind damage.

Plant them out from open ground, and older plants can be shifted during the winter months when they've lost their leaves.

Above: *Halesia carolina*

Left: *Gordonia axillaris* with new foliage.

Teddington, near London, and like many a man of the cloth, he was a botanist in his spare time. Hales was the first person to study the movement of water in plants and also proved that circulating blood exerts pressure. He is also credited with discovering the "medicinal value of fresh air" and worked on ventilators to extract polluted air from factories, hospitals and ships.

Halesia carolina, syn *H. tetraptera*
CAROLINA SILVERBELL

This plant forms a small tree with clusters of white flowers in spring. On a good specimen, the stems can be dripping with flowers. The plants vary from seed and ideally you should use named forms for consistancy. When it is good, it is one of the most beautiful of all hardy flowering trees. Grows naturally from Virginia down to Florida. Height 20 ft (6 m) x 15 ft (5 m). ZONE 4 OR 5.

Carolina = from the state.

Halesia diptera
TWO-WINGED SILVERBELL

Usually a small tree in gardens, *Halesia diptera* has a reputation for being less hardy than others of this genus, which is understandable as it comes from the region of South Carolina down to Florida. It is also considered to be a shy-flowering tree and seems to need a warm climate to flower well. The lovely white, bell-shaped flowers appear in spring and are followed by two-winged fruits. Height 20 ft (6 m) x width 30 ft (10 m). ZONE 5.

Diptera = two wings, referring to the fruits.
(*H. carolina* has four-winged fruits.)

Halesia monticola
MOUNTAIN SILVERBELL

To the casual observer the only difference between this species and *Halesia carolina* is that *H. monticola* is a bigger tree with bigger flowers (around 1 in/2.5 cm long). The flowers are white and bell-shaped and appear in late spring.

The variety *Halesia monticola* var *vestita* has even bigger flowers, as well as leaves covered in a wooly indumentum underneath (*vestita* means hairy, or clothed). There is also a pink-flowered form called **'Rosea'**. All three flower when quite young (in less than 10 years), whereas some flowering trees seem to take an age to come into flower. The fruits have four wings. It is native to the mountains of North Carolina and Tennessee. Being the mountain version, it is hardier than other species and is considered the best *Halesia* for gardens in colder regions. For all, height 40 ft (12 m) x width 25 ft (8 m). ZONE 4 OR 5.

Monticola = from the mountains.

Right: *Halesia carolina* with fall color.

Halesia can be grown in pots, but they are not very happy about it. Mature plants have a reasonable shape without any exciting structure and can have a rather twiggy, messy interior. However, you won't ever need to prune them. If it were a tidier plant it might have more appeal. They have simple, rather plain, leaves though the fall color can be a pretty yellow-gold.

Friends argue over whether this genus name should be pronounced *Hale-sia* or *Ha-lesia*. But perhaps knowing the genus was named for Stephen Hales is a help. Hales reached the ripe old age of 90 before his death in 1761. He was curate of

Hardenbergia

CORAL PEA
Fabaceae

This plant is potentially a super climber for walls and trellises near the entrance to your home and for patios. And if you are a lover of blue flowers—and most of us are—it will captivate you. Like many evergreen climbers, it is not hardy, but this can be alleviated by attaching it to a warm wall or using trellis to grow the plant up and away from ground

frosts. If your climate is really cold, then I'm sorry but you will have to grow it as a conservatory plant. However, it is well worth the effort.

Like most climbers it likes its roots in the shade and tops in the sun. Unlike many climbers it is not too vigorous and doesn't require the same vigilance as, say, jasmine. Being a legume it is not too fussy about the soil, growing in light or heavy ground as long as the drainage is reasonable and the soil is acidic to neutral.

Wind is tolerated by the plant, but the leaves become ragged and burnt and so even though the plant is surviving it is no longer beautiful. Caterpillars, scale insects and aphids can be a problem.

The climber can be pruned back after flowering, but it depends on how vigorous it has been the previous summer. Don't ever be tempted to shift a mature plant. When purchased from nurseries, however, they do transplant easily from pots. They can also be grown as a luxurious ground cover on banks.

Hardenbergia = named for Countess van Hardenberg (c. 1800s).

Hardenbergia comptoniana

The long, narrow, dark green leaves of this vigorous climber set off the 6 in (15 cm) long racemes of purple or lilac flowers that appear from early spring into midsummer. Grows naturally in western Australia. Height 10 ft (3 m) or more. ZONE 9.

Comptoniana = origin obscure.

Hardenbergia violacea, syn H. monophylla
PURPLE CORAL PEA

This is the tougher of the two species and its stunning purple flowers in long showy racemes appear in late winter and go on into

Above: *Hardenbergia comptoniana*

spring, giving a long-lasting display. It has deep green, narrow, single leaves. Native of southern Australia, Queensland and Tasmania. Height 6 ft (2 m) or more. ZONE 9 (8 with protection).

Violacea = violet colored.

Hebe

Scrophulariaceae

This genus is named after the Greek goddess of youth, who was the cup-bearer of Olympus and the daughter of Jupiter (who later became wife of Hercules), so it has a lot to live up to. With a background like that you'd expect them to be tough, and they are. Native to New Zealand, these shrubs grow wild on the seashores and high mountains of this windswept country. Any plant that grows happily in these conditions is fantastic for gardeners, and hebes are ideal for drafty places where you need a tough, dense evergreen. They have become a garden and municipal planting standby in some regions as they tolerate exposure to hot sun, wind and salt, as well as industrial and car pollution. This is not to say that they must be treated badly. As with all plants, they will perform much better given good soil and less extreme conditions.

Apart from their usefulness as garden plants, it is the stunning spikes of flowers, around thumb- to finger-length, that make this genus stand out. Each spike is made up of hundreds of lop-sided flowers with one petal up and three down—rather like pea flowers. The spikes are held aloft above the bush in opposite pairs and a whole bush covered in bloom can be quite a sight, with bright colors ranging from pale mauves and white, to strong purples, reds and blues. Pairs of flowers open successively up the stem, further extending the flowering period.

Hebes like an open, sunny and breezy site and tend to lose their leaves if they are crowded. Too much humid shade and they do not flourish or flower well. Some of the smaller cushion varieties are ideal for rockeries and small patios. In general, the silvery-gray leaf types or the whipcord varieties are hardier to cold. The whipcord varieties have tight, nuggety foliage like plaited string or cord, a bit like an erica or calluna.

One of the best things about hebes is they have a neat and tidy habit. A typical plant is a dense, rounded, evergreen bush with attractive leaves. Even the way the leaves are held on the stems is orderly. The leaves are in opposite pairs, and the pairs are at right angles to each other so that they form a cross when seen from above. Some species have long, slim, grass green leaves, others have leaves in shades of purple or maroon, and many species have stunning silver or gray foliage. While some species can grow to 16 ft (5 m), the ones we usually see in gardens are knee- to waist-high.

As soon as most of the flowers are spent, it is a good idea to take the shears to the bush and trim it lightly all over, thus keeping a better shape and making it bush up more. They can get rather leggy and sparse if not trimmed, and are inclined to die out from the middle if allowed to grow too fast. If your plant is already sparse, you can take it with the loppers and cut the stems back to stumps. Most times the bush responds by growing a new coat of leaves and looks surprisingly good, but be aware

Above: *Hebe albicans* with *Hebe pimeliodes* at the back.

that just occasionally it kills the shrub off. In other words it is "kill or cure," but thankfully it is usually the latter.

Pests include a black spot-type disease that is devastating to some species and non-existant in others. The disease seems to prefer the dark purple- and red-flowered forms the most.

A peculiarity of hebes is their thick mat of roots just under the surface. In this regard they are very much like rhododendrons and, like them, they can be easily dug up and transplanted to another site. It usually pays to trim back the top of the bush to compensate for the loss of roots in the shift. As a further bonus, weeds struggle to get a toehold among the dense roots and the shade supplied by the canopy of leaves.

Hebe = Greek goddess of youth.

Hebe albicans

A dense little mound of a plant with pale gray-green, waxy leaves. Small clusters of white flowers appear near the tips in spring or early summer. Native to New Zealand. Height 24 in (60 cm) x width 36 in (90 cm). ZONE 7.

Albicans = glistening white.

Hebe cupressoides

It is not surprising that this species is called *cupressoides*, as the dense, dark green, whipcord stems look just like sprays of *Cupressus*, that is until the white or pale lilac flowers appear in early summer. From New Zealand. Height x width 4 ft (1.2 m). ZONE 6.

Cupressoides = like a *Cupressus*.

Hebe hulkeana

Possibly the best species for flowers, with the long sprays of delicate white, with just a hint of pink or lilac, appearing in late spring and early summer. It is not such a tidy bush, however, and it often has an open, rangy habit. It is very drought-tolerant and reasonably frost-hardy too. Grows naturally in New Zealand. Height x width 24 in (60 cm). ZONE 7 OR 8.

Hulkeana = named for T. H. Hulke.

Left: *Hebe* 'Oratia Beauty'

Above: *Hebe* 'Autumn Glory'

Hebe pinguifolia 'Pagei'

A hardy prostrate or ground-cover shrub with tough, little, blue-gray leaves. It is worth growing for the foliage alone, but the clusters of white flowers are a wonderful bonus in early summer. Height 12 in (30 cm) x width 36 in (90 cm). ZONE 7.

Pinguifolia = fat or plump foliage.

Hebe speciosa

This has to be one of the best flowering hebe species (*speciosa* means beautiful). The big, bold, thumb-sized leaves are glossy and dark green, often with a hint of purple, and the 4 in (10 cm) long flower spikes look like bottle-brushes in deep red or purple. It is an ideal plant for gardens near the sea, but not hardy enough for colder inland areas. Native to New Zealand. Height x width 4 ft (1.2 m). ZONE 8 OR 9.

Speciosa = beautiful.

Helianthemum

ROCK ROSE, SUN ROSE
Cistaceae

Helianthemums look as if they belong at the beach. In fact they do grow well near the sea, but they are just as happy in cold inland sites, providing they have lots of sun and really good drainage. They almost seem to thrive on poor fare and neglect. Start to feed them or coddle them and they quietly slip away and leave you wondering what used to fill that space. They grow in open mountain, and sometimes coastal, areas across parts of Asia, North and South America and Europe, especially around the Mediterannean.

Most helianthemums are low, even prostrate, ground-cover shrubs, and the ongoing mass of coin-sized flowers all summer makes them perfect garden plants. There are numerous hybrids, which vary in appearance; some are compact with shiny green leaves, while others are more open with grayish or silver leaves covered in soft hairs—all are evergreen.

The range of flower colors is from soft yellows and white through to pink, red, scarlet and orange. Add to this the fact that

some are double flowers and you can see there is a tremendous range available. All they need to thrive is sun and good drainage. They don't mind if the soil is acidic or alkaline, and they cope with wind and storms.

Like all plants in this family, rock roses hate being shifted, so transplant young specimens with care and don't be tempted to move them again. A light trim with the shears after flowering or perhaps early in the spring is a good idea to keep them dense and bushy. They flower on new wood, so the time to prune depends on your climate. In cold regions, it is probably better to prune in spring before they think about flowering as you won't have enough warm weather for them to regrow if you prune them late summer.

It can be tricky keeping them free of weeds because they are low-growing and not quite dense enough to suppress the weeds, so start with a weed-free site and mulch them well.

Helios = Greek for sun; *anthos* = flowers.

Below: *Helianthemum nummularium* cultivars

Helianthemum apenninum
WHITE ROCK ROSE
Thin, gray leaves accompany white, anemone-like flowers, with a boss of bright yellow stamens in the center. This species flowers in midsummer and forms a low-growing mat, making it ideal for banks and rockeries. Native to Europe. Height 16 in (40 cm) x width 24 in (60 cm). ZONE 6.

Apenninum = after a mountain range in Italy.

Helianthemum canadense
FROSTWEED
Bright yellow, single flowers appear in early summer on a small shrub with thin, green leaves covered in gray hairs underneath. This species is native to Canada and the eastern United States. Height 12–16 in (30–40 cm) x width 24 in (60 cm). ZONE 5.

Canadense = from Canada.

Helianthemum nummularium
A low-growing shrub that grows up and then tumbles out across the ground, forming a perfect ground cover. The greeny leaves are white or gray below and the button-like yellow flowers only last a day, but a succession of them opens from midsummer onward. Native to Europe. Height 12–16 in (30–40 cm) x width 24 in (60 cm). ZONE 6.

The clone **'Amy Baring'**, found in the French Pyrenees, is most commonly seen in gardens, as it has deeper yellow flowers and a more compact growth habit. Height 12 in (30 cm) x width 24 in (60 cm).

Nummularium = like money wort.

Hibiscus

Malvaceae

The flowers of *Hibiscus* are so outstanding in color, size and form that we would all grow them if we could. Unfortunately, not everyone has the climate for most of these exotic beasts. If there is one thing they like in abundance it is sun, sun and more sun. The heat that comes with it is also essential, but heat alone without the sun means they don't flower as well and are not as healthy. Even the very hardy *H. syriacus*, which grows to zone 5, always looks much better and is laden with flowers in a hot continental-type climate. So if your climate is marginal and you want to grow hibiscus then you'll have to find the hottest, sunniest spot (or grow them in containers). Dry places under the eaves of buildings are ideal, especially as the reflected heat from the wall increases the annual temperature by at least a zone. Choose a sheltered site away from cold or damaging winds.

Most hibiscus are evergreens, others are deciduous and some die down altogether. There are even annuals and biennials, so it is hard to generalise about their shape or habit. They are not fussy about soil or acidity, and some will grow in very hard, poor soil, and a few in swamps or even water.

Hibiscus = from an old Greek name for marshmallow, a related plant.

Hibiscus moscheutos, syn H. palustris
COMMON ROSE MALLOW, SWAMP ROSE MALLOW
It is cheating a tiny bit to include this plant in the "woody" plant series, but they do build up a woody base. Lush soft stems emerge

Above: *Hibiscus moscheutos*

each spring and are topped with huge flowers—bigger than your outstretched hand (up to 8 in/20 cm across)—and then they die back down to this woody base in the winter. The flowers can be white, pink or shades of red. Found naturally in the eastern states of the U.S.A., like most hibiscus they thrive on summer heat. Height 8 ft (2.5 m) x width 3 ft (1 m). ZONE 5.

Hibiscus coccineus is similar.

Moscheutos = mallow rose.

Hibiscus rosa-sinensis
CHINESE ROSE, HAWAIIAN HIBISCUS, ROSE OF CHINA
Somehow I always pictures these bright-red flowers behind the ear of a beautiful dusky maiden. Travel brochures for exotic locations

Above: *Hibiscus rosa-sinensis*

always seem to have a pretty girl with a hibiscus flower in her hair. The name means Chinese rose, which is also the common name, and it is a sub-tropical shrub from south China. In the warmer parts of the world numerous different-colored hybrids and forms are available, though the species itself is a simple single, scarlet flower 4 in (10 cm) across. Give them as much heat and sunshine as possible. The next essential ingredient is perfect drainage. It's often said they are more likely to die from cold, wet soil than from frosts. Height 8–15 ft (2.5–5 m) x width 5–10 ft (1.5–3 m). ZONE 9.

Rosa-sinensis = China rose.

Hibiscus syriacus
ROSE OF SHARON

One of the oldest shrubs in cultivation, it has been grown in Europe for over 400 years and cultivated in China for thousands. Chinese people have used the leaves for making a kind of tea and the flowers are eaten as a tasty morsel. Named by Carl Linnaeus, it was mistakenly called *syriacus*, as if from Syria, when in fact it comes from Asia.

Even though they are deciduous and hardy, these plants love hot summers and perform much better in a continental climate. They are happy in any soil and quite drought-tolerant once established, although the flowering display will be better if you can keep the soil moist or mulched.

It is a great city plant, coping with both neglect and pollution. The upright bush is 10–12 ft (3–4 m) and usually clothed to the ground with branches. It is quite flexible and wind-hardy. You can prune severely if necessary, and it is possible to transplant even aged bushes if you cut back the top to compensate for the loss of roots. They flower on new growth, which allows pruning in spring.

Each flower only lasts a day, but the bush continues flowering from midsummer until the first frosts. The flowers come in a range of colors including red, white and blue, often with a red or purple throat. This colored blotch usually runs into the petals, creating an ink-spot effect. There are double forms, but I think they lack the charm of the singles and they are more prone to bud rot.

Above: *Hibiscus syriacus* 'Red Heart'

In cool, wet climates *H. syriacus* hybrids are often poor in flower and sometimes the buds go moldy with botrytis, rather like roses. Height 10–12 ft (3–4 m) x width 6 ft (2 m). ZONE 5.

Syriacus = from Syria.

Popular *Hibiscus syriacus* cultivars include: **'Blue Bird'**, its beautiful blue flowers have a dark eye in the center of the flower. **'Diana'**, a lovely large, single white. **'Helene'**, a very large, semi-double, white-flowered cultivar with just a hint of pink and a red blotch in the center of the flower. **'Pink Giant'**, has pink flowers with a red central blotch. **'Red Heart'**, has large, white flowers with a red center. **'Woodbridge'** has rosy pink flowers with a red eye. For all, height 10–12 ft (3–4 m) x width 6 ft (2 m).

Above: *Hibiscus syriacus* 'Blue Bird'

Holodiscus

Holodiscus discolor
OCEAN SPRAY
Rosaceae

The graceful, arching shrub is particularly useful as the creamy white plumes of flowers hang gracefully from the tips of the stems in midsummer, a time when few shrubs seem to flower. A smell like musty cupboards or wholemeal flour is obvious when you get close to the blooms. It was first discovered by David Douglas in California in 1827 and initially classified as a *Spiraea*.

The bush grows fairly upright at first, to around 10 ft (3 m), and gradually fills out to become a graceful, arching shrub. It does get wider as it gets older and may need to be kept in check. A bit of judicious pruning after flowering keeps the bush tidy, but it is not going to look dreadful if you forget to prune it.

The small oval leaves have a grayish, downy surface and are white beneath. This is an ideal plant for sunny edges in a woodland garden or perhaps near the back of a herbaceous border where the flowers will coincide with the perennials. The rank smell of the flowers may be another reason to plant them at the back of the border. Give it a dark background to show off the creamy flowers.

It is very hardy, coping with cold, poor soil and drying winds. It won't mind an occasional drought and likewise is happy in wet regions. There are no pests or diseases of note. With the fibrous root system, you can move the plant any time during winter, when there are no leaves, and its semi-suckering habit means that it is possible to divide a portion to create a new plant. Native to western North America. Height x width 10–12 ft (3–4 m). ZONE 5.

Holos = entire and *discos* = disk; *discolor* = different colors.

Above: *Holodiscus discolor*

Hydrangea

Hydrangeaceae

For me, hydrangeas are the most marvellous flowering shrub on the planet—there is such diversity of leaf and habit as well as sheer flower power. They are also easy to grow, and I'm a fan of anything that wants to be in my garden.

The hydrangeas we see in cultivation are all deciduous shrubs and generally quite hardy. Reliable, easy-care plants, they provide us with fabulous summer color when most shrubs are looking dull. Not only do they provide show-stopping flowers from midsummer onward, they make the most wonderful cut flowers. Hydrangeas grow in virtually any soil, be it acidic or alkaline, and some even grow in wet places, which is most unusual. Add to this the fact that many will grow in shade as well as sun and some are suitable for pots and tubs and you can begin to see just how versatile they are.

Hydrangea = Greek word "hydros," meaning water and "angeion," meaning a vessel, because of the cup form of the seed capsule. (The genus name is nothing to do with their love of water, as is thought by some.)

Hydrangea arborescens
SMOOTHLEAF HYDRANGEA, SILVERLEAF HYDRANGEA, HILLS OF SNOW, SEVENBARK
Native to eastern parts of North America, this was the first hydrangea species in cultivation. It has soft pale green leaves and, in summer, white lacecap flowers 6 in (15 cm) across appear. Height x width 10 ft (3 m). ZONE 3.

There is a splendid cultivar called **'Annabelle'** with huge pompom-like heads of white flowers up to 12 in (30 cm) across.

Left: *Hydrangea arborescens* 'Annabelle' just as the flowers open to white.

Above: *Hydrangea aspera* var *villosa*

This cultivar is often tricky to establish, acting at first like a perennial plant, dying down almost to ground level each winter, before eventually growing into a woody shrub. It needs a sheltered site but is very hardy to winter cold. Height x width 10 ft (3 m). ZONE 3.

Arborescens = from Latin for tree-like.

Hydrangea aspera var *villosa*, syn *H. villosa*

This is the best garden plant of the many forms of *Hydrangea aspera* found in Asia. The leaves are long, pointed and hairy and quite different from how we imagine hydrangeas ought to look. The pink and mauve lacecap flowers appear in late summer and will send you into ecstasies. It is able to cope with more heat and drought than most hydrangeas, but it must have good drainage. An alkaline soil is acceptable. Native of China. Height x width 4–12 ft (1.2–4 m). ZONE 7.

Aspera = rough; *villosa* = hairy, because of the hairy leaves and stems.

Hydrangea macrophylla

BIGLEAF HYDRANGEA, FLORIST'S HYDRANGEA

This is the plant we all think of when someone mentions hydrangeas. They have big leaves and flat, lacecap flowers or big, round, mophead flowers. Hydrangeas are full of surprises, and despite its big leaves, this species is robust and wind-hardy (some even grow on coastal cliff-tops). Most will grow in sun or shade, and don't mind wet soil. This is part of the reason I love hydrangeas. So few shrubs want to grow in shade, especially such floriferous plants, and growing in wet soil is just a no-no for virtually every shrub. So if you've got a boggy bit of ground and wondered what you could grow in it, try one of these hydrangeas.

They will grow in acidic soil, where the flowers will be blue, or in alkaline soil, where the flowers will be pink or red. The white flowers stay white whatever the soil. That is until the fall, when they take on lovely shades of pink or in some cases a pale green. Having given you color for four months of summer, you can cut them and get another six months of indoor color.

Such wonderful floriferous shrubs are rare and being such easy-care plants they should be used, especially as they flower in summer when we spend more time in the garden. There are so many cultivars available, you can have any color from soft pink to

red, white, powder blue and dark blue or purple. Native to Japan. Height x width 3–7 ft (1–2.2 m). ZONE 6.

Macrophylla = big leaves

Above: *Hydrangea macrophylla* 'Red Emperor'

Hydrangea macrophylla cultivars

'Blue Prince' This is the best small blue mophead with tight, round heads of intense cobalt blue in an acidic soil. A small waist-high bush with small leaves. Height x width 3 ft (1 m).

'Enziandom' (syn 'Gentian Dome') has huge round flowers in rich dark blue. Like most of the blues, it needs an acidic soil and takes a few years to develop the best blue colors, as the plants take time to accumulate aluminum from the soil. The more acidic the soil the more aluminum released and made available to the plant—the bluing factor. Height x width 6 ft (2 m).

'Générale Vicomptesse de Vibraye' A beautiful soft powder-blue mophead with repeat flowers through summer. The flowers often turn pale green in the fall. It has pale leaves and an arching habit. Height x width 5 ft (1.5 m).

'Immaculata' The best small bush with white mopheads. It performs best when grown in shade to prevent sunburn to the flowers. Height x width 3 ft (1 m).

'Libelle' A beautiful white lacecap with lovely contrasting blue inner flowers. Height x width 5 ft (1.5 m).

'Merritt's Supreme' Big bold heads that can be rosy pink or, in acidic soil, a rich maroon. In the fall, the flowers take on metallic blue shades. Height x width 6 ft (2 m).

'Nightingale' (syn 'Nachtigall') The best blue lacecap, with large, flat flowers in rich sky blue. The healthy foliage sets off the flowers to perfection. Height x width 5 ft (1.5 m).

'Pompadour' has big dense heads of frilly, soft pink flowers. It produces good cut flowers. Height x width 5 ft (1.5 m).

'Princess Juliana' Probably the best tall white mophead. An

Above: *Hydrangea macrophylla*—mopheads and lacecaps.

'Rotschwanz' (syn 'Redstart') Rich maroony red lacecap flowers with a propeller-like twist in each sepal. The inner flowers are red and white. Unique. Height x width 5 ft (1.5 m).

Hydrangea paniculata

The usual form of this species that we see in gardens is **'Grandiflora'** or the pee gee hydrangea. It has huge (up to 12 in/30 cm) creamy white flower heads from midsummer that gradually turn to pink in the fall. They are both wonderful summer cut flowers or dried flowers at this fall stage.

When you mention the word "hardy" to a gardener they will immediately think of "hardy" in terms of their conditions. It may be hardy to frost and cold if you live inland, or if you live near the sea, hardy will mean wind-tolerant. This plant is the hardiest hydrangea around; that is hardy to cold, as it will grow to zone 3. However, it is also the one most prone to wind damage. The leaves are soft and delicate and easily bruised, plus the stems are brittle. The big flower heads are so weighty it makes them even more liable to damage by high winds. Shelter is therefore the first essential to grow this plant, and, ideally, you should choose a sunny spot with reasonable drainage.

Prune it like a buddleja by developing a short, stout trunk as the only permanant part of the plant and pruning each stem hard back to just a couple of buds in late winter. Native to China and Japan. Height x width 6–10 ft (2–3 m). ZONE 3.

Named cultivars like the big, dense-flowered **'Pink Diamond'** and **'Unique'** are worth seeking out, as are the more open and lacy types like early-flowering **'Praecox'** and **'Kyushu'** or the late-season **'Tardiva'**. All have white flowers eventually

Above: *Hydrangea macrophylla* 'Immaculata'

upright, tidy bush with neat, rounded heads in pure white turning pale green or even red in fall. Height x width 6 ft (2 m).
'Red Emperor' has round dense heads of rosy red that even try to stay red in acidic soils, but it performs best in neutral or alkaline soil. Height x width 5 ft (1.5 m).
'Rheinland' Superb cherry red large mopheads. Height x width 6 ft (2 m).

Above: *Hydrangea paniculata* 'Grandiflora'

turning pink, especially 'Pink Diamond'. Typically they grow to around 6 ft (2 m), although 'Kyushu' tends to be a bit smaller.

Paniculata = panicles of flowers.

Hydrangea petiolaris, syn *H. anomala* subsp *petiolaris*
CLIMBING HYDRANGEA

Among all the showy "bighead" hydrangea flowers, it is easy to miss this gem. The pretty, white, lacecap flowers are like a froth hovering above the waxy, rich green foliage in summer, and this plant also turns heads because it is a climber. Many new to the art of gardening are amazed or disbelieving of a climbing hydrangea, but this Japanese and Korean native will climb tree trunks, buildings or anything strong enough to hold it up. It has clinging roots, like ivy, and eventually the plant becomes very heavy and so flimsy support is just not strong enough. Happy in sun or shade and any kind of well-drained soil, it has the added plus of being cold-hardy. Height up to 50 ft (15 m). ZONE 4.

Petiolaris = with stalks or petioles.

Hydrangea quercifolia
OAKLEAF HYDRANGEA

Although not quite as easy to grow as the robust *H. macrophylla*, this is not a difficult plant and a well-drained soil in sheltered sun or semi-shade with plenty of summer heat is all that is required. Ideally you will add a mulch of bark chips to keep the fibrous roots cool and moist. As a reward you will have big foamy panicles of white flowers all summer, turning to gentle shades of pink in the fall. They are excellent cut flowers, either fresh in summer and as dried flowers once they have turned pinky.

This hydrangea is blessed with fall leaf color as well, and not just a hint of color, but fabulous burnished reds, maroons and purples. Plant in full sun for the best colors and you will also get a better crop of flowers. Place in a mixed border or a sunny spot on the edge of clearing in a woodland garden. For city dwellers, their graceful arching habit is an asset when planted in a tub. Make sure the potting mix you use is free-draining as they are prone to root rot.

Native to southeastern United States. Height 6 ft (2 m) x width 8 ft (2.5 m). ZONE 5, with hot summers to ripen the wood.

The white, double flower form **'Snowflake'** is stupendous and the smooth, white, single flower **'Snow Queen'** is an improvement on the wild plant. Both height 6 ft (2 m) x width 8 ft (2.5 m). ZONE 5.

Quercifolia = oak leaf, from the similarity with the red oak from eastern North America.

Hydrangea serrata, syn *H. macrophylla* subsp *serrata*
TEA OF HEAVEN, BLOOD ON THE SNOW

These woodland plants are smaller and less robust than *H. macrophylla*, though there are similarities. The flowers are either lacecap or mophead, like their larger-leafed cousins, and some have the ability to change flower color as summer progresses, being white in late spring through to pink and then red and finally by fall they are a rich red. They are sometimes refered to as "blood on the snow" because of the way the red supplants the white. They need sunlight to perform this color change but if they are in too hot or sunny a spot the flowers will crisp and dry up. So they need a special place in your garden to perform at their best. It *is* worth the effort to find the right spot. The real surprise is that they will perform this annual color change regardless of your soil. So unlike other hydrangeas, they are not programmed to alter flower color according to the acidity of the soil.

They like an open, free-draining soil, being more fussy in this regard than *H. macrophylla*. Powdery mildew is the only real disease problem. Native to Korea and Japan. Height x width 4–6 ft (1.2–2 m). ZONE 6.

Some attractive cultivars to try in your garden include:
'Blue Deckle', a lovely low-growing lacecap in soft powder blue. A wonderful tub plant. Height x width 3–4 ft (1–1.2 m).
'Glyn Church', a new cultivar named by Corinne Mallett of France. It is an arching shrub with small, round, creamy mopheads that come white then pink and finally red-wine as summer progresses. Height 4–5 ft (1.2–1.5 m) x width 6–7 ft (2–2.2 m).

Left: *Hydrangea quercifolia*

Above: *Hydrangea serrata* 'Glyn Church'

'Miyama-yae-Murasaki' is a neat, wide-spreading, small shrub with fantastic double blue flowers around the rim of the lacecap. Height x width 4 ft (1.2 m).

'Preziosa' is a mophead version that goes through the same color changes as 'Grayswood'. Even the new stems and leaves have a reddish tinge. The constantly changing flower colors will have you entranced all summer. Height x width 5 ft (1.5 m).

'Shirotae' is a white double lacecap in similar fashion to 'Miyama-yae-Murasaki'. The flowers take on a red tinge as summer progresses. A small, compact plant ideal for mass planting. Height x width 4 ft (1.2 m).

Hypericum

ST JOHN'S WORT
Hypericaceae

'Grayswood', a beautiful lacecap flower with large white petals surrounding the smoky blue "true" flowers in the center of the petals. The white petals gradually change to pink, then red and finally red-wine by fall. It has long, pointed leaves and forms a bush around 5 ft (1.5 m) high and the same wide. Ideal for woodland gardens or a semi-shady spot.

'Kiyosumi', a small, upright bush with rather narrow serrated leaves edged in red. The two-tone flowers are white with a red edge (picotee) and are truly amazing. Height x width 5 ft (1.5 m).

I like hypericums. Some gardeners are scathing about them because they are commonplace, almost too easy to grow and a few (very few) have become garden escapes. On the positive side, being easy to grow should always be seen as a bonus. They flower for long periods—some of them never stop—and this is often seen as a negative too, because people get bored with perpetual-flowering plants.

Another thing I like about hypericums is that they are easy to identify. Even though there were more than 300 species at last

Right: *Hydrangea serrata* 'Blue Deckle'

count, you can see a new hypericum and instantly recognize the saucer-shaped, golden yellow flowers. Some have a glistening sheen to the blooms, as if they've been brushed with fairy dust. Mind you the fairies would be kept busy with the sheer profusion of flowers. The size of flower varies with species but there are only marginal differences in color. Hypericums are one of those genera that prove botanists are correct when they say plants modify their leaves and bush shape to suit a given climate (say mountain or seashore), but the flowers remain the same as they are short-lived and have no need to modify their structure. Thus seemingly different plants can be classified as the same genus because the flowers are basically the same. In the wild, hypericums grow across vast areas of Europe, Asia and North America. Most are deciduous, depending on the climate. They are usually tidy in their habits and a few are good ground covers.

A site in full sun gives maximum flower numbers, but these plants will grow in part-shade. Any soil is acceptable, including those that are strongly alkaline. Even wet or windy sites don't pose a threat of death, though it may debilitate them. Many have adapted to drought and most are cold-hardy. If you have a problem spot where it is hard to find a suitable shrub, then hypericum could be the answer. The only difficulty is blending the hot yellow color with other plants. As they mostly flower in summer when other shrubs are only leafy this isn't usually a problem.

I have seen older bushes moved but they sometimes resent the shift and you may need to cut back the bush to relieve the pressure on the smaller root system. You can prune them drastically and it is often a good idea to rejuvenate the plant if it gets weak and thin. Most have an even, rounded outline and keep a good shape without interference. Some gain more ground by suckering like clumping bamboo, while a few creep like the more invasive bamboos.

Occasionally hypericums are attacked by caterpillars and thrips, and diseases such as black spot and rust.

Hypericum = Greek for heath, referring to the plant or its location.

Hypericum calycinum
ROSE OF SHARON, AARON'S BEARD
A brilliant evergreen shrub in the right place and a curse elsewhere. It creeps by underground rootstock and often invades

Above: *Hypericum leschenaultii*

where it is not wanted. It has been overused by landscapers in some regions and thus is out of fashion. This shouldn't detract from what the plant is good at and that is providing a dense ground cover for sun or shade, and, unlike most ground-cover plants for shade, this one has brilliant flowers. In fact, the bright yellow, saucer-shaped flowers will "razzle-dazzle" you from midsummer to mid-fall.

I have seen it growing well in the dry, dense root mat of an established yew tree, and conditions don't come much tougher than that. If you are worried that it will invade your garden, use it in areas isolated by concrete. It is disfigured by thrips and rust in warm regions and may need an occasional prune with shears to tidy up raggedy or injured growth. It is from eastern Europe and Turkey. Height 24 in (60 cm) x width 3 ft (1 m). ZONE 5.

Calycinum = calyx-like flower.

Hypericum 'Hidcote'
Named after Hidcote Manor garden in the Cotswolds of England, one of the best-designed gardens in the world. The plant itself is superb too, a star among an already good genus. It is a super evergreen plant, covered in flowers all summer. The flowers are among the largest in the genus (2½ in/6 cm across), big and yellow, forming a perfect cup of gold. It is tough, hardy and grows around head-high with a tidy habit. It is attacked by thrips in warm regions. Although it is considered to be a hybrid, no one is sure of its parentage. Height x width 5 ft (1.5 m). ZONE 6.

Hypericum leschenaultii
This is a great plant if you have a mild climate. An upright, evergreen bush, it is covered in bold golden flowers most of the year. I have one in a tough site under a plane tree and it's never without

Left: *Hypericum calycinum*

a few flowers, even in midwinter. They are big flowers, too, about the size of a cookie. You can prune annually for size and shape, but I prefer to leave it for four or five years and then prune it drastically. It also seems to be resistant to thrip, another reason I'm so fond of it. This species was collected in Java in 1805 by French botanist Jean Baptiste Leschenault de la Tour, hence the name. Height 6 ft (2 m) x width 4–5 ft (1.2–1.5 m). ZONE 9.

Hypericum hookerianum is similar and possibly a little hardier.

Indigofera

Fabaceae

Indigoferas include some of the best garden plants you will find. All in all, it is a huge genus with literally hundreds of herbs and shrubs from across the tropics and sub-tropics. The hardy ones are usually deciduous and are valuable summer-flowering shrubs. Summer is often such a difficult niche to fill in a shrubbery, other than with the ubiquitous rose and fabulous hydrangeas.

The best garden species of *Indigofera* have tiny pinnate leaves and masses and masses of pea-like flowers in pinks and purple hues on long spikes or racemes. They flower on new wood produced during the summer, so if you need to tidy the bush prune it in spring before the new growth starts. Some are cut back by cold winters, but a quick trim in the spring and all is well again.

Most need full sun to thrive and are capable of growing in drought-prone regions. Having said that, they are just as happy in warm, wet regions. Any well-drained soil will suffice, and like most legumes they will grow in poor rocky or sandy sites.

Seemingly impregnable to pests and immune to soil problems, it is tempting to ask why they are not more popular. They can be a bit tricky to transplant as container-grown specimens are likely to have roots spiraling around the base of the pot. These roots need to be teased out to the shape of a starfish when transplanted if the plant is to survive. With the exception of *I. decora*, they should never be shifted once put in their permanant home. Most are grown from seed, though they will grow from cuttings, and *I. decora* is divided almost like a herbaceous plant.

Like many legume shrubs, the long, narrow stems are liable to fall over in strong winds as they are top-heavy. It pays to prune them quite a bit when they are young to keep them bushy and reduce this problem. A stake would be useful for the first summer or two.

Indigo = a blue dye and *fero* = to bear, because *Indigofera tinctoria* has been used for centuries as a blue dye plant.

Indigofera amblyantha

A great summer-flowering shrub with neat pinnate leaves typical of legumes and showy racemes of upcurved flowers in the darker shades of pink to light rosy red. While the individual flowers are small, the overall display is very effective. Flowers appear from midsummer until the first frosts of winter. Its main claim to fame is it is hardier than most other indigoferas. It is deciduous, low-growing, even semi-prostrate at times. Originally from China. Height 5 ft (1.5 m) x width 8 ft (2.5 m). ZONE 6.

Ambly = blunt and *antha* = flower.

Indigofera decora

"Decora," meaning decorous, is an appropriate name for this delightful garden shrub. The alternate pinnate leaves have a lovely clean look, and tucked in underneath the axils of the new leaves are the long spikes of rosy pink flowers. They are hidden to some extent by the foliage, but enough of the flowers emerge to make a

Below and right:
Indigofera decora

Above: *Indigofera dielsiana*

show. Better still, grow it at eye level on a bank or the top of a wall where the flowers can be more easily admired. The flowers are typical of a legume, with wings and keel, and are in various shade of white to pink to puce. They open in succession from base to tip giving a long flowering season from midsummer.

This shrub forms a small, neat bush and fits easily into any garden. It suckers a little, but it's not going to take over, and should it get a bit tatty, you can slash it to ground level and let it start again with fresh new growth. Typical new growth is 8–12 in (20–30 cm) long with smooth brownish stems. It's evergreen in warm climates but generally thought of as deciduous. It quickly regenerates and grows a bit like *Hypericum calycinum*. Grow it in full sun or part-shade. It is capable of withstanding drought and would make an interesting ground cover, being especially useful for difficult sites. Another plus for this plant, it is pest-free.

Robert Fortune (1812–1880) found this pretty Chinese native in a Shanghai garden in 1846. Many of the plants Fortune collected were from nurseries and gardens on the eastern seaboard of China, as it was difficult to travel inland at that time. Height 24 in (60 cm) x width 36 in (90 cm). ZONE 7.

Decora = decorous, beautiful.

Indigofera dielsiana

This is another of my favorite shrubs. True, it can be rangy and open, but to me that only adds to its charm. If this habit isn't to your liking, it is easily remedied—like all indigoferas it responds well to heavy pruning. Flowering begins in summer with a fairly short spike of bright pink flowers. As time goes by, the older flowers fall off but the spike carries on flowering for the remainder of the summer and into fall, getting longer and longer. The bush has a lovely arching habit and a thin, airy look, with its long, thin, pinnate leaves with opposite little leaflets.

These easy-care plants don't know how to stop flowering and they will grow just about anywhere as long as they get enough sunlight. Give this plant enough room to display the arching stems with their rockets of flowers. It was collected in Yunnan, China, by George Forrest and named after Friedrich Diels (1874–1945), Director of the Berlin Botanic Garden. Height x width 6 ft (2 m). ZONE 6.

Indigofera potaninii is similar.

Indigofera heterantha, syn *I. gerardiana*

This bush of open habit has bright purplish-pink flowers that appear *en masse* all summer. It is an ideal shrub for a hot, dry site, and is tidier than some others species. An occasional winter prune will keep it this way. It is sometimes grown against a wall in very cold regions. Native to the Himalayas. Height x width 6–10 ft (2–3 m). ZONE 6.

Hetero = one sided or unequal and *antha* = flowers.

Iochroma

Solanaceae

While *Iochroma* are definitely shrubs, often growing to 10 ft (3 m) or more, both high and wide, they are not exactly woody. I can't imagine anyone would ever manage to get a block of wood from one, so in some ways they are like a huge herbaceous plant. The stems rot in a very short space of time if they are cut and left on the ground, just like any perennial.

They hail from Central and South America, and yet grow surprisingly well in some cooler regions, to such an extent they have even naturalized in places. I'm amazed at this because they are very frost-tender. I have seen them totally blackened by frost, but, providing the soil doesn't freeze too much, the plants survive this and come away again in the spring. The danger from frost comes in the first winter, when the plant hasn't had time to build up a strong enough root system to recover. So if you are trying this plant in a cool region, plant them early in the summer and feed and water the plant to build up a decent-sized rootstock by winter. Any good free-draining soil will do—the better the drainage the less risk of frost damage.

Iochromas are evergreen, but strong winds can defoliate them as well as frost. They are happy in full sun or quite dense shade, and it may be that you can use shade cover to keep off

Below: *Iochroma cyaneum*

Above and right:
*Iochroma
gesnerioides*

Easy to transplant from pots, older specimens can be shifted if you prune them back to stumps. They can play host to spider mite and whitefly in some regions, but generally they are easy-care plants.

Ion = Greek for violet and *chroma* = color.

Iochroma cyaneum, syn *I. tubulosa*

What the flowers lack in size they make up for in color. The narrow flowers are an intense blue, like some tropical bird or fruit, and appear mainly in summer. It's not a temperate-looking color somehow. The plant forms an ungainly, wide-spreading shrub, so is possibly a candidate for the back of a border. Native to Colombia, Ecuador and Peru. Height 10 ft (3 m) x width 6 ft (2 m). ZONE 9.

Cyaneum = blue, referring to the color of the flowers.

Iochroma gesnerioides, syn *I. fuchsioides*, *I. coccineum*

The showy orangy red, tubular flowers of this species are mass-produced all summer. Each cluster can have twenty-five pendulous flowers and they often appear at every leaf on the new stems. They will flower more or less all summer, as long as new growth is being made. This bush probably has the best overall shape of the genus, with a fairly tidy, upright habit, and large, hand-like, bright green leaves. From Central America. Height 10 ft (3 m) x width 6 ft (2 m). ZONE 9.

Gesnerioides = like a *Gesneria*, a tropical or indoor plant with long, red flowers.

Iochroma grandiflorum

This species is appropriately named, as it has the largest flowers of the genus. They are big, finger-length trumpets in purple-blue and these pendulous flowers often appear in one long display from early summer until winter. Like a herald's trumpet, they start narrow and flare out toward the end. The large tropical-looking leaves are bigger than a hand and have a fleshy texture not unlike tomatoes, to which they are related. The bush grows up and out like an umbrella, so allow for a height by width of at least 10 ft (3 m). Plant up on a bank where you can admire the arching habit of the bush and the mass of hanging flowers, which rival any fuchsia. Native to Ecuador. ZONE 9.

Grandiflorum = big flowers.

Isoplexis

Scrophulariaceae

A very small genus from the Canary Islands and nearby Madeira off the coast of Spain. They are in fact a type of bushy foxglove, and when you see the flowers, you will recognize the connection. Only two species seem to be in cultivation. These unusual plants will grow in virtually any soil and site but they are killed by hard frosts. They will survive a few degrees of frost, however.

Iso =equal and *plexus* = plaited or braided, refers to the flowers looking as if they've been plaited onto the stem.

Isoplexis canariensis

A small shrub just over waist-high that starts as a single stem with small, finger-sized, dark, evergreen leaves. At the top of this thin

frost and strong winds. They will be torn to shreds by gales, but quickly recover in the same way as fuchsias.

Most are big, rangy shrubs. The plants benefit from a severe prune in spring before the new growth emerges, so regardless of your winters, it is probably a good idea to give them a haircut. Flowers are produced on new growth, and so drastic pruning enhances rather than diminishes the floral display. And what a display it is, because although the individual flowers are quite small, the total flower numbers are vast. Each flower is long and thin, like a short pencil.

Left: *Isoplexis canariensis*

stem will be a flower spike. The following season the bush branchs out from below last year's seed heads to form a half-standard bush about 3 ft (1 m) wide. Eventually it becomes a round-top bush about 5 ft (1.5 m) high and wide.

The flowers look exciting from every which way. From above they are narrow, tapering spikes of orange, and if you plant them on a bank you can look up into the flowers with their intricate inner markings. Wherever you plant one it will draw the attention of visitors because it is so unusual and pretty. The flowers last for months and months, with new flowers opening at the top of the spike and old ones dropping off. I've always had a preference for plants that drop their spent flowers cleanly as I hate looking at dead or bedraggled flowers hanging limply on a bush.

The plant is prone to wind rock, so choose a fairly sheltered and warm site. Apparently in the wild they grow in gullies where they are sheltered from wind and only get sun for maybe half the day. Initially, I planted all of mine in a very sunny, hot, dry border. They grew well enough but then started to seed naturally around the garden and to my surprise they seemed to choose the shadier spots, and some even came up in swampy places. The plants growing naturally in the shade always look healthier and happier than the sun-baked ones. Although it seeds around the garden, it is never likely to take over. It seems they are drought-tolerant too, so as gardeners we have incredible leeway regarding how wet or dry the conditions are. They also grow in acidic or alkaline soils.

Transplant young plants from pots, and although it is possible to shift older plants I don't recommend it. You can prune if you need to, but they have a good natural rounded shape so it's unlikely you'll need to find the secateurs. Native to the Canary Islands. Height x width 5 ft (1.5 m). ZONE 9, possibly 8.

Left: *Isoplexis sceptrum*

Isoplexis sceptrum

This species has fleshy grass-green leaves as big as a wide-spread hand. They have an odd sticky texture like tobacco leaves and a short leaf stalk, so they cling closely to the stem to form a whorl or spiral. The flower spikes are similar to but slightly larger than *I. canariensis* and come in a softer apricot color. This species is sometimes attacked by whitefly and prone to root rot, so it's more tricky to grow than *I. canariensis*. However, it does share the same ability to grow in sun or shade. From the Canary Islands. Height x width 5–6 ft (1.5–2 m). ZONE 9.

Sceptrum = sceptre.

Jacaranda

Jacaranda mimosifolia
JACARANDA
Bignoniaceae

Jacaranda is the kind of tree people go into ecstasies about. Even those who never usually notice trees will rave about this one—when it's in flower of course. The flowers are a wonderful shade of purple-blue and absolutely cover the surface of this wide, spreading tree in summer. Unfortunately, this shape of tree is always prone to wind damage because it's twisted and turned by storms until the branches eventually break. The plants can be trained to be more upright, but they are still prone to damage. However, once seen in flower everyones wants to own one.

There is another drawback, however, and that is its need for a warm climate (summer heat). It is not just a case of needing to be frost-free, that's not enough. To perform at its best, the summers must be long and hot. Being deciduous in colder climates, they will take a few degrees of frost providing they get enough summer heat to ripen the wood. In some hot climates they are almost evergreen, but still seem to drop their leaves before flowering.

Below: *Jacaranda mimosifolia*

The terminal heads of purple-blue, foxglove-like flowers usually appear before the leaves in late spring/early summer. They look like *Paulownia* flowers, only smaller and neater. The lovely ferny foliage has a soft, tactile look about it and the leaves are bipinnate, meaning that there are leaflets coming off of leaflets.

The soil needs to be free-draining, but otherwise anything will do and they are tolerant of drought. You can transplant jacarandas in winter when they have lost their leaves. This is also a good time to prune them to the shape you want. Full sun is an obvious requirement because of their desire for heat, and it is necessary for the most flowers. Height 50 ft (15 m) x width 30 ft (10 m). ZONE 9.

Jacaranda = local name in its homeland of southern Brazil and northern Argentina; *mimosifolia* = leaf like a mimosa or "sensitive plant."

Kalmia

Ericaceae

Kalmias are super-hardy evergreen plants—some of them grow at the tops of mountains while others survive swamps or living in dense shade. They are often tricky to grow in gardens, requiring an acidic, peaty soil with good drainage and adequate sunlight. Sometimes copying the conditions of the wild can result in disappointment. The plant growing in a swamp or dense shade has adjusted from a seedling, whereas when we plant a garden-center bush in those conditions it will probably give up and die. Treat them like rhododendrons and give them a mulch and water regularly. Like rhododendrons, they can be attacked by weevils and leaf spots.

Kalmia = named after Peter (or Pedr) Kalm (1715–1779), a Finnish pupil of Linnaeus who traveled widely in North America collecting plants.

Kalmia angustifolia
LAMBKILL, SHEEP LAUREL, WICKY
This is a small evergreen bush with showy and cute small, rosy-red flowers. It grows to less than waist-high and spreads at the roots to form a thicket. You can propagate it and give a piece to a friend by dividing the rootstock. It grows naturally in swamps, but is just as happy in dry places as long as the soil is acidic. The leaves are poisonous to animals, hence the common names. There is a richer form called **'Rubra'** which has darker red, longer-lasting flowers. Native to eastern North America. Height 24 in (60 cm) x width 5 ft (1.5 m). ZONE 7.

Angustifolia = narrow leaves.

Kalmia latifolia
CALICO BUSH, MOUNTAIN LAUREL
Dark, glossy, evergreen leaves and a rounded shape mean that this species looks good all year. Then, in late spring, it becomes absolutely stunning with a mantle of soft lolly-pink flowers. The fist-sized heads are made up of dozens of flowers, each one looking like the underside of an opened umbrella. These flowers sit right on top of the plant, so they are very pretty and seem to last for weeks without getting battered or bruised. If you get close, you'll notice that they are quite pleasantly scented, rather like soap.

This wonderful plant can be tricky to grow and gardeners have their theories about what they need to do well. Some would say they need a cold climate, though I would disagree having seen

Above: *Kalmia latifolia*

them growing magnificently in a zone 9 region. Others say they must have high rainfall, yet I've seen them survive extreme droughts year after year once established. Nearly everybody agrees they need an acidic, free-draining soil. This is understandable as kalmias grow naturally in woods and on mountain tops all through the eastern states of the U.S.A. Like most mountain plants, they are wind-hardy, but that's no reason to plant them in tough, windy sites if you want your plant to thrive. They will endure extreme cold, however, being one of the most hardy evergreen shrubs.

In the wild, kalmias grow in full sun as well as in the shade of big forest trees. I've seen them growing out of the cracks in huge rock faces, which probably accounts for their drought tolerance. In a garden setting, I would suggest full sun if you have a cool climate because they do seem to need summer heat to do well. Typically it becomes a very neat, rounded shrub and it is unlikely that you will ever need to prune it, though it will cope if you do.

They are easy to transplant because, like the related rhododendrons, they have a mass of fibrous roots near the surface. Plants with this kind of root system love to have a mulch of bark or woodchip to keep the roots cool and suppress the weeds. Avoid any cultivation around the plant as it damages these surface roots. Apart from the surface root system, there are other similarities with the closely-related rhododendrons. Kalmias don't like late frosts, they need deadheading to prevent them putting all their energy into making seeds and they are prone to vine weevils, leaf spot and leaf blight.

Kalmia latifolia is the state flower of Pennsylvania. There are several other species of *Kalmia* native to North America but none are as exciting as the calico bush. Height x width 10 ft (3 m). ZONES 3 TO 9.

Kalmia latifolia cultivars
'Carousel' A striking flower with white inner petals within a wheel of reddy purple. It also has good healthy dark green foliage. Height x width 4 ft (1.2 m).
'Elf' Soft shell-pink buds open to almost white but with just a hint of pink. It forms a low, dense bush. Height x width 3 ft (1 m).
'Freckles' Really cute white flowers with flecks of purple inside. Height x width 5 ft (1.5 m).
'Nipmuck' An unusual name for an unusual flower. The deep red buds surprisingly have very pale pink inner petals, creating an interesting contrast. The pale foliage sometimes turns purple in the cool months. Height x width 4–5 ft (1.2–1.5 m).
'Olympic Fire' is a seedling of 'Ostbo Red' and probably even better, with larger flowers and wavy-edged leaves. Height x width 5 ft (1.5 m).
'Ostbo Red' The rich red buds are simply stunning and open to reveal the pink interiors, thus creating a two-tone red and pink effect. Height x width 5 ft (1.5 m).
'Pink Charm' is highly rated for the dense heads of deep pink flowers and because it flowers at a young age. Height x width 3 ft (1 m).
'Pink Globe' This cultivar has good, healthy, large leaves and excellent rich pink flowers in a tight round truss. Height x width 5 ft (1.5 m).

Above: *Kerria japonica*

Above: *Kerria japonica* 'Pleniflora'

There is also a double-flowered form with spiky crowded flowers that is more upright and vigorous than the single, but I think it lacks the single's simple appeal. It was this double form, *Kerria japonica* **'Pleniflora'**, that William Kerr first introduced to Europe from China in 1804. For some reason, he imagined it was a Japanese plant and thus it was called japonica. Botanists in England were puzzled by this double-flower *Kerria* because it had no reproductive organs. It could not be classified until thirty years later, when John Russell Reeves sent home the single-flower version from China.

Kerria japonica is very easy to grow and not at all fussy about soil, growing equally well in sand or clay, acidic or alkaline conditions. Even an occasional inundation of water doesn't seem to bother it. Better still, it seems to grow well in shade, even under old pine trees. It can look a bit raggedy there, but it is easy enough to trim. Sunny sites are quite acceptable too, and it's hardy to cold and wind. High or low rainfall areas are fine and it is drought-tolerant.

The stems are quite unusual, being round, smooth, shiny and green. It is usually a fairly dense shrub, wider than it is high. In fact the stems that touch the ground will send out roots so the plant commands more space. It is very easy to transplant, and even old plants can be shifted, though it is easier to start afresh. Native to China. Height 6 ft (2 m) x width 8 ft (2.5 m). ZONE 4.

'Snowdrift' A dense bush with good dark foliage showing off the white flowers. There's just a hint of red inside the flowers when you look closely. Height x width 5 ft (1.5 m).
'Tiddlywinks' A neat dwarf plant with a good dense habit and pink flowers. Height x width 3 ft (1 m).
'Tinkerbell' Another miniature with rich pink flowers and it flowers as a young plant. Deep green, healthy foliage. Height x width 4 ft (1.2 m).

Latifolia = broad leaves.

Kerria

Kerria japonica
Rosaceae

Kerria is a problem plant—by that I mean what is a gardener to do with it? They really have just one claim to fame: the vibrant splash of yellow so early in the spring that it shouts "hurray, summer is on its way." Like many, I quickly tired of this plant, but slowly and surely it is coming back into favor with me (and other gardeners too).

During the summer months the plant disappears from view with fairly bland, thumb-sized, grass-green leaves, and in winter the bare stems are just a tangle. But with the first hint of spring, suddenly it is out there blazing away, smothered in bright golden-yellow, buttercup-like flowers. It gladdens the heart for a day or two, and then we tend to think "Oh that old thing."

Koelreuteria

Sapindaceae

Koelreuterias are wonderful deciduous shade trees and, in time, become real character trees with twisty gnarled branches and attractive rough bark. Typically they grow to around 30 ft (10 m) but can be much wider, say up to 60 feet (20 m). They seem to grow quite slowly when young and do take many years to reach maturity, when they take on that wonderful old character look. Young plants seem to have twisty ungainly stems and it is often hard to train them to a single leader. Perhaps it is better to allow them to grow how they like and develop more character.

Above: *Koelreuteria bipinnata*

Koelreuterias need an open site, full sun and preferably hot summers. They will cope with poor soil and compaction, and with their added ability to cope with pollution and drought they make an ideal city tree. Winter cold holds no terrors, as they seem to enjoy a continental climate. Grown mostly for their golden yellow flowers in big wide panicles up to a foot long and wide (30 cm), these showy heads are much more freely produced in a hot or drought-prone climate. The pinnate leaves are quite handsome and often turn a rich golden yellow in the fall.

> *Koelreuteria* = named after Joseph Gottlieb Koelreuter (1733–1806), Professor of Botany at Karlsruhe University, Germany.

Koelreuteria bipinnata

This lesser-known species comes from western China. Ultimately a wide-spreading tree, it seems better suited to impatient gardeners as it grows and flowers faster and accepts more diverse climates than other species of this genus. It flowers late in the season, close to fall, and the flowers are similar to *Koelreuteria paniculata*. The seedpods are attractive too, with inflated, bladder-like pods. Height 30 ft (10 m) x width 50 ft (15 m). ZONE 7.

> *Bipinnata* = bi or doubly pinnate.

Koelreuteria paniculata

GOLDEN RAIN TREE, PRIDE OF INDIA, VARNISH TREE
Given time this fine spreading tree, with its huge panicles of golden flowers followed by big, bladder-like fruits, can be the most beautiful plant in your garden. It is a fabulous character tree with twisting, gnarled branches, but there is a catch. You need a climate with hot, dry summers for it to shine in all its glory. Free-draining soil and low rainfall suit this plant to a tee. During the warm summers the flowers appear, and any tree flowering in mid-summer is valuable. The flowers give it its common name of golden rain tree. The pinnate leaves are large and reasonably attractive and they do show a good golden yellow color in the fall.

As well as hot summers, these plants like cold winters. In mild winter regions, or places without sufficient summer heat, koelreuterias survive rather than thrive. They are, however, able to withstand city pollution and are not particular about soil type,

Above: *Koelreuteria paniculata*

other than needing good drainage. Take care when shifting or planting out because they can be a bit temperamental at this stage. Diseases include black spots and root rot.

If you plant one, you'll need some patience because it is some years before it flowers, and even longer before it will become a "character" tree. No pruning is necessary as the natural outline of the tree is nicely rounded. Koelreuterias are not really suited to small suburban gardens as they grow too slowly and eventually too big. They don't like windy sites, and usually I would say don't grow them too close to the sea. I have, however, seen good specimens right beside the sea in Asia. The tree hails from northern China. Height x width 30 ft (10 m). ZONE 5 TO 8.

There is a later-flowering clone called **'September Gold'**. Height x width 30 ft (10 m).

> *Paniculata* = panicles.

Kolkwitzia

Kolkwitzia amabilis
BEAUTYBUSH
Caprifoliaceae

Not many people know this plant, which is a shame because it is certainly worthy of acclaim—I know I couldn't live without one in my garden. At first glance you might think it a *Deutzia* or perhaps a *Weigela*. It is in fact closely related to *Weigela* and has the same style of trumpet-shaped flowers, but it has chosen to take on the garden world single-handedly and is in a plant genus all of its own.

When you see one smothered in flowers in late spring you will be hooked. The arching branches are festooned with soft pink trumpets. It puts me in mind of tinsel decorations on a Christmas tree. Rosy pink buds open to whitish pink tubes like

little faces and there are apricot spots in the throat. It is a reasonable cut flower, and perhaps could be used as a foil for roses. In a garden setting it looks pretty as a specimen plant or in a mixed early-summer border with roses and philadelphus.

Because of the wonderful flowers, I can overlook the fact the bush has a rather nondescript look about it for the rest of the summer. It is deciduous and a rather cluttered twiggy affair in winter. Don't be tempted to tidy or prune it in this drab winter phase because you will be cutting off all the flower buds. You can prune it after flowering, because it will have a whole summer to produce new growth and more flower buds. The bush itself is upright, typically not much over head-high, though you do see vast bushes of it from time to time.

It is hardy to cold yet still manages to grow well in warm, frost-free areas. Full sun is ideal but part-shade is fine. It has soft, rather delicate, leaves so it is really a woodland plant or should at least have a sheltered part of a suburban garden. It is not at all fussy about soil, coping with dry or wet, acidic or alkaline, and even heavy clay. For those of you with limestone soil, this bush should really be near the top of your wish list because such lovely flowering bushes capable of growing on such soils are scarce. It can safely be transplanted at any size during winter, but be patient because it does take a few years to establish and flower properly.

This plant was introduced from China by E. H. Wilson (1876–1930) for the Veitch Nursery in England in 1901. For years it was not popular with gardeners because some of the seedlings were poor. It is worth seeking out the named clones such as **'Rosea'** or **'Pink Cloud'** as they are more colorful with

Below: *Kolkwitzia amabilis*

their richer pink blooms, and more floriferous. The genus is named for Richard Kolkwitz, a professor of botany in Berlin, Germany, early in the 20th century. For all, height 10 ft (3 m) x width 12 ft (4 m). ZONE 5.

Amabilis = lovely.

Laburnum

GOLDEN CHAIN TREE
Fabaceae

For many people the highlight of spring is when the laburnums flower. In cooler regions this is the most showy of all the spring-flowering trees, so much so it has been used on a grand scale for street planting. It looks superb when you see a whole avenue of them in full flower.

They are reasonably wind-hardy, as you would expect of a successful street tree, and not fussy about soil or city pollution. Like so many legumes, they grow in virtually any soil, being equally comfortable with acidic to very alkaline, and sand to heavy clays. Although this suggests that they are easy to grow, I should add a proviso—if you have the right climate. They do like cool or cold winters and a moist climate. Given too mild a climate, they sulk.

Take a bit of extra care when transplanting, as they have stringy roots that may spiral around the pot. Just unwind these roots and spread them out. It's not a plant I would move again later, though I have seen them shifted successfully. It's likely to be a prime tree in your garden, so choose the right spot first time.

These sun-lovers form neat mophead trees with attractive green trunks and, with this good natural shape, they rarely need any pruning. There are no serious pests and diseases apart from stem borer in some regions. Some people are nervous about using them because all parts of the plant are highly toxic.

Laburnum = ancient Latin name for this plant.

Laburnum alpinum
SCOTCH LABURNUM
The plant grows wild on the eastern side of the European Alps, thus its species name. It has very showy pendulous chains of

Above: *Laburnum* x *watereri* 'Vossii'

Above: *Laburnum anagyroides*

yellow flowers in early summer and is considered by connoisseurs to be the best of the laburnums. It forms a tidy, rounded tree. Height x width 25 ft (8 m). ZONES 5 TO 8.

Alpinum = alpine.

Laburnum anagyroides, syn *L. vulgare*
COMMON LABURNUM

A fast-growing deciduous tree from southern and central Europe, it is early-flowering, with short chains of canary-yellow flowers. The flowers are not particularly well-presented and are short-lived compared to other species. It also has less attractive leaves in dull gray-green compared to the shiny deep green of the other two mentioned here. Height x width 25 ft (8 m). ZONE 5, 6 TO 8.

Anagyroides = like the genus *Anagyris*, a strongly scented shrub.

Laburnun x watereri (*L. alpinum* x *L. anagyroides*)

This is the laburnum we see most often in our streets and gardens. The initial hybrid was raised by the Waterer nursery in Surrey, England. It has attractive, smooth, trifoliate leaves and wondrous chains of yellow flowers up to 20 in (50 cm) long in late spring. The cultivar 'Vossii' was raised in the Netherlands from the same parentage and is the standard form you are likely to get when you ask for a laburnum. These hybrids produce few seeds compared to the other two types. This is a real bonus as the seeds are poisonous and seed production debilitates the tree. Height x width 25 ft (8 m). ZONES 5 TO 8.

Lagerstroemia

Lythraceae

Given a continental climate, or at least hot summers, this is one of the best flowering trees you can own. Masses of curly-edged flowers, like rosettes, emblazon the stems in late summer. Each flower is crinkled like crepe paper, hence the common name for some species. Not only are the individual flowers stunning, they come in big, dense cones, creating a stunning array. The flowers are stupendous, though the colors—cerise, pink, puce and purple—can be a little harsh and hard to blend.

It has unusual leaves for a hardy plant as they are waxy and glossy with a definite tropical look. They often have a hint of red and can be good for color in fall too. Having said that, the bush often looks straggly and may need pruning to make a dense tidy bush or else thinning to enhance the trunks. When you see a young plant, the stems look stalky and brittle and not very appealing; and yet given a few years' growth they sort themselves out and have majestic, smooth, peeling trunks. These tactile trunks usually have the twin colors of soft gray-brown and rich warm brown, and the trunks alone make these trees worthy of a space in your garden.

They are usually an upright stalky tree or large shrub, and are naturally multi-trunked, though you can train them to single leaders or a particular shape. There are many dwarf forms available these days that will fit easily into any suburban garden, and they can be grown in pots and tubs.

Only two or three deciduous species are commonly grown in cultivation, but there are evergreen species too. Grow them in full sun for the best performance as they are real sun- and heat-lovers. They are reasonably wind-tolerant, but choose a sheltered site if you can. Any pH or quality of soil is fine as long as it is well drained. Generally they cope well with drought, but do need moisture at flowering time.

When the Swedish botanist Carl Linnaeus introduced binomial (two names) Latin, the idea was that each name would be descriptive, so you could differentiate plants by their descriptive names. However, he got carried away and named lots of plants after his friends and colleagues, such as this one, which is named after Magnus von Lagerstroem (1696–1759) of Gothenburg, Germany.

Lagerstroemia fauriei

Studying plants is a peculiar pastime. You think you've seen everything when you suddenly come across a new plant that takes your breath away. I had this experience recently when I saw this species for the first time in North Carolina. It has not been in cultivation all that long, as it was brought back from its native Japan by John Creech in 1956. Being from the Japanese mountains, it is much hardier to cold than the other species. Also the white flowers appear much earlier in the summer than most. The real highlight of *Lagerstroemia fauriei* is the trunks, with their peeling bark in shades of purple and mahogany.

Lagerstroemia fauriei is resistant to powdery mildew, which attacks *L. indica*, and some of this resistance has been passed onto the hybrid forms. The species is named after Urbain Jean Faurie (1847–1915), a French missionary and plant collector who spent many years in Asia. Height x width 25 ft (8 m). ZONE 6.

Below:
Lagerstroemia fauriei

Two top selections of *Lagerstroemia fauriei* are: **'Townhouse'**, with white flowers, dark red bark and, as the name suggests, it is

Above: *Lagerstroemia indica*

small enough to plant in a city garden. Height 15 ft (5 m) x width 12 ft (4 m); and **'Fantasy'**, with similar white flowers, handsome ochre-colored bark and a very upright multi-trunk habit. Height 15 ft (5 m) x width 10 ft (3 m).

Lagerstroemia hybrids

The flowers of *Lagerstroemia fauriei* may not be as stunning as *L. indica*, but there are new hybrids between the two, combining good color with some of the cold-hardiness and resistance to powdery mildew of *L. fauriei*. These hybrids include dwarf bushes as well as the usual large shrubs.

'Apalachee' has beautiful lavender flowers, rich, dark green, healthy foliage and cinnamon trunks. Height x width 15 ft (5 m).

'Chickasaw' is a true dwarf with rosy lavender flowers. The rich dark green leaves turn into showy bronze in the fall. Height x width 2 ft (60 cm).

'Muskogee' is a vigorous tree with lavender flowers and red fall color. Height x width 20 ft (6 m).

'Natchez' has creamy white flowers and superb russet brown and gray bark. Excellent burnished fall colors. Height x width 15 ft (5 m).

'Pocomoke' is another true dwarf, with rich rosy pink flowers. The new leaves are maroon becoming green and then bronze in the fall. Height x width 3 ft (1 m).

'Sioux' is a strong pink set off against healthy dark green leaves turning orange and reds in the fall. Height x width 15 ft (5 m).

'Tonto' is the closest to true rich red and simply stunning. Excellent fall colors in maroon shades. Height x width 10 ft (3 m).

'Tuscarora' is a fast-growing tree with crimson flowers and lovely mottled bark. Height x width 15 ft (5 m).

Lagerstroemia indica
CREPE MYRTLE

Although the name suggests this species is from India, it is native to north China and Korea. The flower colors tend toward harsh, strident shades and so need to be carefully blended with other plants. Fall leaf colors are good in some regions, the simple glossy leaves changing to burnished colors. Prune in winter to tidy the bush, especially as the spent flower heads look ugly. The tree will recover from drastic pruning and this often leads to increased floral displays. Dry, hot summers not only initiate more flowers but ripen and harden the wood sufficiently for the bush to survive colder winters. In mild, humid regions the plant is not as cold-hardy or as floriferous. Height x width 25 ft (8 m). ZONE 7.

Lagerstroemia speciosa (giant crepe myrtle, pride of India, queen's crepe myrtle) is a more tropical version with much larger flowers up to 3 in (8 cm) wide. The leaves turn burnished reds in the fall, though it can be evergreen in some regions. Native to tropical Asia. Height 30–80 ft (10–25 m) x width 15–30 ft (5–10 m). ZONE 9.

Speciosa = showy.

Lagunaria

Lagunaria patersonii
NORFOLK ISLAND HIBISCUS, COW ITCH TREE,
QUEENSLAND PYRAMID TREE
Malvaceae

Imagine a small round-headed tree so dense and evergreen you can't see through it. Actually "evergray" would be a better description of this tree's battleship-gray, waxy leaves. They are oval to arrow shape going to a point, quite fleshy to touch and as tough as nails. This is one of the most wind-hardy plants on Earth. Not surprising really when you consider it grows naturally on Norfolk Island hundreds of miles off the east coast of Australia and literally miles from anywhere.

The lovely cup-shaped flowers are like lustrous pink mini-hibiscuses, about 1½–2½ in (4–6 cm) across. They appear from midsummer onward and last for weeks, sometimes months. There are named forms with much richer, darker flowers than the species, such as **'Royal Purple'**. Brown pointy seedpods contain small, hard, black seeds and lots of fine fluff. Beware of this fluff, as it is very itchy on the skin.

The tree loves to be out in the open in hot sun and doesn't like being crowded by other plants. Grow it as a specimen tree, preferably on its own, as it doesn't blend very well with other trees and shrubs. While most books describe it as tolerating light frost I know from experience that given long hot summers it will cope with frosts to -12°C without any damage. It grows happily in wet or dry climates and seems unperturbed as to soil, coping with whatever it is given as long as the drainage is good.

Transplant only young specimens from pots and don't be tempted to shift bigger plants. They are totally free of any pests or diseases. Height 50 ft (15 m) x width 25 ft (8 m). ZONE 8, given hot summers.

Lagunaria = Andres Laguna (d. 1559), after whom the genus is named, was a physician and botanist to Philip II of Spain. He was given the task of setting up the first botanic garden in Spain at Aranjuez; *patersonii* = Lt. Col. Willian Paterson, Governor of Tasmania from 1804 to 1808. He was the first to send the seeds of this tree to England.

Lantana

SHRUB VERBENA
Verbenaceae

Is this plant a saint or a sinner? Well it all depends on where you live. In hot climates, lantanas are definitely pests, covering whole hillsides in Hong Kong. In cooler climates, they are well-behaved, small bushes, flowering for long periods, and in really cold climes they have to be grown as conservatory plants. Even in regions where they are commonplace, you have to be impressed by their flowers. Round heads the size of a cookie are packed with flowers in bright yellows, reds, orange or mauve. Lantanas are evergreen, sun-loving shrubs with a reasonably tidy, dense habit and rough, corrugated, rasping leaves. Any free-draining soil will suffice and they are extremely drought-tolerant. They cope with wind, even coastal salt-laden winds, so they definitely earn a place in seaside gardens, providing color nearly all summer long. They are useful, too, in pots or tubs, or at the tops of walls and banks. They are also just right for narrow borders and difficult, drafty places around the house.

Transplant them from pots in winter but don't shift them again. You can prune them back with loppers occasionally if you want to tidy or lower them but they usually have a neat habit anyway. If there is one thing I can't stand about lantanas, it's the smell of the bush. You don't even have to crush a leaf, just brush past it and the smell overpowers you and is headache-making. Not everybody feels this way, and some say it is a pleasant smell. There are no pests or diseases to speak of.

Lantana = an ancient name for viburnum; the leaves are similar to some of the rougher-leafed viburnums.

Lantana camara
This is the common lantana, with two-tone, strongly scented flowers, usually in a mix of orange and yellow, but they can also be pink and yellow or red and yellow. There are single colored forms too, in pure yellows and red. The flower heads are 1–2 in (2.5–5 cm) across. **'Chelsea Gem'** is one of the most well-known in orange and yellow.

Above: *Lagunaria patersonii*

Right: *Lantana montevidensis*

Right: *Lantana camara*

Lantana montevidensis, syn *L. delicatissima,* *L. sellowiana*

WEEPING LANTANA

A creeping plant ideal for the top of a wall as it will trail down to cover bare blocks or bricks. Like all lantanas it thrives on hot, dry sites. The small mauve to rosy lilac flower heads are only half the size of *Lantana camara*. It seems to flower all year, or at least all summer. South America. Height 1–2 ft (30–60 cm) x width 3–4 ft (1–1.2 m). ZONE 9.

Montevidensis = from Montevideo in Uruguay.

Lavatera

MALLOW
Malvaceae

Lavatera are a mixture of annuals, herbaceous perennials and soft sub-shrubs (which allows me to include these wonderful flowers in this book). Teeming with flowers all summer, these easy-to-please soft shrubs will blitz the opposition with a never-ending display of flowers. The pliable stems are laden with large megaphone-style flowers from early summer through until fall. The soft, hairy leaves are evergreen, or nearly so, depending on the climate.

Any free-draining, warm soil will suffice, and reduce the likelihood of root rot. Other attacks may come from aphids and caterpillars. Provide a little shelter and these plants will flourish. As they grow very quickly, they often become top-heavy, hence the need for shelter from strong winds. Their preference is for full sun, but any well-lit site will do. Mallows are ideal plants for

The species grows naturally from Central America up into Texas and the Carolinas. It grows around waist-high, though it can reach three times this. As it generally grows wider than it is high, it can be clipped into a standard moptop shape. The ordinary bush needs an occasional trim to keep a neat, tidy habit and is more inclined to get straggly when given rich, lush growing conditions. Height x width 3–9 ft (1–3 m). ZONE 8 OR 9.

Camara = a place name.

a shrubbery or as brilliant additions to a herbaceous border, where they add extra height as well as color. They also look good with roses—try them as a backdrop to a formal rose bed.

They are easily grown from seed or the cultivars from cuttings, and then easily planted out from pots. Do not attempt to transplant one later, however, as it will die. These evergreen, wooly shrubs are often short-lived anyway and can be killed over winter by cold, or wet feet, or rocking out of the ground during a storm. If you prune them occasionally to keep the proportions modest they are more likely to survive longer.

In the wild they have a wide distribution. Most of them are from Europe or Asia, but one comes from the islands off California.

Lavatera = after the brothers Lavater, 17th-century Swiss naturalists and physicians.

Lavatera arborea
TREE MALLOW

All through the summer months, this upright, soft shrub is covered in soft purple flowers with a darker blotch in the center. The leaves look gray because they are covered in downy white hairs. An ideal plant for coastal regions if given some shelter. Native to western Europe. Height 6 ft (2 m) x width 5 ft (1.5 m). ZONE 8.

Arborea = tree-like.

Lavatera assurgentiflora

Found naturally on the Santa Barbara and Santa Catalina islands off the Californian coast, this species is wind- and salt-hardy. It has soft, hairy, lobed leaves and usually grows to head-high, but it can be much higher. The clusters of flowers appear in midsummer on upturned stalks and are a strong cerise-pink with deeper pink veins. Height 6 ft (2 m) x width 5 ft (1.5 m). ZONE 9.

Assurgentiflora = flowers ascending in clusters.

Lavatera maritima, syn L. bicolor, L. maritima var bicolor

A lovely Mediterannean shrub, its pale pinky lilac flowers have prominent red veins and a central red blotch reminiscent of gera-

Above: *Lavatera maritima*

niums. It flowers all summer long. The leaves are wooly. Western Mediterranean. Height 5 ft (1.5 m) x width 3 ft (1 m). ZONE 6.

Maritima = maritime or seaside.

Lavatera thuringiaca
TREE LAVATERA

A beautiful soft shrub worthy of a place in every garden. This European native is almost evergreen and has velvety leaves and pale lolly-pink flowers all summer. Height x width 10 ft (3 m). ZONE 6 OR 7.

'Barnsley' is a lovely white form, or should I say almost white as there is just a hint of pink in the petals and a red spot at the center of the flower. A fairly new plant on the garden scene, it is deservedly popular with its mass of flowers all summer. The variety **'Kew Rose'** has deeper pink-veined petals. For both, height x width 10 ft (3 m).

Above: *Lavatera thuringiaca* 'Kew Rose'

Leonotis

Leonotis leonurus
LION'S EAR, LION'S TAIL
Lamiaceae

*L*eonotis looks magnificent in the summer with bold, upright spikes of fuzzy orange flowers. Then I look again in the winter and wonder if it deserves space in my garden. Although it is evergreen, it gets very scruffy in winter and needs a good haircut to keep it tidy and manageable. The flowers occur in a whorl or circle around the stems, and then there is a gap of bare stem and another whorl of flowers, with the oldest flowers at the base.

Its multiple pencil-thick stems are very upright and hold the narrow hairy leaves in spiral fashion all the way up the stem. The plant has two saving graces: one, the brilliant orange flowers last for weeks, if not months, in high summer; and, two, the ability to grow in poor soil and windy sites. Another possible site is under huge nourishment-robbing trees. I've seen them planted right up to the trunks of big, old trees, but it has to be where the sun can beat down on them.

They transplant easily from pots, but don't try to shift them again later because they'll die. It is easier to start again with cutting-grown plants.

It forms an upright shrub around head-high, and is usually wider than it is tall. The bush will cope with quite severe wind, though occasionally whole branches get blown out, especially if the plant is allowed to get leggy. Full sun is essential, and although it will cope with considerable drought and dry, sandy soils, it will just as easily grow in wet regions and in heavy clays. It seems happy enough in alkaline soil and is certainly content in very acidic soil.

Typical of the Lamiaceae family it doesn't seem to be attacked by any pests or diseases. This family includes many of the aromatic herbs such as salvia and lavender. *Leonotis*, too, has quite a strong smell when you're cutting the stems and perhaps the odor puts off any bugs. It's not unpleasant, more a medicinal sage-like smell. Height x width 6 ft (2 m). Generally a zone 9 plant, this South African native will grow against a wall or a similar protected site in zone 8. I've seen it growing in the open in London and covered in snow for days at a time without coming to any harm.

There are white flower forms available, but personally I find them boring, especially when the species itself has such a vibrant color.

Below: *Leonotis leonurus*

Leon = lion; while *otis* = ear and *urus* = tail.

Leptospermum

TEA TREE
Myrtaceae

*L*eptospermum are tough evergreen bushes from New Zealand and Australia. Grown for their mass display of round flowers, the species have single rose-like flowers and the doubles are like the crepe myrtle, with frilly-edged blooms. The leaves are usually small, often almost needle-like, and can be sharp to touch.

They are great plants for the back of a border or as part of a screen where you need some tough, wind-hardy specimens. While they will withstand strong winds once established, they are liable to be flattened when young. Top-heavy young plants seem to get blown over at ground level. It might pay to stake the plant until the roots are well established, say around two years, and you can help the plant be less top heavy and more bushy by frequent light pruning with the shears in this early phase.

Full sun is essential and they grow in a variety of soils from good moist loams through to heavy, dry or stony ground. They are capable of withstanding quite severe drought once established. Acidic or neutral soil is required.

Young pot-grown plants establish easily if you make sure the roots are spread out. Don't try to move a plant once it is established. They are hardy enough to grow in inland areas with mild frosts as well as by the sea.

Leptos = Latin name from the Greek "leptos," meaning slender and *sperma* = seed, because they have thin, slender seeds.

Leptospermum petersonii
A big, upright bush with shiny, green, needle-like leaves. Older bushes often have an open arching habit though it is upright and compact when young. They can be trimmed to keep a tidy habit or

Below: *Leptospermum scoparium* 'Nichollsii'

Above: *Leptospermum scoparium* 'Red Damask'

you can leave them alone for a more natural look. The mass of single, white, rose-like flowers appear in summer. It is a good hot-climate plant as the flowers never burn. Plant one near a path so you can enjoy the fabulous lemon-scented foliage—crush a leaf as you pass. Native to Australia. Height 10 ft (3 m) x width 6 ft (2 m). ZONE 8 OR 9.

Leptospermum scoparium

TEA TREE, MANUKA

Captain James Cook was one of the first sea captains to keep his crews free of scurvy—a killer disease caused by lack of Vitamin C. Wherever his crews came ashore they had to eat some greenery. In New Zealand he made them brew up a tea from the leaves of this plant and the name has stuck ever since.

The bush comes in two basic shapes: one is semi-prostrate and is a useful ground cover, and the other, more typical one, is narrow and upright. The upright version is an ideal garden plant giving height, shape and form with a bonus of flowers in the spring. Just a light trim after flowering is all that is needed to keep the dense habit. Their nature is to keep growing, gradually getting more sparse and open. They are evergreen but the leaves are tiny and create more of a haze of foliage.

Most trees grow about head-high, though they keep that same narrow upright habit of growth. There are some even smaller bushy ones around waist-high and some beautiful trailing types, ideal for covering unsightly banks and walls. One of the great attributes of leptospermums is their ability to grow in hostile situations in clay, or on hot, dry banks.

The small, round flowers are typically single with five petals in a circle and the size of a small coin. Quite a few of the cultivars have double flowers with frilly edges. The colors range from white to pink to rich reds and crimsons. They are becoming popular with the cut-flower trade as they are a long-lasting cut flower.

Black sooty mold on the stems is caused by a scale insect living on the plant. Otherwise, it is an easy-care shrub. Native to New Zealand and Australia. Height 6–20 ft (2–6 m) x width 6–15 ft (2–5 m). ZONE 8.

Scoparium = broom-like after *Cytisus scoparius*.

Some popular cultivars include:

'Crimson Glory', a tidy, upright plant with grayish foliage and rich red, double flowers. Height 10 ft (3 m) x width 6 ft (2 m).
'Nichollsii' with rich bronzy foliage and deep red flowers. Height 10 ft (3 m) x width 6 ft (2 m).
'Red Damask', a Californian hybrid with double deep red flowers. Height 10 ft (3 m) x width 6 ft (2 m).
'Ruby Glow', with double rosy red flowers appearing in late winter to early spring. An upright shrub with dark reddy foliage. Height 5 ft (1.5 m) x width 3 ft (1 m).

Leucadendron

Proteaceae

I am cheating a bit by including these as flowers when in fact the colorful part we get excited about are showy bracts around the true flower hidden within. *Bougainvillea*, *Clematis* and *Cornus* are not true petal flowers either, but that is how we

Above:
Leucadendron
'Safari Sunset'

Right: *Leucadendron*
argenteum

conditions. For this reason they are brilliant seaside shrubs where there is a constant breeze—salt-winds hold no terrors for them. You can grow them in high rainfall areas providing the drainage is good. Give them a free-draining soil that is acidic, or tending that way. Sandy and rocky sites are fine, and even clay is acceptable if it is free-draining. They love to grow on banks.

When you plant one, take care because they hate being moved and don't ever try to shift one later. They are a bit garish and can be difficult to blend with other shrubs, so often look best in isolation. You can prune them after flowering as long as you are not too ruthless. Don't cut back into old wood or below the current season's growth. Alternatively, you are pruning the bush when you cut stems for a vase, and later you can trim the remaining spent flowers to keep the bush nicely rounded.

Occasionally a caterpillar chews the edges of young leaves or bracts before they firm up and scale insects can also be a pest. Root rot is the biggest threat and can kill a plant in days. Typical of the Protea family, leucadendrons hate fertilizers or animal manures.

Leukos = Greek for white; *dendron* = tree.

Leucadendron argenteum
SILVER TREE
This species is grown purely for its fabulous foliage, which is nigh on unique in the plant world. Each narrow, finger-length leaf is covered with thousands of soft, silky hairs. The cone-like flowers—yellowish green on male plants and greenish silver on females—are found at the tips of the stems and appear from spring to summer. This bush is the largest of the genus, forming an upright pillar of a plant. It thrives near the sea and needs a breezy site, but may be toppled by strong gales. It is often short-lived and can die overnight from root rot if it gets too wet around the roots or the roots are damaged by wind rock. Native to Cape Peninsula, South Africa. Height 30 ft (10 m) x width 10 ft (3 m). ZONE 9.

Argenteum = silver.

Leucadendron laureolum
A dense, head-high bush with gray-green leaves and yellow or gold flowers. The males have long, narrow bracts and the female plants have chunkier, more robust heads. As with all leucadendrons, you have to propagate from cuttings to get the clone you want. This species is more tolerant of alkaline soils. Originates from Cape Peninsula, South Africa. Height 6 ft (2 m) x width 4–5 ft (1.2–1.5 m). ZONE 9.

Laureolum = laurel leaf.

Leucadendron salignum
An upright evergreen shrub that grows from waist- to head-high. The stems are red, the narrow, glossy leaves are green and the stems are topped with exciting red bracts enclosing the cone-like flowers. There are green and yellow forms too. Cape Peninsula, South Africa. Height 4–6 ft (1.2–2 m) x width 4–6 ft (1.2–2 m). ZONE 9.

Salignum = willow, as in *Salix*.

Leucadendron 'Safari Sunset' is a hybrid between *L. salignum* and *L. laureolum*. It is a bigger, more robust plant with bigger leaves, bigger flower heads, produced from summer through to winter depending on the climate, and decked in stunning deep red bracts. Being a hybrid it seems to have increased vigor and resilience to wind, weather and soils. It is an excellent cut flower, as the stems last for weeks, if not months. Height 8 ft (2.5 m) x width 6 ft (2 m). ZONE 9.

think of them. Most leucadendrons have smooth, seemingly plastic leaves, and the first time you see them you have to touch them to make sure they are real. There are species with silvery gray hairs covering the leaves and these are wonderfully tactile, e.g. *Leucadendron argenteum* has beautiful, silky, silver leaves.

The true flowers are found in small, tight cones at the tip of the stem, and male and female flowers are located on different plants. Most are excellent as cut flowers, because the waxy leaves are easily transported without wilting and the stems last for weeks in a vase.

All of the leucadendrons hail from the Cape Province of South Africa, growing either on the mountains or the coast. They are emphatic about what they like and don't like, and you ignore this at their peril. They love full sun and an open, breezy situation. Likewise they hate cold, wet feet and humid

Leucospermum

Proteaceae

The stunning, futuristic-looking flowers of leucospermums come in orange, reds and yellows. Each head is like some spikey sea anemone with upturned tendrils. The heads are large (up to 6 in/15 cm) and very showy, yet they seem to mingle easily in seaside gardens along with spiky agaves and masses of daisy flowers. Somehow, though, these plants are difficult to blend in with more conventional gardens. They flower in summer as seems fitting for a seaside plant.

Leucospermums are evergreen South African shrubs with stiff, waxy leaves and a slightly wayward habit of growth, so they usually end up being wider than they are high. This can be a problem when planting them in a shrubbery because they take up so much room. The alternative is to plant them at the top of a bank or on top of a wall, where we can use their tendency to grow down rather than up to our advantage.

They are real sun-lovers and can't abide shade. On the plus side of the ledger, they will grow in coastal gardens right by the sea shore, coping with the salt-winds, scorching sun and dry soils. Strong winds can, however, be the death of them, if the plant gets too top-heavy. Better to let them spread sideways, giving them more stability in the wind.

They will grow in high rainfall areas too, providing they have plenty of air movement around the plant and the drainage is good. Soft, muggy, humid conditions or poor drainage lead to leaf diseases or root rot. These are the main threat to the plant, other than severe frosts. They cope with light frost, providing the plant gets enough summer heat and warm soil. The other threat comes from root disturbance. Once you've planted your leucospermum don't ever move it again.

You can prune them lightly, and this can extend the life of the plant as they are often short-lived if not pruned. One option is to take the flowers for indoor cut flowers and thus prune the plant in the process. The key is not to cut back into old wood, so any cut you make must be within the last year's growth. It's easy enough to see each annual growth as the pattern is bare stem, whorl of leaves, bare stem, whorl of leaves, etc. As cut flowers they last for a long time in a vase, and this is reason enough to grow them. Even if you've never seen the bush, you've almost certainly seen the flowers in florists' shops.

Leukos = Greek for white; *spermum* = seed.

Leucospermum cordifolium, syn L. bolusii, L. nutans

The most well-known and easiest to grow of the leucospermums, its glowing heads of rich orange are fantastic. Appearing from early spring to midsummer, they last for weeks and weeks. It has thumb-sized, twisty, gray, slightly hairy leaves and a dense habit. Native to South Africa. Height 6 ft (2 m) x width 6 ft or more (2 m or more). ZONE 9.

Cordifolium = heart-shaped leaves.

Leucospermum reflexum
ROCKET PINCUSHION
This species gives a more upright bush than most and the styles of the red flowers initially face skyward, only gradually turning to face the ground. Hence the name *reflexum*, meaning reflexed or bent backward. The flowers appear from early spring to early summer and the narrow leaves are covered in soft, gray hairs. From South Africa. Height 10 ft (3 m) x width 6 ft (2 m). ZONE 9.

Lonicera

HONEYSUCKLE
Caprifoliaceae

Lonicera are a funny mix of shrubs and climbers that seem to bear little relationship to each other. For instance, *Lonicera nitida* is a dense evergreen shrub used for hedges and *L. korolkowii* is a shrub with glaucous blue leaves and small pink flowers. Then there are all the deciduous and evergreen climbers. One thing they do have in common, however, is that they are all very easy to grow and have attractive, very often fragrant flowers. Some of the climbers grow too easily, and have become naturalized in warm climates.

Loniceras will grow in virtually any ground, be it acidic or alkaline, sandy or clay. Try to ensure the drainage is reasonable, but otherwise don't worry. They are all best transplanted from

Right: *Leucospermum cordifolium*

Above: *Lonicera* x *brownii* 'Dropmore Scarlet'

container-grown nursery plants, and while you could move a shrubby deciduous type in winter, it would be risky to move the evergreen or climbing loniceras.

All loniceras can be pruned to keep them tidier, depending on the shape you are trying to create. Most prefer full sun but cope with shade, and a few of the climbers insist on shade, so it's difficult to make hard-and-fast rules for this genus. Nearly all species are cold-hardy, but again, being a diverse group, some are almost tropical.

Apart from an occasional aphid attack, they are healthy, easy-care plants. Considering they have soft leaves, most are also quite wind-hardy, especially the climbers. Beware, these climbers can be tenacious killers of innocent shrubs. The strong vines twine around the stems constricting the flow of sap until the poor shrub gives up. Ideally, the climbers should be given a trellis or some independent means of climbing and not allowed into any nearby shrubs.

Lonicera = named for Adam Lonitzer (1528–1586), a German botanist and physician.

Lonicera x brownii 'Dropmore Scarlet'
(*L. sempervirens* x *L. hirsuta*)
SCARLET TRUMPET HONEYSUCKLE

A lovely climber with bright orangy red, trumpet-shaped flowers that appear in summer and last over a long period. The leaves are bluish and perfoliate, meaning pairs of leaves join around the stem to form one leaf. This deciduous vine has the cold-hardiness of

Lonicera hirsuta but unfortunately did not inherit the pest-resistance of *L. sempervirens*, and so is often attacked by aphids. But this is the only drawback of this plant, if you don't mind the lack of scent. Height 15 ft (5 m). Very hardy to ZONE 4.

Brownii = origin obscure.

Lonicera x heckrottii
(*L. americana* x *L. sempervirens*)

A vigorous scrambler/climber with dazzling, showy flowers. Seen from above, the flowers form a star of rosy purple tubes opening to golden orange trumpets. The flowering season is long, starting in summer, and as an added bonus, the flowers are fragrant. Height 15–20 ft (5–6 m). ZONE 5.

Heckrottii = origin obscure.

Lonicera hildebrandiana
GIANT BURMESE HONEYSUCKLE

This is the "granddaddy" of the genus, with the biggest flowers of them all. An evergreen tropical climber, it will adapt to frosty climes if given hot, baking summers to ripen the wood. It was discovered in Burma in 1888 and named in honour of H. H. Hildebrand, a plant collector of the time. It has lush green, oval leaves, about finger-length in size, and vigorous stems capable of pulling down any flimsy support with sheer weight of growth. The magical flowers open creamy white, though no one ever seems to notice this stage because they are captivated by the older flowers, that have turned to apricot and are blessed with a heavenly scent.

Above: *Lonicera* x *tellmanniana*

The flowers are huge by comparison to other species (3–6 in/ 8–15 cm long), as seems fitting for such a gigantic plant. It is tricky to propagate, though it will grow for some from stem cuttings and root cuttings. Height 60 ft (20 m). ZONE 9.

Lonicera korolkowii

This plant was a hit at the Chelsea Flower Show, London, England, a few years ago, but like many overnight successes it has been working hard for years to get some attention. The Confederate gray-blue leaves are most unusual and topped off with contrasting pink flowers in the spring. The flowers sit prettily on the tips of the stems. A dense, twiggy bush with an arching habit, it is generally quite tidy. The species comes from Turkestan. Height 10 ft (3 m) x width 15 ft (5 m). ZONE 6.

> *Korolkowii* = named after General Nikolai Iwanowitsch Korolkow, the local Governor of the region at the time the plant was discovered in the 1870s.

Lonicera sempervirens

TRUMPET HONEYSUCKLE, CORAL HONEYSUCKLE

Handsome, shiny, gray-green leaves and long, tubular flowers in a rich orangy red appear on this evergreen climber in summer and fall. It is an easy-care plant for a trellis and pest-free. It hails from the eastern states of the U.S.A. Height 12 ft (4 m). ZONE 4.

> *Sempervirens* = evergreen.

Lonicera tatarica

TATARIAN HONEYSUCKLE

A big, upright shrub with grayish-blue leaves that is laden with pink, spidery flowers in late spring to early summer. The name *tatarica* means infernal, or "of the infernal regions," as it comes from the land of the Tartars in central Asia. Native to southern Russia and central Asia. Height 10 ft or more (3 m or more) x width 8 ft (2.5 m). ZONE 3.

Right: *Lonicera tatarica* 'Hack's Red'

Choose the **'Hack's Red'** variety with its showy purple-red flowers or **'Arnold Red'**, with the darkest red flowers of all. 'Hack's Red' forms an upright bush with a reasonably tidy shape (if not, this is easily remedied by judicious pruning). It is a slightly twiggy, stalky bush with smooth gray stems and small, heart- to oval-shaped leaves in gray-green. Pairs of flowers appear just above the new leaves and the flowers are like a bird's foot, with three petals one way and one going the other way. The petals are curved in a long boat shape and the color is intense cerise-purple with bright yellow stamens. For both, height 10 ft or more (3 m or more) x width 8 ft (2.5 m).

Lonicera x tellmanniana (*L. tragophylla* x *L. sempervirens*)

This plant can be grown as a bush or as a climber and copes especially well with shade. In fact it seems to need shade to grow properly. Lovely apricot flowers with a subtle scent appear in late spring through to midsummer and overtop the gray-blue, rounded leaves. Height 15 ft (5 m). ZONE 7.

> *Tellmanniana* = origin obscure.

Loropetalum

Loropetalum chinense
FRINGE FLOWER
Hamamelidaceae

I have just dashed outside to pick a flower from this plant in the depths of winter (albeit a zone 8 winter!). This species has been regarded as frost-tender by much of the gardening world and I think it is one of those shrubs capable of tolerating cool winters if it gets enough summer heat to toughen up the growth. By contrast, mild summers produce soft growth more liable to frost damage. It also appears that gardeners are now prepared to give it a go because they want the new colorful varieties.

Above: *Loropetalum chinense* 'China Rose'

But I'm getting ahead of myself, let me first describe the original wild plant. It is evergreen with mottled leaves, thus making a contrast of the pale green new leaves with the older darker ones all the more special. It is a winter-flowering shrub and the flowers appear on the tips of new growth. Although the thin, strap-like, creamy white petals look just like a *Hamamelis*, the rough-textured leaves give you the clue that it is not so. These small, oval leaves are ridged and furrowed with a hard, leathery feel.

It forms a big, round, dense mound of a bush. The stems are horizontal and weeping at the tips. Each stem comes out and tumbles over the lower or inner branch, so it creates a perfect dome of foliage. It eventually reaches 6 ft (2 m) in cultivation, so it fits easily into most gardens. However, it's unlikely to be a top priority for most gardeners and would look somehow out of place in a small suburban garden. Ideally, it belongs in a sheltered woodland garden. Full sun or good light is necessary for a dense cloak of foliage, but it will tolerate some shade.

It prefers an open, free-draining, acidic soil, such as you might choose for a rhododendron. They are, however, much more drought-tolerant than rhododendrons, so a wet or dry climate suits. In the wild they grow on sun-baked cliffs and so they are used to wind, heat and drought. No pests bother it, so it is an easy-care plant. Just choose the right site and leave it alone to perform every year for the rest of your life. These plants can also be grown in pots and tubs or trained as a standard, enhancing the natural weeping habit. Native to China. Height x width 10 ft (3 m). ZONE 8, or even 7 with hot summers.

This plant has been lingering on the fringes of the garden world for decades (it was introduced from China in 1880 by Charles Maries) and then, when the new red flower varieties came out of China in the 1990s, suddenly everybody coveted them. Now it looks set to become a top-selling plant. There are a number of red- and pink-flowered clones becoming available such as **'Blush'**, **'Burgundy'**, **'China Pink'** and **'China Rose'**. The flowers are more ostentatious and even the foliage is more exciting in red, bronze and burgundy.

Loro = thong; *petalumn* = petal; and *chinense* = from China.

Right: *Loropetalum chinense*

Magnolia

Magnoliaceae

The leaves of the popular deciduous magnolias have two prime attributes. The first is the large convex shape and clean, green finish. The second, more important one, is the good sense to stay out of sight while the flowers are blooming. I'm sure the plant doesn't do this for our benefit, but it certainly adds to the spectacle. The outer sepals and inner petals all look the same and are known as tepals. It is hard to find a better flowering plant and yet it is one of the least sophisticated and oldest on the planet. Magnolias are thought to be the oldest of the true flowering plants, appearing after the conifers. Some of the larger-leafed species have a habit of flowering with the leaves and thus the flowers are often overlooked.

Magnolias are a mix of evergreen and deciduous trees and large shrubs from Asia (especially China and Japan), eastern North America and Mexico. They are surprisingly good city trees, putting up with atmospheric pollution, and they perform very well in heavy, cool, moist soils. I have a theory that plants with thick, fleshy roots, such as magnolias and ash trees, actually prefer dense, heavy soils to the lighter fluffy loams.

The fleshy roots should never be allowed to dry out and magnolias hate having their roots disturbed, so either plant them in a woodland situation, in a lawn or put a mulch on top of the ground around them. They don't like thin or hot, dry soils and they generally don't like lime. On these soils the leaves often look anaemic. A few of them will tolerate lime, however, namely *Magnolia acuminata*, *M. delavayi*, *M. kobus* and *M. wilsonii*.

All magnolias flower and grow best in full sun, though they will tolerate some thin shade. A sheltered position is essential for the wellbeing of the plant and to prevent wind-blast on the flowers. Although the tepals are fleshy, the flowers are quite vulnerable to wind and hot sun. Magnolias usually have a good natural shape and rarely need pruning, but will cope if you feel the need. They can even be cut back to stumps and will regenerate quite easily. Most of the deciduous types have a clean, open habit that is pleasing summer or winter.

Magnolia = named after Professor Pierre Magnol (1638–1715), an Italian botanist, author and teacher.

Magnolia campbellii

A big, upright tree only suitable for large gardens and those with patience, as they can take many years to begin flowering. However, they are truly stunning when they do flower. The huge flowers have a tidy, upright, tulip-shape initially, opening up to a saucer-shape 12 in (30 cm) across. The tree can have both shapes at any one time. They come out very early in the spring so the buds may be frosted in colder areas. The standard garden type is pink and yet in the Himalayas the white form is the most common. Native of Nepal, Sikkim (India), Bhutan. Height 50 ft (15 m) x width 30 ft (10 m). ZONE 7.

Campbellii = named after Dr. Campbell, a British diplomat who had some hair-raising escapades in Sikkim and north India in the 1840s.

Magnolia campbellii cultivars and hybrids

'Charles Raffill' A cross made from two forms of *Magnolia campbellii*, it has big, rosy pink to purple flowers. It can take many years to flower for the first time, but has the advantage of flowering later in the spring and so avoiding frosts in some climates. Height 50 ft (15 m) x width 30 ft (10 m).

Above: *Magnolia campbellii*

Left: *Magnolia 'Iolanthe'*

flowers are slightly less intense in color, but the combination of open flowers and emerging buds is charming. The stems are dark purply brown, and smooth with little gray raised bumps or lenticels (breathing holes). The leaves come a long time after the flowers and are the size of a small hand and often palish green. Many magnolias have a slightly anaemic look to them, which can be due to the soil not being acidic enough. They also sometimes appear this way in colder climates; it is as if the sap isn't flowing fast enough to maintain the plant with all its needs. Often this just occurs in spring. Height 10 ft (3 m) x width 8 ft (2.5 m). ZONE 6.

Two lovely hybrids to look for are: **'Sayonara'**, its beautiful creamy white flowers having a hint of pink at the base. It flowers late in the season and so avoids frosts in many areas. Height 12 ft (4 m) x width 8 ft (2.5 m); and **'Susan'**, with big, bold, tulip-like flowers sitting upright on the bare branches. The blooms are deep violet to purple-red with white inside. Height 10 ft (3 m) x width 6 ft (2 m).

Liliiflora – flower like a lily

Magnolia x loebneri (*M. kobus* x *M. stellata*)

Intermediate in height between the two parents, these hybrids make large, dense shrubs, much denser than most magnolias. Typically the bush is around 10 ft by 10 ft (3 m x 3 m) after ten years, but does eventually get much bigger (up to 30 ft/10 m).

The bush tends to be cluttered, both in the number of stems and the almost too many flowers, thus losing some of the simple beauty of other magnolias with less flowers. The fragrant, star-shaped flowers appear before the leaves in midspring and are tinged with pink. The form **'Leonard Messel'** has more purply pink in the flowers (height 25 ft (8 m) x width 20 ft (6 m)) and **'Merrill'** is a pure white form (height x width 25 ft (8 m)). All ZONE 5.

Loebneri = named for Max Loebner, who bred the plant in the 1920s.

Magnolia sieboldii, syn *M. parviflora*
OYAMA MAGNOLIA

Different from most magnolias, the white flowers on this species hang down rather than sit up like tulips. It is a wide, spreading, hardy shrub and ideally in a garden situation it should be planted on top of a bank or wall so you can appreciate the nodding flowers. The blossoms appear from late spring through to late summer,

'Iolanthe' A *Magnolia campbellii*-type hybrid with huge lavender-pink blooms. It has the advantage of flowering as a young plant and has an attractive upright habit. Height 15–20 ft (5–7 m) x width 12–15 ft (4–5 m).
'Lanarth' Has rich pinky purple flowers, but it can take years to flower. Height 50 ft (15 m) x width 30 ft (10 m).
'Star Wars' Stunning raspberry pink flowers and laden with blooms from a young age. Height 15 ft (5 m) x width 10 ft (3 m).
'Vulcan' A real color break with rich wine-red flowers of size and substance. It flowers young, but can have some small dull flowers in the first few years. It settles down to produce outstanding blooms. Height 12 ft (4 m) x width 8 ft (2.5 m).

Magnolia liliiflora 'Nigra'
LILY-FLOWERED MAGNOLIA
The neat emerging buds in early summer have a slight curve and a pointed tip, like a bird's beak, and are bright papal purple. It is equally exciting when the flowers open, with the wavy petals twisting this way and that to form a haphazard pattern. The open

Above: *Magnolia 'Susan'*

Left: *Magnolia* x
soulangeana

are fragrant and usually have a red center—sometimes bright red, sometimes rather pale. Native to Korea and Japan. Height 25 ft (8 m) x width 40 ft (12 m). ZONE 6.

Sieboldii = named after Baron von Siebold (1797–1866), who spent many years botanizing in Japan.

Magnolia x *soulangeana* (*M. denudata* x *M. liliiflora*)
SAUCER MAGNOLIA

Named in honor of the Chevalier Soulange-Bodin, who first raised them in 1820 in a garden at Fromont near Paris, this species is usually an upright bush at first, spreading with age. Thick stems are shiny browny purple and the leaves are bold rich green, the size of your hand or more. Large chalice-like flowers appear in spring, before the new leaves, and invariably have purple or red at the base of the tepals, the color thinning out toward the tops to be paler pink or white. The inside of the tepals is white and if you cut them for a vase the flowers open right out to reveal a beautiful porcelain-white inner. Height x width 30 ft (10 m). ZONE 6.

There are lots of lovely cultivars:
'Alexandrina', with a very upright habit, it is ideal for small gardens. The purple-pink tulip-like flowers have a white base. Height 15 ft (5 m) x width 12 ft (4 m). **'Lennei'** has dark purple-red flowers with white inside. Height x width 20 ft (6 m). **'Rustica Rubra'** has rosy red outer tepals and the flowers are scented like ice. Height x width 20 ft (6 m).

Magnolia stellata
STAR MAGNOLIA

This is surely the best and most compact magnolia for small gardens. In time it becomes quite a large bush but it is only going to

Above: *Magnolia stellata*

be 6 ft (2 m) x 6 ft (2 m) after 10 years, so it is easy enough to fit in a smaller garden. The bare gray stems are covered in lovely tactile, furry, gray flower buds during winter, opening to wide, flat, starry flowers in spring. The tepals are widely spaced, giving the star effect indicated by the common name. The flowers are nicely scented too. Native to Japan. Height 10 ft (3 m) x width 12 ft (4 m). ZONE 5.

Stellata = star, referring to the shape of the flowers.

Above: *Malus
floribunda*

Malus

CRABAPPLES
Rosaceae

Good old reliable crabapples have been a standby in gardens for centuries, called upon to perform every spring and then conveniently forgotten until the the "crabs" appear later in the year. They just seem to fade into the background during summer, which means they look presentable but no longer stunning. Except, that is, for a small group with purple-red foliage that is able to claim our attention for longer. They reappear in the fall when we cannot help but notice the fruits or "crab apples."

Flowering crabs are just like fruiting apples in that they make a small, mophead tree suitable for suburban gardens. Typically they are wider than they are high and so make an ideal shade tree for a lawn. Some shade trees are so successful at making shade they also kill the grass beneath. Crabapples don't do this, so you can have a neat lawn right up to the trunk.

They are easy to grow in most soils and climates. On the downside, they are prone to the myriad pests and diseases that apples get, but thankfully they don't seem to be plagued by them or need regular spraying to keep them healthy. They do have the prime advantage, like apples, of growing both in very alkaline soil and acidic soil. They will grow in clay soil, too. Whatever the soil type, a cool, moist soil is best, and you may struggle to grow them well in very hot, drought-prone regions.

Like apples, they can be grafted onto rootstocks with the ability to change their tree size and soil tolerances. Apple or *Malus* rootstocks have been selected to change the overall size of the tree and even its tolerance of certain soils and pests. Of course they are deciduous, just like apples, and generally the fall color is nothing to rave about. One day it has leaves and the next time you notice the tree is bare.

They are not as "clean" and open-looking as a cherry and instead have a rather messy, twiggy look through winter. *Malus* put up with cold, wet winters, being one of the hardiest trees around. Winter is the time to transplant them as they are dormant, and you can shift any size tree if you have the manpower. Ideally, plant the tree in full sun for health. They will put up with an occasional storm or regular light winds, but don't choose too windy a site.

The flowers are just like apple blossom, as you'd expect, and the clusters of white flowers with a hint of pink appear on bare twigs in spring. So familiar are they, we often talk about apple blossom to describe some other flowers and use them to decorate curtains, wallpaper and plates, etc. There are variations, including red, purple and strong pink flowers.

Malus = ancient Latin name coined by the Roman poet Virgil.

Malus x *arnoldiana* (*M. baccata* x *M. floribunda*)
A beautiful small tree with an arching, graceful habit. In spring, the masses of red buds open to fragrant, soft pink blossoms fading to white. Fruits are yellow, maturing to red. This species is named after the Arnold Arboretum in Boston. The parent plant, *M. baccata*, is even hardier than the hybrid, and has pure white, fragrant flowers. Height 15 ft (5 m) x width 25 ft (8 m). ZONE 4.

Malus floribunda
JAPANESE CRABAPPLE, JAPANESE FLOWERING CRABAPPLE, SHOWY CRABAPPLE

A beautiful Japanese species and the name says it all—*floribunda* means an abundance of flowers. They are beautiful flowers, too, emerging from rosy red buds like fat pearls to reveal blush-pink and white blossoms. Each node has a spray of five to eight flowers, so it is a very floriferous small tree. The small yellow fruits are, however, not as wonderful as some *Malus* species. Height x width 30 ft (10 m). ZONE 5.

Malus ioensis
PRAIRIE CRABAPPLE

The common name and species name refer to its homeland of Iowa and central parts of the United States. It has scented, soft pink flowers, downy leaves and interesting peeling bark. The form usually seen is the double-flowered ***Malus ioensis* 'Plena'**. This deliciously scented plant has big double flowers like water lilies. Both prefer an acidic soil and are not as easy to grow as some species. They seem to perform best in warm or hot summer climates. For both, height 30 ft (10 m) x width 25 ft (8 m). ZONE 2.

Above: *Malus ioensis* 'Flore Pleno'

Malus 'Profusion'

This is a stunning plant in every way, with purple-red new growth, rich red-wine-colored flowers borne in "profusion" in spring, as the name suggests, and topped off with small red crabapples in the fall. An easy and robust plant for the garden. Other purple crabapples include **'Eleyi'**, **'Lemoinei'** and **'Royalty'**. All are quite similar, with height x width 30 ft (10 m). ZONE 4.

Malus sieboldii, syn *M. toringo*
TORINGO CRABAPPLE

A beautiful, semi-weeping bush with lovely, clean white, fragrant flowers in spring. The petals are rounded and put me in mind of a philadelphus. The plant doesn't get very tall or wide, around 10 ft (3 m) both ways, and so it is suitable for smaller gardens. From Japan. ZONE 5.

Sieboldii = named after Baron Philipp von Siebold (1797–1866), who collected plants in Japan.

Metrosideros

POHUTUKAWA, RATA
Myrtaceae

Which do you want first, the good news or the bad news? The bad news is only those gardeners in warm climates near the sea need apply to grow these wonderful plants. And the good news? Well, not only do they grow near the sea, but some can be grown right up close to the shore, coping with the worst storms and gales the ocean can deliver. All the *Metrosideros* have thick, waxy leaves; some with a shiny top surface and others in a dull blacky-gray camouflage color. The leathery leaves deflect wind, and salt deposits are easily washed off. If you bend a leaf in half it scrunches as it breaks, almost like plastic, showing just how strong they are. Most have new leaves

covered in soft, white down protecting the newly developing leaf until it has hardened and some retain this wooly protection underneath the old leaves.

Some species of this genus are climbers and others begin life as a vine, eventually strangling the host tree and becoming a forest giant in their own right. However, from an ornamental point of view, the coastal bushes and tree types are the best. Most of them form rounded, dense, evergreen bushes or trees. They are not fussy as to soil and some naturally grow on cliffs, seemingly living on fresh air. The roots are invasive and will rip up asphalt and concrete paths so plant them with care. They are easy to transplant and even huge trees can be moved by crane if you cut the tops back to compensate for the loss of roots. Most

Above: *Malus* 'Eleyi'

Left: *Metrosideros excelsa*

Above: *Metrosideros collina* 'Tahiti'

types can be pruned for shape and even drastic pruning only elicits more growth.

Once established these plants handle hot sun, drought, sandy soils and wind. Leaf roller caterpillars can attack the young developing leaves and show up as large notches when the leaf matures. The worst enemy for this tree is definitely frost.

Metrosideros are found throughout the South Pacific, with the biggest concentration of them in New Zealand. In Hawaii they are thought to be sacred to Pele the goddess of volcanoes because the red flowers are the color of lava. I think any goddess would be proud to have such sparkly bright red flowers as her emblem.

Metro = heartwood; *sideros* = iron, and ironwood is an appropriate name because the timber is particularly hard and heavy.

Metrosideros collina 'Tahiti'

Only introduced to cultivation in the 1980s, this wonderful bush is perfect for seaside gardens. It forms a dense shrub between waist- and head-high, and is loaded with brilliant balls of red flowers and tactile furry new leaves. It can flower more than once a year and often flowers intermittantly all year; alternatively, it has one or two blazes of color. It copes with hot sun, drought and salt-wind but abhors frost. It's also a good tub or patio plant. Height 3–6 ft (1–2 m) x width 6 ft (2 m). ZONE 9.

'Spring Fire' is another Pacific Island type with bigger, orange flowers and is somewhat taller. Height x width 6–10 ft (2–3 m).

Collina = of the hills, as these plants are found on mountains throughout the Pacific.

Metrosideros excelsa, syn. M. tomentosa

POHUTUKAWA, NEW ZEALAND CHRISTMAS TREE

In its native New Zealand, this magnificent tree is known by both the Maori name, pohutukawa, and its European name, New Zealand Christmas tree, as it flowers at Christmas (early summer in the Southern Hemisphere). The streets of many northern seaside towns are ablaze with color at this time when vast numbers of pohutukawa come into flower. The scented balls of bright red stamens shimmer in the sunlight and attract nectar-feeding birds. The juvenile plants have a glossy, more frost-tender leaf and so propagating adult plants with their hardier foliage increases the frost-hardiness. Really old trees have long beards of aerial roots and if you cut off a branch with these roots attached you can have an instant tree. You may need to cut off the foliage just to make it more manageable and transportable. Height x width 70 ft (20 m) or more, but it takes many years to reach these gigantic proportions. ZONE 9.

Excelsa = beautiful.

Metrosideros kermadecensis

A very similar plant to *Metrosideros excelsa* except that it forms a smaller, more compact tree and has smaller leaves. The disappointing thing about this species it that although the flowers are lovely, it often flowers intermittently and rarely has the impact of the pohutukawa. There are also some popular variegated forms with yellow and green leaves that contrast beautifully with the red flowers. The name refers to its island homeland, the Kermadecs, which are north of New Zealand. Height x width 20 ft (6 m). ZONE 9.

Michelia

Magnoliaceae

Michelias are really magnolias by another name. The only thing separating a michelia from a magnolia is the fact their superb flowers are all along the stems in the axils of the leaves whereas magnolias have a single flower at the tips of the stems. And like the magnolias *Magnolia grandiflora* and *M. delavayi*, the species in cultivation are evergeen. Michelias are very easy to grow if you have the right climate. Most need a mild zone 9 to 10 climate, though they will grow in warm, sheltered parts of zone 8. Like so many plants, they will tolerate colder winters if given scorching hot summers and I was reminded of this when I saw several "tender" michelias growing in Korea, where they have horrendously cold winters.

This genus is named after Pietro Antonio Micheli, a 17th-century Florentine botanist. Most people call them "Mike-elia," when it should probably be "Michelle-ia," but my attitude to Latin has always been as long as two people understand each other it's fine, never mind about the pronunciation.

They are happy in any acidic or neutral soils as long as the drainage is good. Heavier clay soils with good drainage also pose no problem, because like magnolias they seem to thrive in denser soils. They vary in their need for sun and ability to handle wind, as some need shade and shelter and others are tough.

Above: *Michelia yunnanensis*

The only disease I've ever seen is occasional black spot on the leaves after prolonged periods of rain (magnolias are also attacked by black spot at times). The roots of both *Michelia* and *Magnolia* have a distinctive smell and tend to be thick and fleshy with no apparent hair roots. Like the magnolias, they should never be allowed to dry out and most don't like dry soils or lime. Easy to transplant from pots, they need no special attention. Most can be pruned, including severe pruning if necessary, but they usually have such a good, tidy, upright shape it is not needed.

Michelia doltsopa
WONG-LAN

This has long been one of my cherished plants, ever since I first set eyes on one back in the 1970s. It forms a huge bush or tree in no time and is an ideal "instant" tree for the garden. The leaves are large and rather tropical-looking, about the size of your hand. They are dark green above and can be gray or covered in rusty brown hairs underneath. The clone **'Rusty'** is especially furry beneath the leaves.

While the tree looks good for 11½ months of the year, it will suddenly scare the pants off you in spring when it has finally finished flowering because it will suddenly drop 90 percent of its leaves and you'll think it is dying. Just as you're wondering what to do next, the new leaves emerge and all is well (for a further 11½ months, until it decides to give you another shake-up). Most evergreen trees drop a portion of their leaves every year, sometimes in one hit, but more likely throughout the year; *Michelia doltsopa* is one of the few to do it all at once.

Left: *Michelia doltsopa*

While the leaves are attractive, the real treasure is the flowers. We can almost set the calender by ours, as it starts flowering on the shortest day of the year. It's amazing to have such a floriferous tree flower at that time, but it gets even better. The tree remains in flower for at least two months, and more often for three, and the big (4 in/10 cm), white, ostentatious flowers are deliciously scented. It's a rich, heady mix of sugar and cinnamon and floats on the air. Sometimes you can be on the other side of the garden and suddenly get "bowled over" by the scent on the breeze. The flowers emerge from big, furry buds and the petal numbers vary according to the clone. It has the good habit of dropping the spent flowers fairly cleanly. The bush sensibly flowers later in the spring in cool climates.

Michelia doltsopa doesn't like constant winds and this is especially true of the clone **'Fragrant Cloud'**. The tree tends to be bare and distinctly one-sided if grown on a windy site. It needs full sun to produce the vast array of flowers. They are fairly easy to transplant, but not so easy to propagate and therefore they are usually grafted. Choose a moist, sheltered site with plenty of room as it eventually becomes a big tree. Introduced from western China by George Forrest in 1918, it also grows in the warmer valleys throughout the Himalayas where doltsopa is a local name. Height x width 30–50 ft (10–15 m). ZONE 8 OR 9.

Doltsopa = a local name for the plant.

Michelia maudiae

A typical *Michelia* with white, scented flowers in the axils of the leaves. As a summary, this is a case of damning with faint praise, because in truth if you could have one of these in your garden, you would. There are only two things stopping you. One, it's not easy to come by, and two, it is considered tender by most experts because it hails from the Hong Kong region of southern China. But like a lot of plants from that area, they are hardier than once thought. A number of plants from this region actually cope with the hot conditions in Hong Kong, rather than demanding them. I have it on the good authority of two plantsmen who live in cold-

Right: Michelia maudiae

winter climes, one in Korea, that this plant is "bone-hardy." You'll hope that it is because the superbly scented, white flowers have a ring of petals like a saucer with a central cone of white in the middle. The overall effect is like a mass of large white butterflies sitting in the bush in spring. This is enhanced by the contrast with the shiny, black-green leaves, about the size of a small hand. It becomes a large, upright bush or small tree. Height x width 15–25 ft (5–8 m). ZONE 8, possibly 7.

Maudiae = named for B. Maude, author of the *Botanic Garden* (1825).

Michelia yunnanensis

This is my chance to brag, as I like to think I grew the first plants of this species outside of China. In 1986 I received a batch of seeds from the Kunming Botanical Institute in Yunnan, China. We grew over 40 different seedlings and selected the best. They do vary considerably from seed and the flower size can be from thumbnail-size (¼ in/18 mm) up to 4 in (100 mm) across. The white flowers open along the stem from the inside first, with the flowers near the extremities of the shoot opening last. There are up to fifteen to twenty flowers per stem. Some have cup-shaped flowers and others are flat and open. The powerful lemony scent can be overpowering at times and fleeting at others. Even the flower buds are exciting, like little furry creatures sitting in the bush waiting to do their thing. In warm climates they flower for a month in early spring but sensibly wait till late spring in colder places. The leaves are thumb-sized and usually dark green, but seedlings vary from blacky green to almost smoky gray-green.

It quickly becomes a head-high, upright, dense bush, but can be twice this height. However, you can prune them if they get too big for their chosen site. This species thrives on heat and drought and yet is just as accommodating when grown in wet regions or dry shade. The bush grows naturally on the hot, baked hills around Kunming, so blistering sun and drought pose no threat. They flower much better when grown in full sun, but will cope with dense shade and drought, which holds great possibilities for landscaping around buildings and under the eaves.

They are reasonably wind-hardy and generally a tough plant, as evidenced by the fact they will grow in tubs and pots. Height x width 6–10 ft (2–3 m). This species seems to be more cold-hardy than most, too, at ZONE 8 (or up to 6 if given hot summers).

Yunnanensis = from Yunnan Province, China.

Mitraria

Mitraria coccinea
Gesneriaceae

This lonely little treasure is the only known plant in the genus, but it does have some choice relatives, including saintpaulias (African violets) and gloxinias. This is one of the few woody plants in the family and by rights it should be more popular. All it needs is a cool, moist site and it will repay you with a shower of little orange red flowers with pouches like baby squid.

It is evergreen and has small blacky green leaves. Being a sprawly plant, it is best treated as a climber. Plant it against a bank in a shady dell and let it scramble up so that the flowers tumble down toward you. The flowers first appear in late spring, and continue for weeks, if not months, sometimes coming intermittently, and other times in a flush of flowers.

Left: *Mitraria coccinea*

It needs an open soil with plenty of leaf mold, preferably with an acidic or neutral pH. It prefers cool, moist, shady sites. It naturally occurs near the Magellan Straits at the bottom of South America, and was introduced by William Lobb for the Veitch Nursery in England in 1846.

The long, thin stems are quite brittle, so it doesn't like wind and also hates too much heat or drought. It's generally hardier than commonly supposed and growing it in shade helps to protect it from the worst of frosts. It is possible to grow the plant with the foliage in the sun as long as the roots are cool and shaded.

It is easy enough to transplant from containers, but it would be tricky to extricate the long stems from the ground if you wanted to move it at a later date. The plant may need an occasional prune in late winter to tidy it up.

Height 6–10 ft (2–3 m). ZONE 8 or 9.

> *Mitra* = mitre, like a bishop's mitre, from the shape of the seed pod;
> *coccinea* = scarlet.

Neillia

Neillia thibetica, syn *N. longiracemosa*
Rosaceae

Here is a plant you don't see very often, but it has its uses. On first glance you would say that the leaves are from the related blackberry. The shiny rich green leaves are rugose, or contoured with valleys and sub-valleys. They are heart-shaped with neat serrations around the edges. As they age, they lose that lovely shininess and fade to a flat green. The new young stems are red and at the tip of each new growth around midsummer

the plant puts out a finger-length raceme of pink flowers. Each head has twenty to forty little, pink, tubular flowers and the overall effect is not unlike some of the smaller *Aesculus*.

The plant tends to ramble and scramble and does sucker too. It is definitely not a shrub for tidy gardeners or small city plots, but it is a useful ground-filler for bigger woodland gardens. It is happy in sun or shade, coping with quite dry shade, making it

Below: *Neillia thibetica*

Above: *Nerium oleander* 'Pauline Gregory'

The flowers appear *en masse* on the tips of the stems from midsummer onward, until the first frosts or cold spell. The petals glisten in the sun and seem very tough regardless of hot sun or winds. Single flowers the size of a coin have a spiral or twist in the base of the petals as if someone has been spinning them around. There are doubles, too, and in a great range of colors, from hot reds and pinks through to more subtle pinks, apricot or white. The long leaves are dark green, tough and hard and shaped like a long willow leaf. Take care when you handle them, however, as the leaves and sap are very poisonous.

The bush has an upright habit with strong cane-like growths, and a whippy nature that allows them to bend in the wind. The outline of the bush is rounded, but you can prune them drastically if necessary and they will regenerate quite happily (just be careful of the poisonous sap).

They will put up with acidic, alkaline, wet, dry, compacted or any other soil. But although they survive in virtually any soil, they will appreciate and grow best in good, fertile, free-draining conditions. Likewise, they cope with salt-winds, drought or pollution, but what they must have is hot summers and plenty of sunlight. Neriums will take light frosts if the summers are hot enough. Native to eastern Mediterranean, possibly western China (they were possibly spread by the early traders). Height x width 6–10 ft (2–3 m). ZONE 9.

Nerium = from the Greek word "neros," meaning moist or near water because they grow in or near stream beds from the Mediterannean through to China; *oleander* refers to their likeness to olives or *Olea.*

Nerium cultivars
'Franklin D. Roosevelt' A tall plant with double apricot to orange flowers. Height x width 10 ft (3 m).
'Mrs Roeding' An arching bush with double apricot to soft salmon pink flowers. Height x width 6 ft (2 m).
'Pauline Gregory' Single flowers in bright pink. Height x width 6 ft (2 m).
'Petite Pink' A very compact bush ideal for small gardens and tubs with single, pink flowers. Height x width 3 ft (1 m).
'Professor Martin' Glowing red, single flowers that make a great display all summer. Height x width 6 ft (2 m).

even more useful. It is reasonably cold-hardy as it comes from Tibet (note the old spelling for Tibet in the species name) and was collected in 1904 by the indefatigable E. H. Wilson (1876–1930). He also collected the only other species you are likely to come across, **Neillia sinensis**, which has white flowers.

It is easy to grow in any soil, including alkaline, as you would expect of a plant from the rose family. There are no significant pests and it is easy to transplant in winter. It can also be divided like a *Kerria*. An occasional winter prune to tidy it is sensible. It was named after Patrick Neil, who was secretary of the Caledonian Horticultural Society, Scotland. Height x width 6 ft (2 m). ZONE 6.

Thibetica = from Tibet.

Nerium

Nerium oleander
OLEANDER
Apocynaceae

A super-tough plant in every regard except one—it won't take heavy frosts. In every other way, you can mistreat this plant and it won't die. In warmer parts of the world, you often see them on the most barren and difficult sites: by the sides of roads, with the roots restricted by concrete or in poor, heavy, compacted soil. They even survive city dust and grime, but they do look so much better when looked after. By contrast, gardeners in cool regions cherish them. I have seen them in Munich, Germany, where they grow them in huge baskets under glass then lift them into prime city locations by crane for the summer months. It is easy to understand why they are so popular: they have handsome foliage and flamboyant flowers on a tidy, upright, evergreen bush.

Above: *Nerium oleander* 'Professor Martin'

Above: *Nerium oleander* 'Punctatum'

'Punctatum' An upright vigorous plant with single, soft pink flowers. Height x width 10 ft (3 m).
'Sister Agnes' A superb single white that is fragrant too. It has the ability to shed spent flowers and not hang on to drab, burnt flowers as do some of the whites. Height x width 10 ft (3 m).

Olearia

DAISY BUSH
Asteraceae

Olearias are one of the more bizarre plants on the planet. They are daisies—nothing special about that, daisies are quite common. They are also woody—again, many plants are woody. But put the two together and you have a "woody daisy", which is seriously weird as far as most of the botanical world is concerned. Not so down in New Zealand, where there are a multitude of shrubby daisy plants including woody *Senecio* and *Brachyglottis*. There are also around 100 species of *Olearia*, mostly from New Zealand and a few from Australia and Tasmania.

Olearias in the wild grow on sea shores, coastal cliffs and mountain tops. Nearly all of them grow in full sun and exposed, windy places. As gardeners we can use this twin ability because wind and coast-hardy shrubs, particularly those that have wonderful flowers, are a scarce commodity. The mass of bright daisy-like flowers can completely smother the foliage.

Their name comes from the similarity with olive trees (*Olea*), as both have tough, leathery leaves. Being evergreen also helps them to cope with wind. Ever-gray might be a better description, however, because like so many coastal plants a lot of them have gray or whitish leaves. Some have simple, smooth leaves and others have wavy-edged, almost scalloped leaves.

Many coastal shrubs are just that and will not grow inland in frosty places. Olearias are different, and most of them will tolerate light frost. Some, such as *O. ilicifolia* and *O.* x *haastii*

cope with frosts to -12°C. Most of them are drought-hardy but fade away in shade or in a close, humid atmosphere. Generally they are big, upright bushes and fast-growing, so they are ideal for an instant screen to deflect the wind or hide a neighbor's view of your house. Most have a tidy habit but can be pruned if necessary.

They can be grown in any soil provided the drainage is good, because olearias hate wet feet. They cope surprisingly well with extremes of acidicity and alkalinity, as well as clay soils. Many are very tolerant of city pollution. I've even seen them covered in grime from car exhausts without any ill-effect. Some are useful as hedges, though because they can be short-lived, this may leave you with a gap if one or two die out. That's not to imply they are not pretty as a lone bush, as the smothering of daisy flowers is quite a sight. Nearly all olearias are white-flowered, though there are other colors (see the species below).

Transplanting from pots is quite easily done, but it is not a good idea to shift them later. If you must, cut them back quite hard. Also prune hard if your bush becomes straggly.

Olearia = like an olive (*Olea*).

Olearia cheesemanii
Easily the best of the New Zealand species for sheer flower power. A canopy of white daisies totally obscures the leaves in mid- to late spring. It is a tidy, upright bush with very handsome, shiny, gray-green leaves tapering to a point. It's not as wind-hardy as some, but handles more cold. *Olearia arborescens* is similar. Height 12 ft (4 m) x width 10 ft (3 m). ZONE 8.

Cheesemanii = named for T. F. Cheeseman (1846–1923), who published a *New Zealand Flora* in 1906.

Olearia x *haastii*
(*O. avicenniaefolia* x *O. moschata*)
The heads of fragrant white daisies appear in late summer on this dense, upright bush. The oval, leathery leaves are a handsome, shiny, dark green above and white and furry beneath, protecting them from salt-wind and pollution. A naturally occurring hybrid from New Zealand. Height 6 ft (2 m) x width 10 ft (3 m). ZONE 8.

Haastii = named for Julius von Haast (1822–1887), an early explorer of New Zealand.

Below: *Olearia cheesemanii*

Above: *Olearia phlogopappa* 'Pink Gem'

Olearia ilicifolia
MOUNTAIN HOLLY

An intriguing plant with hard, battleship-gray leaves with holly-like spikes along the wavy edges. The scented, white, daisy flowers appear in midsummer. This tough plant is one of the most cold-hardy of this genus and is capable of growing in hot sun or quite dense shade, coping with wet or dry climates. From New Zealand. Height x width 15 ft (5 m). ZONE 7.

Ilicifolia = leaf like an *Ilex*, or holly.

Olearia phlogopappa, syn *O. gunniana*

This is very showy when in flower in late spring and the display lasts for weeks, making it a valuable shrub. It comes in a range of flower colors including pink, white and blue. It is known also as **'Blue Gem'** and **'Pink Gem'**, or sometimes **'Comber's Blue'** and **'Comber's Pink'**. It naturally grows around head-high and has small, narrow, wavy leaves. Give it a light prune with the shears after flowering to keep it tidy and bushy. It is a parent of the similar hybrid, *O.* x *scilloniensis*. From Tasmania and southeast Australia. Height x width 6 ft (2 m). ZONE 8.

Phlogo = wick or flame; *pappa* = obscure.

Paulownia

Scrophulariaceae

Given the right conditions paulownias are magnificent deciduous trees. They have huge leaves, giant flower heads and fragrance too—a great combination of color, drama and scent. Paulownias need two things to thrive: hot summers and shelter. Shelter to protect the enormous leaves from shredding in the wind and heat to make them grow luxuriantly and ripen the wood. While paulownias tolerate cold winters, they need heat or warm summers to flower properly.

Plant in full sun, preferably in a sheltered gully so you can look down on the canopy of leaves and flowers from above. The flowers look so much better against a green background rather than against the sky.

They are not too fussy about soils as long as they are well-drained, and both wet and dry climates seem to suit them. *Paulownia tomentosa* is probably better for cooler, wetter climates, while *P. fortunei* is ideally suited to hotter, drier situations.

The plants in this genus sometimes send up suckers and can therefore be grown from root cuttings. They are easy to transplant when very young, and they grow fast, becoming instant trees in less than five years. Even in winter they look stately, with their open, clean trunks. Given the timber is so hard, it is surprising that it is also palatable to borer grubs. The timber is very valuable and is commonly used for dowry boxes in Asia. All species are Chinese and are equally content in hot or cold climates given a warm summer.

Paulownia = named after Anna Paulowna (1795–1865), daughter of Czar Paul I of Russia, who became Princess of the Netherlands.

Paulownia fargesii

Big heads of up to forty flowers appear in late spring on the tips of the stems before the new leaves emerge. The spikes of flowers are made up of big, fat trumpets, like a foxglove, with each one as long as your finger. The outer part of the tube is pale purple-mauve and the inner is basically white with masses of tiny purple dots on the

Right: *Paulownia fargesii*

flared petals and bigger splashes of dark purple within the tube. Although the colors are strong at close range, the overall effect from a distance is a rather smoky pale mauve. The flowering season is often brief compared to the other species. The triangular leaves are smaller, smoother and more graceful than other species and it is probably the best species for cooler climates. A mature tree has a neater, tidier look than *P. tomentosa*. Native to China. Height x width 30 ft (10 m). ZONE 7.

Fargesii = Père Farges (1844–1912) was a French missionary based in China.

Paulownia fortunei

This species has big, wide-mouthed flowers 4 in (10 cm) across in off-white with very large purple-black splodges in the throat. However, the fragrant flowers vary considerably in size and color from tree to tree with seedling variation. The flowers smell like sweet custard even after they've fallen to the ground. This species needs hot summers to thrive. From China. Height x width 25 ft (8 m). ZONE 6.

Fortunei = named for Robert Fortune (1812–1880).

Paulownia tomentosa

EMPRESS TREE, FOXGLOVE TREE, PRINCESS TREE, ROYAL PAULOWNIA

One of the most spectacular flowering trees in the world, it is a stunning sight, and one I cherish, every spring. The rich purple-blue flowers are much darker than those of *Paulownia fargesii* and often appear with the new leaves in late spring. As if that is not enough, they have enormous leaves 12 in (30 cm) long that look marvellous in a sheltered site but are easily torn by strong winds. It does, however, tolerate poor soils and air pollution very well. Native to China. Height 40 ft (12 m) x width 30 ft (10 m). ZONE 5.

Tomentosa = wooly, referring to the wooly underside to the leaf.

Philadelphus

MOCK ORANGE
Philadelphaceae

We always cherish plants from our mother's or grandmother's gardens as they bring back memories of our innocent past. My childhood garden was heavy clay soil over limestone, which does not suit many shrubs, but we did have several wonderful philadelphus. Philadelphus, or mock orange, is one of the few shrubs to actually enjoy a high pH, or alkaline soil, and yet it is equally happy in the very acidic soil I am now blessed with.

Even though the wet, heavy, clay soil of my mother's garden never seemed to bother the plants, they are just as happy in a dry climate. In fact, they are a standby in drought-prone regions, so I can say with confidence this plant will grow more or less anywhere.

They are very hardy to cold and cope with a certain amount of wind. They love sun, the more the better, but will grow in semi-shade. So, they are easy-care plants with no need to stake or water, and no pests and diseases to bother them.

The charming festoons of fragrant flowers appear in early summer on last year's wood, so if you feel the need to prune

Right: *Phildelphus coronarius* with *Rhododendron* 'Success'.

then do so immediately after flowering to get as much new growth as possible for next year's blossom. They won't object if you forget to prune them, and my own preference is to leave them alone for five or six years and then give them a hard pruning just after flowering.

The flowers are white, though a few have a subtle pink or mauve center. Some have a fabulous fragrance and others are

Above: *Paulownia tomentosa*

sadly lacking in this regard. They do vary as to the degree of scent and it is worth seeking out the ones with the stronger fragrance. It always seems a travesty to plant a rose or philadelphus with no scent. A bonus is their summer flowers appear after most spring shrubs are a spent force. Another thing in their favor is they flower well every year. Some trees and shrubs have a lazy year, or even only flower well every second year.

Philadelphus are a good cut flower for home gardeners, but they are not available in shops as they don't travel well. They are a great complement to roses in the garden, as well as in a vase. One of the best things about philadelphus is the flowers remain white and don't fade, blotch or burn even in strong sunlight—the flowers are either perfect on the bush or they fall off cleanly. So many white flowers, like those on rhododendrons and camellias, look sublime with the first flush and then retain a portion of muddy, scarred or bruised white flowers to ruin the display. Not so with philadelphus.

The stems are dull gray, so the deciduous bush has no redeeming features in winter, it just looks like a twiggy mass. They transplant readily and you can move an established bush in winter if you really need to. Just cut back the stems to facilitate the move.

Philadelphus are native to North America, both east and west coasts and down into Mexico, and then in China through to eastern Europe. Most are very hardy, deciduous shrubs with a few evergreen types. Most species have an upright habit and you can use them to add height midway through a border or at the back of a mixed or herbaceous border. Their summer flowers make planting with perennials and roses an obvious choice. However, they look equally good in a dense shrubbery with rhododendrons and camellias, adding a light airy feel to the darker, somber tones of the evergreens. The flowering period is weeks rather than days so they give good value and conveniently seem to "disappear" when not in flower.

Philadelphus = named by Linnaeus from the Greek meaning brotherly love, after the King of Egypt Ptolemy II Philadelphus (308–246 BC), who married his sister.

Below: *Philadelphus* 'Sybille'

Above: *Philadelphus* 'Beauclerk'

Philadelphus 'Beauclerk'

A wide, spreading, rather scruffy plant when young, but you will soon forgive it all these foibles when the very large (2 in/5 cm), single, cup-shaped, white flowers appear in late spring and early summer. They are very showy and better than most single roses. Height x width 8 ft (2.5 m). ZONE 5.

Philadelphus coronarius
MOCK ORANGE

This big, upright plant, arching with age, is essential for any large garden. It's going to take up lots of space, but it will earn its keep in late spring/early summer when laden with flowers. Each flower is made up of four petals forming a pure white cup of scented bliss. It's one of the most heavenly scents on earth; slightly citrusy, definitely a sharp, almost icy lemony scent. Even without the showy flowers it would be an essential garden ingredient for its scent alone. Despite its airy, lazy habit, the bush is quite tidy overall, with a rounded shape. The wood is brittle if pushed or broken and yet the plant is quite wind-tolerant and it is hardier than it looks. With its dense, twiggy habit, you'd imagine it would look rather scruffy in the winter when it loses its leaves, but somehow the bush just disappears and you'll only notice it again next spring when, reliable as ever, it is smothered with flowers again. Native to eastern Europe. Height 10 ft (3 m) x width 8 ft (2.5 m). ZONE 5.

There is a lovely yellow-leaf form appropriately called **'Aureus'**. This is a great plant to brighten up a shady corner. The bright yellow foliage gradually greens as summer drifts on. It is ideal for shade, where it will retain its yellow color, as it is likely to burn and scorch in hot sun. The flowers don't show up much being white on yellow but the scent is still enjoyable. Height 8 ft (2.5 m) x 6 ft (2 m). ZONE 5.

Coronarius = crowning as in coronation, used for crowns or garlands.

Philadelphus 'Sybille'

An arching, slightly gangly, deciduous shrub that gets denser and tidier in time. The brown stems become stripy and the leaves have a rather dull look, being hairy on top. While the bush may not be

the neatest, the flowers are sublime. Four large petals open wide to form a flattish, white flower with a rosy streak painted at the base of each petal, creating an intriguing pinky, soft purple center around the cluster of stamens. The petals seem joined to create one perfect cup-shaped flower, but they are just overlapping. Height 4 ft (1.2 m) x width 6 ft (2 m). ZONE 5.

Philadelphus **'Virginal'**

Everyone says this is the best double form and I have to agree. It has been around a long time and it is still hard to beat. The leaves look luscious compared to many; they are heart-shaped with a very distinct point. There are big panicles of snow-white double flowers that are full and very fragrant in early to midsummer. It is a robust, easy plant with a tall, upright habit. Height 10 ft (3 m) x width 8 ft (2.5 m). ZONE 5.

Philesia

Philesia magellanica
Philesiaceae

A couple of the tricks I learnt as a student studying plant names was to learn all the genera with just one or two members rather than waste valuable time learning 200 camellias or rhododendrons. This makes your plant knowledge seem far more impressive, as you know and recognize more genera. We would have plant identification tests and if I didn't know the family name then I'd guess it was going to be the same as the genus name. Well sometimes it works! *Philesia* is one such case. This neat little Chilean shrub has its very own family, the nearest relative being the Chilean bellflower *Lapageria rosea*. The similarity is immediately obvious with the long, red, bell-shaped flowers; the difference being *Lapageria* is a straggly climber while *Philesia* is a tight little bun of a plant with the flowers semi-hidden within the foliage.

It actually comes from the cooler regions of southern Chile and Tierra del Fuego, growing in damp rainforests. Certainly this plant thrives in moist regions, and is unlikely to do well in drier places. It prefers a cool, moist climate with rain all year, and while it doesn't like hard frosts, it does like to be cool.

It's a very low-growing plant (normally 6 in/15 cm, though it can grow up to 3 ft/1 m) with dense, dark foliage. The blacky evergreen leaves are long, thin and pointy, like sharp arrow-heads. It becomes a really dense, low thicket and spreads by underground stems. You might think it was easy to propagate, like most suckering shrubs, but despite the stems growing through the soil, they rarely have side roots and are not easy to strike from cuttings. The only "easy" way to propagate is to have a stock plant for dividing. Like a lot of cool South American shrubs, it is prone to lethal root rot in warm summers but is otherwise free of pests.

Choose a free-draining, acidic soil in a cool, semi-shaded spot. It's worth finding the right situation to keep it alive because it will repay you with beautiful, rose-red, bell flowers much bigger, at 2½ in (6 cm) long, than one would imagine for such a small, compact plant. The flowers come in late summer.

The plant was introduced by William Lobb for the Veitch Nursery in 1847. Height 3 ft (1 m) x width 6 ft (2 m). ZONE 7.

Philesios = Greek for to love or lovely; *magellanica* = for the Portugese explorer Magellan (1480–1521), who led an expedition of five Spanish ships to circumnavigate the globe in 1519.

Phlomis

JERUSALEM SAGE
Lamiaceae

*P*hlomis is not something gardeners lust after. It is more a practical type of plant that is put in the garden to do a job. But having grown three or four different species, I am now realising just how valuable they are as brilliant ground covers and for their seemingly endless display of flowers. These hooded blooms come in an interesting range of colors, from pale yellows to gold, and pale lilac to purple. The plants are low, dense and evergreen, and though initially you may need to put a mulch around them to keep the weeds down, once they are established, they'll do that on their own.

I like easy-care plants and *Phlomis* fits in this category. They are able to grow in wet or dry climates and they are not fussy about acidic or alkaline soil. However, they must have good drainage. They never need feeding or tending. A light trim with the shears occasionally might help, but they have a good natural shape for the most part. Most of them are spready shrubs between knee- and waist-high. Some have upright growth and others are more of a dome shape, but all of them spread sideways.

Below: *Philesia magellanica*

Above: *Phlomis fruticosa*

Full sun is perfect, though a bit of shade is acceptable. Hot sun and drought won't bother them, in fact they thrive on it, and the same is true of windy places. They are very easy to transplant when young, and I can't imagine they would shift later. It would be so much easier to buy more plants, or propagate your own, as they reproduce quite easily.

Their natural home is the warmer parts of Europe, Asia and North Africa, and in many ways they are typical Mediterannean plants with their grayish, furry leaves.

Phlomis = the Greek for wick or flame, as the down was used in lamps.

Phlomis cashmeriana
The whorls of soft purple, hooded flowers appear on this neat shrub in midsummer and can often seem two-tone. The pale gray leaves are very wooly underneath. Native to the Himalayas, particularly Kashmir, hence the species name. Height 36 in (90 cm) x width 24 in (60 cm). ZONE 8.

Phlomis fruticosa
JERUSALEM SAGE
A dense mound of a bush with gray-green leaves somewhat like common sage, but thicker, almost with a pelt-like cover of hairs. In summer, the golden yellow flowers appear on the tops of the bush. They are hooded trumpets and the ends of the flowers face down to the ground, so from above they appear as circles or whorls. From the Mediterannean. Height 3 ft (1 m) x width 5 ft (1.5 m). ZONE 8.

Fruticosa = shrubby.

Phlomis italica
A low, dense plant with gray, wooly leaves. In summer, the upright spikes of flowers appear in subtle shades of pinky lilac. Each spike has a whorl of flowers, then a gap and another whorl of flowers

Phlomis italica

and so on, extending the flowering season over a period of months. The Balearic Islands near Italy are its home, thus the name *italica*. Height 12 in (30 cm) x width 24 in (60 cm). ZONE 9.

Pieris

Ericaceae

Everyone should have at last one *Pieris* in their garden. Although often distracted by their abiltiy to put on a great show of new foliage in the spring with fiery reds or burnished bronze, if they never displayed this leaf color, they would still earn their keep for the mass of white, bell-shaped flowers in spring. Some species are called the lily-of-the-valley shrub for the similarities between them and the ground cover plant of the same name. If you can grow rhododendrons, then *Pieris* will suit your garden, as they like similar conditions and they are very easy for any gardener with acidic to neutral soil. Having a fibrous root system, again like a rhododendron, means that they are easily transplanted at any size and even very old specimens can be moved in winter. They enjoy a cool root run, and a mulch of bark or woodchip is ideal as they dislike having their roots disturbed by zealous weeders. If given a mulch to keep the roots cool, then a hot spot in full sun is fine, otherwise some shade will not go amiss.

They are all evergreen and shapely, rounded bushes. They are very hardy for the most part. I've seen them growing wild near the tops of high mountains surrounded by stunted, hardy birchs and other deciduous plants. As with many mountain plants, they can handle a fair amount of wind, heat and drought. They are just as happy in a mild climate and not one of those hardy shrubs that fail to perform in warmer regions. Unlike the related rhododendron, they are virtually immune to pests and diseases, apart from the occasional problem with root rot. They are prone to occasional thrip and lacewing attack in warm climates.

Pieris = from Piera, a place in northern Thessaly, Greece, reputedly the home of the Muses, who in Greek myth were nine young, beautiful, modest virgins who presided over the fine and liberal arts.

Pieris formosa var forrestii

An upright tidy bush with big, showy, white flowers in long racemes in spring, and, as a bonus, it has particularly good red growth in spring. Height 10 ft (3 m) x width 6 ft (2 m). ZONE 7.

'**Wakehurst**' is a selected form with lovely red new growth in spring and beautiful white flowers. Height 10 ft (3 m) x width 6 ft (2 m). Another to look for is '**Jermyns**', raised at the Hilliers Nursery in England. It has showy red buds opening to white flowers with a red calyx. Height 10 ft (3 m) x width 6 ft (2 m).

Formosa = beautiful; *forrestii* = for George Forrest (1873–1932), who collected this form in Yunnan, China.

Pieris japonica
LILY-OF-THE-VALLEY BUSH

This plant is an ideal garden shrub, being smaller and tidier than *Pieris formosa*. It has the typical lovely glossy foliage and red new growth in spring, but it is the flowers that are the best feature. Massed strings of white flowers decorate the tops of the bush in late winter and spring. Native to China and Japan. Height 12 ft (4 m) x width 10 ft (3 m). ZONE 6.

There are some beautiful selected clones with different-colored flowers including '**Dorothy Wyckoff**', with striking purple buds opening to white with a red calyx. '**Flamingo**', with dark red buds and deep rosy pink flowers. '**Christmas Cheer**',

Below: *Pieris formosa* var *forrestii* 'Wakehurst'

Right: *Pieris
ryukiensis*
'Temple Bells'

Right: *Pieris japonica*
'Christmas Cheer'

plants to perform more than one trick. This little bush not only has a compact nature and bright apple-green foliage, in early spring it is smothered in tiny white bells. The flowers are so profuse you can hardly see the leaves and they "sing," or rattle, if you brush past.

The flowers last a very long time, say four to five weeks, and are followed by trick number two, the bright, burnished red new growth. This show is more fleeting but is pretty good none the less. It pays to deadhead this species, as it is so profuse the seed production will weaken the plant. It comes from the Japanese island of Ryuku. **'Temple Bells'** is a selected clone grown for its profusion of flowers. For both, height 3 ft (1 m) x width 4 ft (1.2 m). ZONE 8.

Ryukiensis = from Ryuku Island, Japan.

whose flowers are a lovely mix of pink and red. The flowers often appear before other cultivars and it seems to be more cold-hardy; and **'Valley Valentine'**, which has rusty red buds and flowers. For all, height x width 6 ft (2 m). A smaller plant is **'Purity'**, with upright flower spikes holding pure white flowers contrasting with the pale green leaves. It is a very compact shrub. Height x width 3 ft (1 m).

Pieris ryukiensis

This fantastic little bush will fit easily into any garden, even the smallest pocket-hankerchief. In small gardens, we always want our

Plumbago

Plumbago auriculata, syn *P. capensis*
CAPE LEADWORT
Plumbaginaceae

In midsummer, the tops of the stems of this evergreen South African shrub are decked with heads of soft blue, phlox-like flowers. They are the most delicious shade of sky-blue and the flowering goes on into the fall. There is a white-flowered form, **var *alba***, but I think it is pathetic in comparison. If you must stray from the simple beauty of the wild plant, go for the rich-blue clone **'Royal Cape'**. The leaves are simple and smooth in pale green and, though evergreen, the plant can look tatty in winter.

In nature, this South African shrub scrambles through and over other shrubs and it will do this in your shrubbery given half a chance, so take care where you plant it. There are two possible solutions to this rangy habit. One is to grow it as a climber against a wall, where it thrives with the extra heat, and clip it occasionally to keep it neat and tidy. Eventually the plant becomes a narrow thicket of stems like a thin hedge, but it will still need some support to stop it falling over. The second possibility is to plant it away from other shrubs. In this setting it will become a wide-spreading plant with an arching habit, or you can trim it to a rounded dome-shape.

This plant loves sun and plenty of heat and, as you might expect, it is quite drought-hardy. In fact it will handle extreme drought and so can be grown in tubs. It seems oblivious of soil type, providing it is free-draining.

It's sensitive to winter frosts, but if you can persuade it to grow fast during the first summer it will have more chance of survival. On a big bush, the extremities will be frosted but the inner stems usually survive and with a good cut back in spring all will be well again. You can give it a light trim or be more severe because the plant regenerates quickly either way. Other than frost, it is an easy-care, pest-free plant.

They transplant quite easily from pots, but I imagine it would resent being shifted again at a later date. It copes with a little shade in a hot climate and breezy sites, too. Height 10–20 ft (3–6 m) x width 3–10 ft (1–3 m). ZONE 9.

Plumbago indica, syn *P. rosea* (scarlet leadwort) has soft red flowers, but otherwise is very similar to *P. auriculata*. It is more sensitive to frost, however, and is probably a zone 10 plant.

Plumbum = lead; *auriculata* = eared, or small-eared, referring to the leaves.

Potentilla

CINQUEFOIL
Rosaceae

Potentillas are a mix of shrubby and herbaceous plants from all across the cooler parts of the Northern Hemisphere. The shrubby species are excellent long-flowering plants that love to be in full sun. They are tough and hardy, and capable of growing in virtually any climate. They put up with a variety of soils, from acidic to alkaline, clays to sand. Just make sure that the drainage is reasonable. They'll take a little wind and some shade, but don't be too cruel.

Potentilla = from "potens," as in potent or powerful because of the medicinal uses of some of the herbaceous species.

Potentilla fruticosa
SHRUBBY CINQUEFOIL
What a wonderful little bush this is: a grow-anywhere, easy-care small shrub with loads of flowers from midsummer onward. The round, saucer-shaped blooms are the size of a small coin (1¼ in/3 cm across) and like buttercups in rich yellow, as well as reds, orange and creams. The bush itself is nothing riveting, but it remains reasonably tidy and can be trimmed every year to keep a neat, rounded dome between knee- and waist-high. The leaves are

small and divided and the bush looks twiggy and messy during the winter months, but they flower on and on for most of the summer so we forgive them.

This is a handy little shrub for those difficult-to-fill spaces between a path and a building. They will handle the shadow of a wall better than leafy gloom. They transplant easily from pots and would probably shift without harm in winter if required as they have a fibrous root system. Native to much of the Northern Hemisphere. Height 3 ft (1 m) x width 5 ft (1.5 m). ZONE 2.

Fruticosa = shrubby, so as to distinguish it from the herbaceous species.

Potentilla cultivars
'Goldfinger' A neat little plant with bold, golden yellow flowers. The flowers are large and smother the bush in summer. It has blue-green leaves. Height x width 2 ft (60 cm).
'Goldstar' Rich yellow flowers borne on an upright bush. It flowers profusely. Height x width 3 ft (1 m).
'Pretty Polly' Pale pink flowers smother this low-growing shrub. It is ideal for ground cover and the front of a border. Height 2 ft (60 cm) x width 4 ft (1.2 m).
'Red Ace' A tidy little mound of a shrub with bright green leaves. The warm orange-red flowers appear in summer. Height x width 2 ft (60 cm).
'Tangerine' A low-growing shrub ideal for ground cover. As the name suggests, the flowers are a vibrant tangerine. Height 2 ft (60 cm) x width 4 ft (1.2 m).

Above: *Plumbago auriculata*

Right: *Potentilla fruticosa* 'Goldstar'

Right: *Protea cynaroides*

Protea

Proteaceae

Named after the Greek god Proteus and a national emblem of South Africa, these wondrous plants have been a favorite of mine for over twenty years. While too tender for most inland areas of Europe and North America, they are stupendous garden shrubs for warm coastal regions. They love to be within sight of the sea and thrive in breezy to downright windy places. Some even cope with seafront locations, with all the storms and salt-spray that entails.

The plants in this genus vary from little ground-hugging bushes with egg-sized flowers up to very large shrubs, and almost small trees. They are all evergreen with big, fleshy leaves, often covered in hairs to protect them from strong winds. The ones typically seen in gardens are sprawly shrubs around head-high. Their branches are so heavy they get bowed down with the weight and can be grown tumbling down over a bank or a wall. If ever you have cause to cut one out, you'll appreciate just how heavy they are, because a single branch can be too heavy to lift.

I know many gardeners who take them completely for granted and regard them as quite boring, but how anyone can look at these flowers and not be entranced is beyond me. The flowers usually emerge in late fall and winter, when very few plants are putting on a display, so they seem to have the stage to themselves. The flowers are also attractive to nectar-feeding birds.

If you have a suitable climate, where would you plant a protea? In a sunny border, tumbling over a wall or, dare I say it, as an isolated lawn specimen. I usually hate seeing shrubs in isolation, especially in a lawn, but somehow proteas lend themselves to this treatment. They don't like their roots disturbed and don't blend easily with Northern Hemisphere shrubs, so an isolated position might be ideal. The protea would appreciate this situation, too, because they are not very sociable plants. By that, I mean they don't like company or being crowded by others.

Plenty of sun, space and breeze are essential requirements, and really good drainage is the next priority. It is debatable which kills them quickest, shade or poor drainage, but both lead to their demise. On the good side, they are extremely drought-tolerant once established and will grow in pure sand or rocky places. The soil must be acidic, and don't *ever* feed them because

that is killer number three for these plants. Like most of the protea family, they hate fertilizers, especially nitrogen and phosphates, as well as animal manures. They cope with quite a lot of cold if in a warm, sunny summer location, but are generally regarded as a zone 9 plant.

Proteas also need regular pruning to extend the life of the plant, otherwise they get top-heavy and either run out of steam or else get blown over in a gale. However, if you prune off the flowers to take indoors for a vase then the pruning is done for you. Each season's new growth will be as long as your forearm and if you cut the flower stems just a couple of inches above where the last season's growth began, you are in effect only allowing the plant to grow 3 to 4 in (8–10 cm) a year. This will greatly extend the life and improve the health of the plant, and keep the bush much tidier.

The flowers last for such a long time, it is possible to let each bloom stay on the bush for two weeks before cutting the flower for another two or three weeks' vase life. A succession of flowers on the bush means you have an extended season of color. They are sold as a commercial cut-flower to supply cold-climate buyers, who lust after them.

Sometimes the leaves are attacked by spots and mildews, but this is less likely if the plant is in a windy, open site. The most devastating disease is root rot, which can kill a plant in just a few weeks. Usually the cause is heavy rain and/or poor drainage. They just love open, free-draining soil. There is another problem with proteas—they hate being shifted. Also, they don't grow happily in containers. Nurseries usually grow them in open fields, which means digging them up to sell, so there is a tricky period before it is finally in your garden. Once planted, don't ever be tempted to shift it to another site because it will almost certainly die.

Although I'm not a fan of staking plants, I'll make an exception for a protea and give it a cane for the first year of its life. Some people recommend putting a big rock over the root ball, next to the trunk, to try and hold it in place and it does seem to help. Sometimes they grow up in a tidy fashion for a year or two before becoming wayward, but more often than not they start to sprawl almost immediately.

Protea = named for the Greek god Proteus.

Protea cynaroides
KING PROTEA

A big, bold, wide-spreading shrub with branches tending to be horizontal, reaching skyward at the tips, where the flowers appear. The huge flower can be bigger than an outstretched hand—up to 12 in (30 cm) across—with pointy, silky, pink petals that shine in the sunlight. This star of petals surrounds a big dome of stamens and looks altogether "other-worldly." Even the leaves are strange, being waxy and paddle-like, spiraling around the thumb-thick, smooth stems. Native of South Africa. Height 6 ft (2 m) x width 6–10 ft (2–3 m). ZONE 9.

Cynaroides = like *Cynara*, the globe artichoke.

Protea neriifolia
The finger-sized evergreen leaves are handsome enough, but it's the hand-sized flowers that grab your attention. The egg-shaped buds are covered in overlapping scales, or bracts, gradually changing to pinkish petals with blacky brown hairy tips, to the really large finger-length petals forming an even-topped circle where the hairy tips all face inward as if peering into the cone-like flower to see what's inside. Inside is a mass of stamens and anthers

forming another huge cone. These flowers look prehistoric to me, and are the epitome of exotic. Even the spent flowers are exciting, as the patterns left in the dried calyx after the seeds have gone are quite delightful. South Africa. Height x width 6–10 ft (2–3 m). ZONE 9.

Above: *Protea neriifolia*

Neriifolia = leaf like a *Nerium*, or oleander.

Prunus, syn *Amygdalus*

FLOWERING CHERRY, ALMOND, PEACH, PLUM, CHERRY LAUREL
Rosaceae

Prunus is such a diverse group of plants that it is hard to know where to begin. While the familiar cherries, apricots, plums and peaches are all part of this genus, so too are the evergreen Portugese laurel (*Prunus lusitanica*) and the cherry laurel (*P. laurocerasus*). However, it is the typical Japanese cherry trees with their froth of pink blossoms in the spring that I want to focus on in this book. In Japan, cherry-flowering season is a special time, and it is easy to understand why, because a stroll under cherry trees in bloom will lift anyone's spirits. Most cherry trees are sensible enough to wait until the threat of frost is past before opening their flowers, though a few come out early, so generally winter cold is no threat to the traditional Japanese cherry tree.

Flowering cherries like deep, fertile soil with good drainage, but they are not worried if it is acidic or alkaline. Full sun is essential, and they relish the heat as long as they have adequate moisture. They will handle a certain amount of wind and the fact they are used as street trees is proof of this. If possible, however, do choose a sheltered site, if only to keep the blossom on the tree for longer. There is still a magic quality about the tree even when the petals are on the ground beneath.

Most flowering cherries form big, wide, spreading trees with a tidy, open structure. Generally the shape is good enough without pruning, but if you must, summer pruning is recommended to reduce the risk of silver leaf disease, which gets into the sap stream and kills the plant. Winter pruning is more risky because there is no sap flow, whereas in summer the heavy sap flow washes away the spores of the disease, a bit like allowing a cut finger to bleed to wash away infection. This is the only life-threatening disease of these trees and recently a cure has been found in the form of injecting plugs of "friendly" Trichopel fungi. The Trichopel fungi fill up all the spaces and won't allow the silver leaf any room to develop, so it works as a physical block rather than attacking the bad fungus.

The trees shift easily with bare roots in winter, but they may need a stake until the new roots have established. Having chosen your spot, try not to move them around. In theory it is easy enough, but they can sometimes go into a decline.

Prunus = ancient Latin name for plum.

Prunus campanulata

TAIWAN CHERRY, CARMINE CHERRY, BELL-FLOWERED CHERRY

This species was once described to me as the "monsoon" cherry. It just loves a monsoon-type wet climate, growing all summer long and forming a seemingly mature tree in just a few years. The strong, lush growths soon turn into very handsome upright, blacky trunks with horizontal bands of gray. In very early spring the bare stems are dripping with carmine bells.

On close inspection, the flowers have a thin, narrow, waxy calyx in raspberry-pink with a circle of carmine petals beneath. The flowers are brimming with nectar and loved by birds and bees alike. It does not like heavy frosts and is not very hardy. It seems to need a temperate climate or at least warm summers. Native to Taiwan and southwest China, and southern Japan. Height x width 25 ft (8 m). ZONE 8 OR 9.

Campanulata = like bells.

Prunus 'Okame' (*P. campanulata* x *P. incisa*)

This plant is a lovely combination of both parents raised by Captain Collingwood Ingram (1880–1981), who was known in the plant world as "Cherry" Ingram because of his love of the genus. This upright plant is ideal for small gardens as it forms a thin, narrow column and in early spring is covered in masses of bright rose-pink flowers. Each flower has a long, thin, red calyx that remains after the petals have fallen and gives the clue as to the

Right: *Prunus campanulata*

Above: *Prunus serrulata* 'Shogetsu'

P. campanulata parentage. The narrow, upright nature of the tree comes from the *P. incisa* parent. The flowers are very popular with bees and to walk under a bush in flower feels like the whole hive is busy above your head. So if you're afraid of bees, choose another plant! Quite good fall color too. Height 15 ft (5 m) x width 6–10 ft (2–3 m). ZONE 7.

Prunus serrulata
JAPANESE CHERRY

While we refer to the range of Japanese cherries as *Prunus serrulata*, many of them are likely to be of hybrid blood. But as they have been cultivated and bred in Japan for over 1000 years, it's bound to become rather complex. Most are big, wide-spreading trees in various shades of pink, with an occasional white, or even green, flower type. ZONE 6.

'Amanogawa' is unusual because it forms a bolt-upright column of a tree, so it is ideal for narrow spaces between buildings. The semi-double pink flowers smother the bush in mid-spring, and they are fragrant. Height 25 ft (8 m) x width 6 ft (2 m). ZONE 6.

'Kanzan' (syn *P.* 'Kwanzan') is one of the most familiar blossom trees of spring, with double flowers in a bright pink. The flowers open a strong pink and then actually intensify in color. It also has a very upright habit. The new spring leaves have a bronzy tinge. It is generally considered the hardiest and toughest of the flowering cherries. Height x width 30 ft (10 m). ZONE 6.

'Mount Fuji' (syn *P.* 'Hosokawa', *P.* 'Shirotae') is one of the best white cherries, with single and semi-double white flowers on long stalks on a spreading tree. The fragrant flowers are an added bonus, and often the soft green leaves emerge at the same time, creating a beautiful contrast. The bush has a very graceful, semi-weeping habit. Height 20 ft (6 m) x width 25 ft (8 m). ZONE 6.

Above: *Prunus serrulata* 'Kanzan'

'Pink Perfection' is a beautiful double with pink flowers in heavy clusters. It also has attractive bronze new growth and excellent fall colors. Height x width 25 ft (8 m). ZONE 6.

'Shogetsu' (syn *P.* 'Shimidsu Sakura') is a graceful, wide-spreading tree ideal for avenue planting. The clusters of pink buds open in spring to reveal frilly pink and white double flowers, becoming simply white with age. It has wonderful fall colors in rich orange and reds. Height 20 ft (6 m) x width 25 ft (8 m). ZONE 6.

'Tai Haku' is also known as the great white cherry. It is a very big, upright tree with large, single, white flowers 2½ in (6 cm) across and reddish new leaves emerging at flowering time in mid-spring. Give it plenty of room and preferably find a dark backdrop to highlight the flowers. Height 25 ft (8 m) x width 30 ft (10 m). ZONE 6.

Above: *Prunus* x *yedoensis* 'Awanui'

'**Ukon**' is a large, upright tree with unusual pale green flowers, sometimes with a hint of pink. The flowers usually emerge at the same time as the new bronzy leaves in mid-spring creating an exciting twin-color effect. Height 25 ft (8 m) x width 30 ft (10 m). ZONE 6.

Serrulata = finely-toothed, as the leaves have serrated edges.

Prunus subhirtella

A small tree renowned for its early, pink, fragrant flowers and excellent fall colors. The beautiful soft pink single flowers appear in early spring, before the leaves. It is debatable if this Japanese cherry is a true species, and some people think it is a hybrid. Height x width 25 ft (8 m). ZONE 5.

'**Fallalis**' is a form worth growing for its habit of flowering at unusual times. As the name suggests, it flowers in the fall, and often again in spring. In some seasons it flowers all through winter. The semi-double, white flowers with a hint of pink appear from pink buds. It is a good cut flower to cheer up the house in winter. Height x width 25 ft (8 m).

'**Pendula**' comes in different forms, some with soft pink flowers, some strong pink, and there are doubles too. The tree has a genuine weeping habit, with branches bending to touch the ground, and because of its tidy habit and superb fall color it is perhaps more likely to be grown for its shape and leaf, than for the flowers. Height x width 25 ft (8 m).

Sub = near or somewhat; *hirti* = hairy.

Prunus x yedoensis (P. speciosa x P. subhirtella)
YOSHINO CHERRY, POTOMAC CHERRY

A lovely Japanese hybrid smothered in single, soft pink blossoms in early spring. As a bonus, they are also delightfully scented. The bush has a spreading habit and in time is a huge tree, so take care where you plant it. The fall colors can be stunning in some years. Height 50 ft (15 m) x width 30 ft (10 m). ZONE 5.

'**Awanui**' is a *yedoensis* seedling bred in New Zealand by Keith Adams, with a total froth of strong, single, pink flowers in spring. Height 25 ft (8 m) x width 30 ft (10 m).

'**Ivensii**' has a weeping habit and pure white, fragrant flowers in spring. Height x width 25 ft (8 m).

Rhaphiolepis

Rosaceae

Rhaphiolepis are a small group of dense, evergreen shrubs in the rose family native to east and southeast Asia. Anything less like a rose, however, is hard to imagine. They look more like dwarf versions of the related photinia. Thankfully they do have several endearing features, not least their ability to grow near the sea. *Rhaphiolepis umbellata* especially will grow right on the seashore where you thought no shrub would survive. The thick, glossy leaves protect them from the hot sun, wind and salt-spray. This is not to say that inland gardeners should not grow these easy-care shrubs. The dense, mounded shape is ideal for giving a garden structure or "body," and the spring flowers in pinks and whites, while not absolutely stunning, are showy enough to merit attention, especially combined with this plant's other attributes. So if you've got a troublesome spot in the garden where you need a waist-high, hardy, flowering evergreen look no further.

Open, sunny and breezy sites are best, but I've seen plenty of good specimens growing in tough, shady spots. Soil type and density seem irrelevant, as they'll grow in anything. They are easy to transplant from pots when young; just take care to unwind any spiraling roots. But don't be tempted to shift them again, because they have tough, stringy roots. Drought is no problem once the plant is established. Without wanting to relegate them to boring utilitarian sites, they certainly are great shrubs for difficult places around buildings and in those small borders where you need a dense, easy-care shrub to stay below window height.

Raphis = needle; *lepis* = scale.

Above: *Rhaphiolepis* x *delacourii* 'Coates' Crimson'

Rhaphiolepis x *delacourii* (*R. indica* x *R. umbellata*)

Named after Frenchman M. Delacour of Cannes, who hybridized this species from *Rhaphiolepis indica* and *R. umbellata*. It is hardier to cold than *R. indica* and I think prettier, and thankfully it inherited some of the wind-hardiness of *R. umbellata*. The new leaves are covered in hairs, protecting them from wind damage until they harden up. There is a group of hybrids under this name and in spring and summer they all have showy pink or rosy flowers in erect little cones. It tends to be more open and upright in its growth habit and may need an occasional trim to keep neat and tidy. Height 6 ft (2 m) x width 8 ft (2.5 m). ZONE 8.

'**Coates' Crimson**' has rosy crimson flowers, while '**Spring Song**' has pink-on-white blooms over an extended period. '**Springtime**' has bronzy new growth and strong pink flowers from late winter to spring. All height 6 ft (2 m) x width 8 ft (2.5 m). ZONE 8.

Rhaphiolepis indica

In spring and early summer, this shrub has small heads of white to pale pink apple blossom flowers with a slight but pleasant fragrance. It grows to shoulder-high, and its tough, leathery leaves have an obvious pointed tip. The new leaves are soft and bronzy and at this stage are vulnerable to attack from caterpillars, and as the leaves expand so, too, do the notches caused by the caterpillars. It is also prone to leaf and black spot. The species originates in China, and not India as the name suggests. Height 5 ft (1.5 m) x width 6 ft (2 m). ZONE 8 OR 9.

Rhaphiolepis umbellata, syn *R. japonica*, *R. ovata*

This is the ultimate in wind-hardy shrubs—if *Rhaphiolepis umbellata* won't grow on your windy site, nothing will. The bold, round leaves are thick and solid, accounting for the salt- and wind-resistance. The summer flower heads of white blooms are slightly scented and appear in umbels, and are nicely presented on top of the bush. They are followed by black berries that are appreciated by birds. Native to Korea and Japan. Height x width 5 ft (1.5 m). Sometimes regarded as a little tender, hot summers will, however, enable it to survive colder winters. ZONE 7.

Umbellata = flowers in umbels.

Rhododendron

Ericaceae

I n gardens we have a fantastic range of colors from white to various shades of pink, red, purple, blue, orange, yellow and multicolors. Of course we grow rhododendrons for their glorious flowers but most are very handsome foliage plants, too, and so earn their keep year-round by providing tidy bushes. The flowering period for each bush is quite short, but by choosing various cultivars you can extend the flowering season for at least two months and longer.

We tend to think of rhododendrons as dense, evergreen shrubs, but the multitude of species within this genus include a number of deciduous types, as well as the popular mollis azaleas, which are technically rhododendrons. And while most rhododendrons are very tidy, rounded mounds of dark foliage,

Above: *Rhaphiolepis umbellata*

some are twiggy, ungainly bushes, and they vary from mighty trees, such as the Himalayan *Rhododendron arboreum* through to tiny miniatures, e.g. *R. lapponicum* at 6 in (15 cm) high. Some smaller species, like *R. impeditum*, grow *en masse* like heather across moorland in western China. Then just when you think you think you've got rhododendrons sorted, someone introduces you to vireya rhododendrons. Vireyas are glossy-leafed tropical rhododendrons from equatorial Borneo and New Guinea. Not only do they have astonishing shiny leaves, but the waxy flowers come in brilliant tropical colors, and just to complete the picture, they also flower two to three times a year because near the equator there are no seasons. Unfortunately these are too tender for most regions, but they do make superb conservatory plants because of their repeat flowering.

You will often hear people say rhododendrons need shade, when what they really need is shaded roots to keep the roots cool. They have a mass of fine fibrous roots near the surface and if these dry out then a number of them die and this allows root rot to attack and generally debilitates the bush. The plant tries to shield its roots from the hot sun by providing an umbrella of foliage. We can help protect the roots of newly planted rhododendrons by providing a thick mulch of woodchip or bark to keep the roots cool and moist, and there will be the added benefit of preventing weeds.

Above:
Rhododendron
'Lem's Cameo'

Weeds are more of a problem for rhododendrons than for other shrubs. We come along with a trowel or hoe and start attacking the weeds and in the process we destroy some of the fine fibrous roots of the rhododendron. Every broken or damaged root is a source of infection and the bush has also lost some of its feeding capacity. If we were to rattle the hoe around a shrub such as *Weigela* or *Philadelphus* it would make no difference to the plant as their roots are deeper. This mat of fine roots does have several advantages; it means that you can plant rhododendrons near the house or by paths as there are no big roots to lift concrete or invade the drains. Another bonus is that rhododendrons at any size can be shifted because the root mat is compact. The only constraint is the size of the bush, but with the help of a crane or a frontend-loader there is no limit. If you dig around in a circle, just a little wider than the spread of the foliage (sometimes known as the drip-line), and for a waist-high bush you only need to go to one spade's depth, you will have gathered enough of the plant's roots.

Rhododendrons need an acidic or neutral soil and good drainage. They also enjoy moist climates and prefer year-round rain. Having said that, they do have amazing powers of recovery. I've seen rhododendrons seemingly at death's door, wilting from prolonged drought, and yet they perk up at the first rain. Perhaps some shade would be valuable if your climate is not moist year-round, as trees will spare them the hot sun during any dry phase. They cope with occasional storms, but don't like regular winds. One severe gale a month is preferable to constant lesser winds that dry out the plant and cause the leaf edges to burn.

When the flowers are spent, it pays to take off the old flower heads using a finger and thumb flick technique. Even though this is a boring and grubby job (the heads are sticky), the plant will repay you with a better floral display next year because left to its own devices the plant will put all its strength into making lots of seeds rather than producing next year's flower buds. This deadheading is really the only pruning necessary for most species. If a bush gets too big, or it gets tatty for some reason, then you can prune the bush more drastically. Most rhododendrons regenerate very well if cut back to bare stumps. The key is to prune the whole bush to the same height. Many gardeners are tempted to prune one side of the bush this year and the other side next year. This fails because the plant concentrates on growing the straggly, tall side and ignores the pruned side.

Pests can be manifold depending on your climate. Mildews, thrips and weevils can be devastating and Phytophthora root rot deadly.

Most of the species were introduced early in the 20th

Above: *Rhododendron* 'Pirouette'

century, even vireyas were in cultivation in the orangeries and conservatories of Victorian England long before the Himalayan and Chinese species. Nowadays, most of the plants for sale are complex hybrids. Regarding zones or climate, they vary so much it is best to take advice from your local nursery or gardening society.

Rhodo = rose or red; *dendron* = tree.

Rhododendron augustinii

Beautiful blue flowers smother this large, upright shrub in spring. Each floret is small, and the flower heads are only 2 in (5 cm) wide, but the sheer number of flowers more than compensate for their small size. The smooth, palish green leaves often have a hint of bronze and are scented if crushed. Can be grown in a suburban or woodland garden. Named after Augustine Henry (1857–1930), an Irishman based in China for many years working as a customs officer. He collected specimens of thousands of plants, many of them new to cultivation. China. Height 6 ft (2 m) x width 4 ft (1.2m). ZONE 6.

Rhododendron catawbiense

MOUNTAIN ROSEBAY

This super-hardy species from the Appalachian Mountains has been used for breeding hardy hybrids since it was first discovered by John Fraser in 1809. The large heads of flowers are usually shades of pinky lilac and appear in late spring and early summer. It is a dense, wide-spreading bush with attractive glossy green leaves. There is a white form, too, **R. 'Catawbiense Album'**. Both height x width 10 ft (3 m). ZONE 4.

Catawbiense = from Catawba, U.S.A.

Rhododendron griersonianum

This red-flowered bush has probably produced more hybrid off-spring than any other rhododendron until the introduction of *R. yakushimanum*. The individual flowers are long and trumpet-like, held in loose fashion. The orange-red flowers appear in late spring. The bush itself is usually wide-spreading and rather open, growing to around head height. The leaves are long, pointed and hairy, or bristly, while the orange-red flowers are produced late in the

spring. Introduced from western China in 1917 by George Forrest, who probably collected more rhododendron species than any other plant hunter. Height x width 6 ft (2 m). ZONE 8.

Griersonianum = named for R.C. Grierson, who worked for the Chinese Maritime Customs Department and was a friend of George Forrest.

Above:
Rhododendron
'Lem's Monarch'

Rhododendron hybrids

Rhododendrons have been hybridized for over 150 years. The first hybrids were based on the American species, such as *Rhododendron catawbiense*. Surprisingly, some of the very first hybrids were vireya rhododendrons, grown in the orangeries of the large houses of Europe. But as more species were introduced from the wild, hybridizers were given more and more opportunity to produce a variety of offspring. The modern hybrids are a complex group of plants and it is getting harder to trace their species background as each generation moves another step away from the wild plants.

Today, breeders look for fashionable colors, such as peachy pinks, and for hardiness and disease resistance.

Good, reliable hybrids include:

'Anna Rose Whitney' Bold, shocking-pink flowers in a dense head late in the season. This is a *R. griersonianum* hybrid. Height x width 10 ft (3 m).

'Crest' has beautiful primrose-yellow flowers and rich green, smooth leaves. The bush tends to be slightly open. A *R. wardii* hybrid. Height x width 6 ft (2 m).

'Dora Amateis' is a wonderful little plant that is absolutely smothered in pure white flowers. The individual flowers are small, but produced in profusion. The mound-shaped, tidy bush has small, narrow leaves. Height 3 ft (1 m) x width 4 ft (1.2 m).

'Fastuosum Flore Pleno' an old, old *R. catawbiense* hybrid. It is still worth growing with its bold, gray-green leaves and double, purple-blue flowers held in loose trusses. Height x width 10 ft (3 m).

'Lem's Cameo' A superb peachy pink, with the flowers held in a tidy head. It flowers late in the season. It also has very attractive bronzy new growth and rich green, shiny summer leaves. Height x width 6 ft (2 m).

'Lem's Monarch' This big, bold shrub has large, handsome, mat green leaves. The huge heads of pinky red and white flowers create a delightful twin-color effect. It is late flowering. Height x width 10 ft (3 m).

'Loders White' A dense, rounded bush with good foliage. The pink buds open to white flowers with a pink edge. Height x width 10 ft (3 m).

Above: Rhododendron 'Mount Everest'

'Mount Everest' The rich dark green leaves look good all year and highlight the pure white flowers held in tight trusses. Look inside the flowers for a deep red spot in the center. Height x width 10 ft (3 m).

'Pirouette' One of the newer *R. yakushimanum* hybrids and a great improvement on the "Seven Dwarfs" group of hybrids. The

Above: *Rhododendron* 'Loder's White'

Rhododendron schlippenbachii
ROYAL AZALEA

It's always a thrill to see a garden plant you know growing in the wild, and seeing this species was a highlight of a plant-hunting trip to Korea a few years ago. I now realise why I struggle to grow it; Korea has very cold winters followed by a slow, steady spring and then hot summers. So if you get fluctuating spring temperatures then this is liable to tempt it into flower early and then the flowers will be frosted. It's a big, rounded bush with pale mauve or soft pink, saucer-shaped flowers. It differs from most rhododendrons in being deciduous, and has scintillating red and orange fall color. It was discovered by Baron von Schlippenbach in Korea in 1854. Height x width 15 ft (5 m). ZONE 5.

Rhododendron wardii

The best of the yellow rhododendrons, and the basis for many fine yellow hybrids. This species was discovered by and named after Frank Kingdon-Ward, who found it in western China in 1913, and is possibly the best of the many rhododendrons he introduced. The leaves are pale glaucous green, rounded at both ends, with a clean simple look. The yellow flowers appear in loose trusses in spring and sometimes have a red throat. It usually grows around shoulder-high but can be taller. Height x width 6–10 ft (2–3 m). ZONE 7.

Rhododendron yakushimanum, syn R. degronianum subsp yakushimanum, R. metternichii var yakushimanum

Considering this plant wasn't introduced until 1934, it has had an amazing impact on the world of rhododendrons. Found growing naturally on the windswept parts of Yakushima Island in Japan, this is a super-tough plant capable of handling strong winds, cold and virtually any climate. Added to which it is dwarf and very dense and compact. It has been used to produce numerous offspring, including the well-known "Seven Dwarfs" group of hybrids. How-

Above: *Rhododendron johnstoneanum* hybrid with *Rhododendron* 'College Pink'

foliage is good and the large flower heads are made up of a mass of frilly-edged flowers in soft pink fading to white. Height 3 ft (1 m) x width 4 ft (1.2 m).

'Trude Webster' This plant is big, bold and beautiful. Huge soft pink and white flowers are held in enormous upright cones and complemented by the large, gray-green leaves. Height x width 12 ft (4 m).

'Virginia Richards' A dense mound with shiny rich green leaves topped off with peachy pink flowers in a loose truss. Height 4 ft (1.2 m) x width 6 ft (2 m).

Rhododendron impeditum

A small alpine plant with tiny scented leaves and masses of small blue or purple flowers in late spring. It is a great little rockery plant and best grown in cold regions, as it doesn't like heat or humidity. Collected in western China by George Forrest in 1911. Height x width 24 in (60 cm). ZONE 4.

Impeditum = tangled or twiggy.

Rhododendron johnstoneanum

The bush, with its slightly hairy, bristly leaves, is smothered in creamy yellow, slightly fragrant flowers grouped in threes and fours in spring. The wide-mouthed trumpet flowers sit tidily on the neat bush. It is easy-care and ideal for small gardens. Height x width 6 ft (2 m). ZONE 8.

Johnstoneanum = named after Mrs Johnston, the wife of the Political Agent in Manipur in 1882.

Right: *Rhododendron* 'Seven Stars', a *R. yakushimanum* hybrid.

Above: An old character plant of *Rhododendron obtusum* 'Amoenum', a parent of some Kurume azaleas.

You will often be told that azaleas need shade, but this isn't necessarily true. High shade is useful if you have dry summers, but full sun in a moist climate is fine. I have hundreds of azaleas in my garden and the best ones are in full sun, in a climate with high sunshine hours and high light intensity. The reason for their success is a deep mulch of bark chips keeping their roots cool. Keep their roots cool, shaded and moist and they are happy plants.

Azaleas don't like wind or hot, dry climates but they cope with high rainfall as long as the drainage is good. Ideally they need a moist climate or regular irrigation, and acidic soil with good drainage topped with a mulch.

Much as I love azaleas, they do seem to host a multitude of pests. Leaf roller and leaf miner caterpillars can nearly defoliate them. Leaf hoppers and thrips can devastate the leaves, while weevil grubs attack the roots and can even ringbark the plant at ground level, sometimes killing the bush. Wet soil or prolonged rain can lead to deadly root rot or Phytophthora. And then there is powdery mildew. The list goes on. Despite all this, most azaleas survive and put on a fantastic show every spring. The key is keeping them as healthy as possible with an open, acidic soil and a mulch and spring feed of acidic fertilizer.

Should a bush ever have a wayward or straggly stem this can be pruned back. They are a surprisingly good cut flower and last for several weeks in a vase, and you can put ungainly stems to good use in this way. The bushes tolerate quite ruthless pruning, to within a few inches of the ground if necessary to rejuvenate the plant. Likewise you can shift established bushes in winter to add "body" to a new border. They have a mass of fibrous roots, allowing gardeners to shift them without harm.

There are hundreds of cultivars ranging from ankle-high to over head-high, though most are around waist-high and grow wider than they are tall. The colors go from white through pale and deep pink, red, mauve and purples. There are some fine doubles too.

The following is a brief description of the rhododendron species that make up the evergreen azalea group.

Rhododendron indicum A Japanese species forming a dense, low, mound of a bush. It is mostly evergreen, but can lose a portion of leaves in cooler climates. The flowers are a wide-mouthed trumpet shape and come in reds and scarlets. Height x width 3 ft (1 m). ZONE 7.

Indicum = from India, as they were wrongly thought to originate from the subcontinent.

Rhododendron kaempferi A low, compact bush that is deciduous in cool climates and semi-deciduous elsewhere. The flower colors range from apricot to orange, and reds and scarlets. Height 3 ft (1 m) x 4 ft (1.2 m). ZONE 5.

Kaempferi = named after Englebert Kaempfer (1651–1715), a botanist who worked for the Dutch East India Company in Japan.

Rhododendron kiusianum From the windy mountain tops of Kyushu Island in Japan, this hardy little evergreen forms a dense, spreading mound. Flowers vary from lilac to purple, and red to crimson.

Introduced by E. H. Wilson (1876–1930) in 1918. He brought back what he thought were the 50 best clones. These are now known as "Wilson's Fifty." Height 3 ft (1 m) x width 4 ft (1.2 m). ZONE 6.

ever, I think the species is far more beautiful than any of the hybrids, with its smooth, leathery leaves that emerge in the spring covered in dense silver or bronzy hairs. The dense heads of white and pink flowers look just like apple blossom—it is so simple and effective. Height 3–5 ft (1–1.5 m) x width 3–7 ft (1–2.2 m). ZONE 5.

Rhododendron sp.

Based on R. indicum, R. kaempferi, R. kiusianum and R. simsii
EVERGREEN HYBRID AZALEAS

Azaleas are a confusing group of plants. For example, the name "azalea" comes from the Greek word *azaleos*, meaning dry or parched, referring to the habitat of *Rhododendron luteum*. This, however, isn't the preference of the garden varieties. Then the name of one species is *R. indica*, where "indica" means Indian, but they mostly hail from Japan and Korea. And technically azaleas don't exist, but that doesn't stop them putting on a fine flowering show every spring! Azaleas have for a long time been classified as rhododendrons, but every gardener still calls them azaleas. It is one of those name changes that just won't stick. They are small, dense, compact plants, ideal for the front of borders, rockeries and often have hose-in-hose double flowers. Apart from the mass smothering of flowers in the spring, azaleas are popular because they are tidy, evergreen shrubs and will fit easily into any garden border. Grown *en masse*, they are hard to beat for a stunning spring display.

Rhododendron obtusum This species has a somewhat confused history. Some say it grows wild on the mountains of Kyushu Island along with *R. kiusianum*. Others say it is a hybrid plant. The original plants in cultivation came back from China with Robert Fortune (1812–1880) in 1844 and it has long been cultivated in China and Japan. It is a dense, semi-evergreen plant with wide, funnel-shaped flowers in shades of red. The form **R. obtusum 'Amoenum'** is hardier and has lavender to purple flowers. For both, height 3 ft (1 m) x width 4 ft (1.2 m). ZONE 6.

Obtusum = obtuse or blunt leaf.

Rhododendron simsii A bold shrub with rich green leaves and vibrant red, funnel-shaped flowers. Evergreen, but can lose some leaves in cold winters. Height 5 ft (1.5 m) x width 7 ft (2.2 m). ZONE 9 OR 10.

Simsii = obscure.

Good cultivars of evergreen azaleas include:
'Apple Blossom' (Wilson's number 9). A low, dense bush with grass-green leaves and pale pink flowers with a white throat. Height x width 3 ft (1 m); **'Buccaneer'** A Glen Dale hybrid from Maryland with orange-red flowers on an upright bush. Height x width 4 ft (1.2 m); **'Goodson's Brick'** Unusual brick red to orange color, the tiny flowers smother the bush and the pale green leaves. Height 4 ft (1.2 m) x width 5 ft (1.5 m); **'Hinode Giri'** (Wilson's number 42.) Masses of tiny, funnel-shaped flowers in bright crimson. Height x width 3 ft (1 m); **'Louise Dowdle'** A Glen Dale hybrid with large pink flowers with a darker blotch in the throat. Height x width 4 ft (1.2 m); **'Vuyk's Scarlet'** A very dense, dark green bush with large red flowers in spring. Often flowers again in fall or winter. Height x width 4 ft (1.2 m).

Rhodotypos

Rhodotypos scandens, syn R. kerrioides
JETBEAD, WHITE KERRIA
Rosaceae

This plant has a certain charm that eventually grows on you. The first few times it flowers, you think it is nothing special, a bit like a white *Kerria* (hence the common name), but nowhere near as showy. They are closely related, the main difference being that *Kerria* have alternate leaves and bright yellow flowers whereas *Rhodotypos* have more attractive corrugated, opposite leaves and more subtle white flowers.

Left: Azalea 'Apple Blossom'

Left: Azalea 'Goodson's Brick'

Above: *Rhodotypos scandens*

are barely missed. We can have vertical and horizontal roses: climbing roses on walls and fences are a familiar sight, as are big, rangy ramblers, and recently, with the new carpet roses, we now have groundcover versions. There are tiny miniature roses that grow in pots or rockeries and allow apartment-dwellers to have some roses on a balcony or windowsill.

Most modern roses cope better with cold than they do with too much heat. Typically zones 6–8 is great, and zones 9–10 all right. People go to elaborate lengths to grow them in cold climes by mounding them with soil, straw or sawdust to keep the base of the plant free from extreme cold. I've also seen rose beds at the equator, but they weren't too happy.

Plant your roses in winter with bare-root plants, but in cold areas (where the ground is very cold) fall- or spring-planting may be better. Roses are usually sold bare-root, often pre-wrapped in plastic, but it is possible to buy potted plants year-round. Just remember to unravel any spiraling roots before planting. Mulch the surface of the soil after planting with crushed bark, or similar, or, ideally, old mushroom compost, as this will feed the plant as well as keep the weeds at bay.

Roses like regular feeding to keep them in tip-top condition, so give them a balanced fertilizer every spring before the new growth comes, and again in summer after the first flush of flowers.

In general, roses are easy to grow. The first and only essential is sun, and plenty of it. Roses need sun to thrive, especially the bush roses. They have a preference for heavy soils and clay is fine, better than sand in fact. On light soils, add plenty of compost or well-rotted animal manure. Roses grow happily in both acidic and alkaline soils, and they will even cope with occasional waterlogging. Alternatively, they withstand moderate droughts, but will need irrigation in very dry climates. Do not water overhead, as it only encourages diseases.

The multitude of pests and diseases that can attack them is the main drawback to growing roses and they often need regular spraying to keep the mildew, black spot and aphids under

However, when you see an established bush covered in shiny white flowers set off against the grass-green leaves you will be a fan.

Like the *Kerria*, this plant will grow just about anywhere and I'm always keen on easy-care plants. It is happy in sun or shade, in wet or dry climates and any soil—in other words, it copes with neglect and whatever you care to throw at it. A quick prune to tidy the bush after flowering is optional. It tends to have a more rigid, almost horizontal habit compared to the lax *Kerria* growth. The bush is also more open and airy and has smooth blackish stems. It's the sort of plant you place where not much else will grow and then enjoy the late spring white flowers as a bonus. No pests and easy to transplant in winter as it is deciduous. This species hails from China, Korea and Japan. Height x width 5 ft (1.5 m). ZONE 5.

Rhodo = usually means red, or more likely rose in this context; *typos* is shape, so the genus name refers to its rose-shaped flowers; *scandens* = lax.

Rosa

ROSE
Rosaceae

Roses are so much a part of our lives and our gardens we sometimes take them for granted. Then someone offers you a bloom or you smell a rose in the garden and you're hooked again. It's a hard-hearted person who can resist a beautiful rose. Not only are they a standby for summer color in our gardens, we also use them as cut flowers, especially to give to friends and family. Most of us have at least a few rose bushes and many gardeners make shrines of them with beds totally devoted to this genus.

Roses can be hard to blend with other shrubs or herbaceous plants, but within the genus there is so much variety other plants

Above: Climbing rose 'Cressida'

Above: Floribunda rose 'Sexy Rexy'

control. Some species and varieties are more disease-resistant than others, so look out for them when buying if you don't want to spray.

Most of the roses for sale in garden centers have been "budded". This is where a piece of the cultivar has been grafted onto a rootstock. Sometimes suckers shoot up from this rootstock and these need to be removed or they will take over the bush. These suckers are usually easy to distinguish with their paler leaves and more numerous leaflets. Being vigorous, they try to grow higher than the rest of the bush. You can cut them off with secateurs, but if you can manage to tear them away from the rootstock they are less likely to regrow. When we cut them off with secateurs we leave a small ring of buds able to resprout, whereas the tearing action removes these lower buds as well.

Most bush roses need winter pruning to rejuvenate the bush. Cut out any old or weak shoots, as well as any dead or diseased branches. Try to create a "vase" of strong shoots with an open center to allow air movement through the plant, which will reduce disease.

Not surprisingly, roses are part of the rose family, but you might be surprised to learn of the vast number of valuable plants in this family, ones we would be hard-pressed to live without, such as apples, pears, plums, peaches, apricots, raspberries and strawberries; and a host of ornamentals, including cherries, *Sorbus*, *Spiraea*, *Cotoneaster* and *Crataegus*.

The following groups of roses have been organised alphabetically and cover the main types popular in cultivation.

Floribunda Roses

This type of rose is the ideal shrub for summer gardens as they seem to be perpetually in bloom. The upright bushes have clusters of flowers at the tops of all the stems, and with a bit of judicious pruning and deadheading you can have flowers all summer.

The individual flowers are not as perfect in structure as those on a Hybrid Tea rose, but they make up in quantity what they may lack in quality. The rich, dark foliage is a perfect foil for the flowers. Height x width 4–5 ft (1.2–1.5 m). ZONE 6.

Rosa floribunda cultivars

'Amazon' Beautiful peachy apricot-colored flowers with a swirl of petals filling the center.

'Avalanche' A neat, compact plant covered in creamy buds opening to ivory white with a caramel center.

'Class Act' A charming rose with flat, open, creamy white blooms with a big central boss of golden stamens. Good healthy foliage. Winner of many awards.

'Eye Paint' A good single red rose with a pale center and silvery

Above: Floribunda rose 'Eye Paint'

Below: Floribunda rose 'Class Act'

Above: Hybrid Tea rose 'Gold Medal'

Above: Hybrid Tea rose 'Amberlight'

summer but are not as floriferous as the Floribundas. Height x width 4–6 ft (1.2–2 m). ZONE 6.

Hybrid Tea cultivars

'**Amberlight**' A lovely fragrant rose with pinky apricot blooms. Good healthy foliage.

'**Gold Medal**' Yellow buds with a hint of pink open to pure gold. Nice smooth petals and good shape flower.

'**Peace**' Released just after World War II, hence the name, this rose has stood the test of time. It is a healthy bush topped with large blooms of yellow with a hint of pink.

'**Tequila Sunrise**' A great name for a great rose. The flowers are a spiral of golden yellow petals topped with hot orange.

'**Voodoo**' Frilly petals in scrumptious coral red. Excellent disease-resistant foliage.

underneath the petals. A healthy, robust variety in flower for months.

'**Playboy**' Yellow to gold petals with a red trim fading to a pinky orange. Flowers over a long season.

'**Sexy Rexy**' Soft pink buds open to reveal layers of even softer shell-pink petals. Profuse flowering and good healthy growth are an added bonus.

'**Sun Flare**' When fully open, a classic golden yellow with a boss of yellow stamens in the center.

Hybrid Tea or HT Roses

These upright bushes are usually taller than Floribundas with rich, glossy foliage, often with a reddy or bronzy new growth. The foliage is deliciously scented on many varieties and the smell of a rose garden in the early part of the day comes from the foliage rather than the flowers. The flowers are bigger with a better shape than that of Floribundas' and are the ones most often used as cut flowers. The flowers can be singles or in groups of three or four on a stem.

The shape of the flowers can be exquisite and some have a knockout scent as well. After the first flush of flowers you will need to deadhead or possibly prune a little to encourage the plant to produce more flowers.

They tend to have several bursts of flowers throughout the

Rose climbers and ramblers

Climbing roses are both a joy and a bane. When they are good, they are brilliant—usually on someones else's wall or trellis—smothered in flowers, with lush, healthy foliage and pretty as a picture. Try them yourself and they never stay where they are put, and you always seem to be pruning or training them.

I think I have found the answer. Grow them on a tripod of three long poles tied at the top (like a tepee). Choose one cane per pole and tie them till they reach the top and let that be the only permanent portion of the plant. Allow the rose to trail and flow down from the top, hopefully covered in flowers, and in winter just cut off everything except the three main stems. You can leave them for two or more years before pruning at all if you wish to have a more relaxed style of growth.

When planting climbing roses against a wall, you will need a more permanent system of nails and wires to contain them, and do make sure the color of the rose blends with the color of the wall. Height up to 30 ft (10 m). ZONE 6.

Climbing rose cultivars

'**Cressida**' One of the English Roses in a subtle cameo pink. The very full flowers are scented. Can be grown as a shrub or climber.

'**Dublin Bay**' Rich deep red flowers that look good enough to eat. It flowers over a long period.

'**Uetersen**' A good healthy plant with attractive foliage topped off with deliciously scented rosy pink blooms in that full, crowded petal fashion of some roses. Not overly vigorous and easy to train.

'**Wedding Day**' A very vigorous climber with a mass of small white flowers. The flowers are held nicely in heads of a dozen or more and open flat to show a central boss of stamens.

Rubus

Rosaceae

Rubus is not a genus we normally associate with flowers, but take a closer look and you will find one or two flowering gems. This huge genus occurs naturally all around the globe and includes species such as raspberry and blackberry. Most are deciduous, but there are evergreen species. However, nearly all do have bristles or sharp thorns.

Rubus = from "rubra," meaning red, because some species have red fruits.

Rubus 'Benenden' (*R. deliciosus* x *R. trilobus*)

A "nice single rose" was my first thought when I spied this plant in an English garden. Then I realised something wasn't quite right. Yes, it is from the rose family, but the leaves look like a raspberry's. And so, for the first time in my life, I was admiring a *Rubus* flower. That's not to say I hadn't seen *Rubus* flowers before, I had just never found them so enticing.

The big, single, white flowers are 2–3 in (5–8 cm) across and they are arranged quite prettily, contrasting well against the grass-green new foliage. Graceful, arching canes are dotted with flowers in late spring and early summer, just as the roses are starting to flower. The flowers open in succession and so the flowering display is renewed every few days.

This hybrid was raised in 1950 by Capt. Collingwood Ingram, better known as "Cherry" Ingram for his love of cherry trees. Thankfully this particular plant is sterile, which is a bonus because some *Rubus* have become naturalized as the seeds are spread by fruit-eating birds. Another thing in its favor is the stems are thornless, unlike many of its vicious relatives.

Above: Two climbers, 'Dublin Bay' (red) and 'Wedding Day' (white).

Left: Climbing rose 'Uetersen'

It is deciduous and cold-hardy, even though one parent is from Mexico, and it is not fussy about soil or pH as long as the drainage is good. The only blight seems to be a root rot, or wilt disease, and this can kill or debilitate the plant. It is especially likely in poorly drained ground or wet, muggy climates. Basically this plant prefers a cool climate, say zone 5 to 8, and is inclined to fade away in warmer areas.

It usually forms a fairly tidy, arching bush around head-high. You can prune it occasionally after flowering to keep the shape tidy and possibly to rejuvenate it when the canes get old.

It is a plant with many possible uses: they look fine in a mixed border, or as a solo specimen in a woodland garden where the isolation can show off the arching habit to good effect. I've also seen it trained as a climber against a wall. It grows readily in sun or semi-shade, and will take a bit of breeze.

The leaves are vaguely like a Canadian maple, soft and felty to touch, or perhaps more like a blackcurrant leaf. It is one of those odd leaves that makes a noise when you rub it between finger and thumb. Each new growth has a flower like a big single rose with five white crinolene petals and a central boss of lemon-yellow stamens. Height x width 6 ft (2 m). ZONE 5.

Left: *Rubus* 'Benenden'

Rubus spectabilis 'Olympic Double', syn R. spectabilis 'Flore Pleno'

In spring, this variety has gaudy purple-pink double flowers rather like a miniature dahlia. While the flowers are pretty, the bush is prickly and has a tendency to sucker and so is really only useful in semi-wild gardens. Height x width 6 ft (2 m). ZONE 5.

Spectabilis = remarkable or showy.

If I had to choose another *Rubus* for my garden, after *R.* 'Beneden' or *R. spectabilis* 'Olympic Double', it would be one of the white-stemmed species, such as **R. thibetanus**. Flowers aside for the moment (as they are generally insignificant on these species), these types have arching stems, usually a purple-brown color, covered in an awesome white bloom that can be rubbed off by hand and weathers away after time and so old stems need to be removed to highlight the new white stems. Native to Western China. Height x width 8 ft (2.5 m). ZONE 7.

Thibetanus = old name for Tibet, from where the plant originates.

Other *Rubus* relatives include the wild blackberry, *R. fruticosus*, and raspberry, *R. idaeus*. I have recently discovered an amazing ground-hugging, creeping type ideal for steep banks called **R. pentalobus** (syn *R. calycinoides*). The saucer-shaped white flowers appear in summer, and are followed by the red fruits typical of this genus. Native to Taiwan. Height 4 in (10 cm) x width unlimited. ZONE 7.

Schizophragma

Hydrangeaceae

I love the two species in this genus for a whole host of reasons. First, they are climbing hydrangeas, and many gardeners are amazed to find such a thing actually exists. Second, the huge, airy, lacecap flowers seem to float out from the plants. Third, and more practically, they are such easy-care climbers. Give them good soil at planting time and leave well alone. In a few years you'll be blessed with wondrous flowers. They are both deciduous and have very attractive leaves.

It is true, the plants do take a few years to establish—they seem to sulk for a year or two before they reach for the sky. I think this is because we often plant climbers in such ridiculously tough sites: at the bottom of walls in damp shade or amongst a whole lot of builder's rubble. Even harder, is at the base of an established tree where all the goodness and moisture in the soil is long gone and where it has to start a desperate search for nutrition and moisture.

Like most climbers, they have an urge to get to the top of whatever structure they are given to climb. So it is best to plant it on a 6 ft (2 m) wall rather than a 60 ft (20 m) tree.

They are hardy, putting up with extremes of cold and summer heat. Wind can tear them from their support sometimes, but otherwise is not a concern. Once established, they are self-clinging, like ivy, gripping tenaciously to bricks or timber. Any structure must be strong and solid and likely to remain for years—they are no good on a flimsy trellis.

Schizophragmas are fine in full sun or part-shade and, like most climbers, their natural inclination is to grow toward the sun, where they flower more profusely. Virtually any soil will do, but it will grow faster given good conditions. They transplant without problems, but it is always better to choose the right place the first time. Be patient while they establish themselves, and don't expect flowers straight away. In only a few years, you'll be rewarded with a fantastic plant covering your wall or fence without having it take over.

Schizo = I cut; *phragma* = a wall. Thankfully, this doesn't mean it is going to cut your wall in half, rather it is a reference to the splitting of the seed capsule walls.

Schizophragma hydrangeoides
JAPANESE HYDRANGEA VINE

In midsummer, big, slightly fragrant, creamy white, lacecaps of flowers 10 in (25 cm) across appear on this woody climber. This species has reddish-tinged, heart-shaped leaves with a sawtoothed edge and reddish leaf stalks, and is the more attractive of the two species for foliage. There is a a form called **'Roseum'** with rose-

Right:
Schizophragma integrifolium

Far right:
Schizophragma hydrangeoides 'Roseum'

colored bracts and another form, **'Moonlight'**, with silvery blue leaves and prominent veins. Originates from Korea and Japan. Height 40 ft or more (12 m). ZONE 5.

Hydrangeoides = like a hydrangea.

Schizophragma integrifolium

A strong-growing vine that has more grayish, furry leaves than the *Schizophragma hydrangeoides*. Like this species, the huge, creamy, lacecap flowers appear in midsummer and are also slightly fragrant. This plant loves summer heat. From Central China and Taiwan. Height 40 ft or more (12 m). ZONE 7, or to zone 5 with summer heat.

Integrifolia = whole or entire, because the leaf has no serrations around the edge.

Sinojackia

Sinojackia rehderiana
Styracaceae

Now here is a deciduous shrub that deserves to be more popular. The flowers appear in mid-spring, long before the related *Styrax* have come on the scene. It is easy to grow, robust without ever threatening to take over a garden, and has dainty, white, bell-shaped flowers that dangle gracefully beneath each branch. These appear in such profusion that even a small specimen seems laden with flowers. The flowers appear all at once and so provide one big show. By comparison, some of the *Styrax* tend to flower in dribs and drabs over a long period and therefore lose some of their impact. If the plant has a fault, it might be the long-winded name, which I'm sure puts people off.

The glossy leaves start to emerge with the flowers and add substance to the flowering display rather than diminishing it. The fully grown leaves are finger-length, glossy on top and brilliant grass-green and, while the trunks and stems seem a bit brittle, the overall structure is quite strong. *Sinojackia* tend to form a slightly open bush; each branch is only slightly up from the horizontal position, which is why the flowers are held in such

easy view. The flowers look best from below, so if the bush is tall enough or planted on a bank, you can enjoy walking underneath them.

The bush is not particularly dense and so is ideal to shade rhododendrons from hot sun. The overall shape of the bush is a wide pyramid. Sinojackias are hardy and grow happily in cold climates (zone 6), yet are equally happy in warm zones 9 and 10 climates. They seem to be quite tolerant of drought and yet thrive in a wet climate.

A breezy site is acceptable, and full sun is best, although tall woodland shade is fine. They are not too fussy about soil as long as it is acidic or neutral. They have a good fibrous root sytem and are easy to transplant from pots or from open ground. You'll never regret planting one because it won't take over the garden, and the roots won't get in the drains.

The spring blossom will delight you and you'll find garden visitors are intrigued by it. You can show off your new-found knowledge by rattling off the name *Sinojackia rehderiana* as if

Left: *Sinojackia rehderiana*

*Above: Sophora
tetraptera*

especially in places where they need the extra heat to thrive, as most of them like warm summers. Cold winters are not usually a problem if they have enough summer heat to ripen the new wood. Breezy and even windy sites are fine despite their soft, delicate appearance.

Most are drought-tolerant and they have tough, stringy, searching roots. Transplant them when young because they do not like being moved. They are often multi-trunked bushes or trees and if you want a tidy-shaped bush, it pays to train them when young. Removing older branches results in a wound that takes years to heal.

Sophora = old Arabic name for a leguminous tree.

Sophora davidii, syn *S. viciifolia*

A large deciduous shrub with white pea-like flowers that are blue at the base. These appear in late spring to early summer in racemes 6 in (15 cm) long. It has neat, pinnate leaves and gnarly trunks. It seems to need hot summers to perform well and could perhaps be classed as an interesting rather than stunning plant. Native to China. Height 8 ft (2.5 m) x width 10 ft (3 m). ZONE 6.

Davidii = Père David (1826–1900), a French missionary to China.

Sophora japonica

JAPANESE PAGODA TREE

This is a handsome, rounded, deciduous tree with a liking for hot summers. It will survive cold winters providing it gets the prerequisite summer heat to ripen the wood. Like many *Sophora* it is reluctant to flower as a young plant, a disappointing habit in these days of "instant gratification". The small, fragrant, tubular flowers are almost white, with shades of yellow and green, and festoon the tree in 12 in (30 cm) long panicles in late summer given a hot summer climate. But, be warned, they can fail to appear in regions with cooler summers.

The lovely pinnate leaves, with lots of tiny, dark green leaflets, are held until late in the year but rarely provide any great fall color. The plant is not fussy regarding soil and is reasonably tough in the wind. The only problem is a canker disease, but they do tolerate city pollution well. In time it forms a mighty tree and so is bested suited to large gardens. The cultivar **'Regent'** is the same as the species except it has a much tidier habit, grows faster and blooms earlier. Native to Korea and China. Height 60 ft (20 m) x width 45 ft (15 m). ZONE 5.

There is a lovely weeping form appropriately called **'Pendula'**, the height of which is determined by the height it is grafted onto a seedling rootstock. If you want a low mound, choose a graft at say 5 ft (1.5 m), but if you'd prefer a weeper you can walk beneath for secrecy or shade then choose a graft that is much higher. It really needs a prime spot on its own, say as a lawn specimen, to be appreciated for its novel shape.

Japonica = from Japan, but in the early days of European plant gathering in Japan it was assumed all the plants found there were native. As it turns out, many had been introduced from mainland China, as is the case here.

Sophora tetraptera

KOWHAI

In its homeland, the national flower of New Zealand is a stunning sight in spring. It is commonly used as a street tree because of its relatively compact size and because it is capable of withstanding poor soil and windy, even coastal, conditions. For such a delicate-looking leaf it is remarkably wind- and salt-tolerant.

The flowers bring double joy as they encourage nectar-feeding birds into the garden. At first glance, the golden flowers form a

you've been growing it all your life. There is a sister plant called **S. xylocarpa** that is more-or-less identical. Both are native to eastern China. Height x width 20 ft (6 m). ZONE 6.

Sino = Chinese; *jackia* comes from John George Jack (1861–1949), Professor of Dendrology in Massachusetts; *rehderiana* = from Alfred Rehder (1863–1949), a German botanist who became curator of the herbarium at Arnold Arboretum, Boston, and wrote a famous manual of trees and shrubs.

Sophora

Fabaceae

*S*ophora are a wide-spread group of trees and include evergreen and deciduous species. The cultivated species are grown for their showy flowers. Some are pea-like with wings and others are tubular. They have pretty pinnate leaves and usually a good semi-weeping habit so the trees are worth growing for foliage. Some of them can be grown as wall shrubs,

tube, but on closer inspection you'll see they have the typical legume pattern of two wings and a keel. Nectar-feeding birds have long tongues to delve into the tube and seek out the nectar. Each individual flower is 1–2 in (2.5–5 cm) long, and in isolation they do not amount to much. However, a whole tree covered in blossoms is a sight to behold. Although the tree is technically evergreen, they do often lose their leaves just before flowering and so the flowers are more prominent.

The flowers are followed by chains of seeds in a long, twisted, four-sided, brown pod, that, when opened, reveals the hard, shiny, golden seeds. The trunks are often twisted affairs and have great character, easily fitting into an Asian-style garden. There are various named forms with bigger or brighter flowers, and there is a prostrate form also, **Sophora tetraptera var prostrata. S. microphylla** is similar but has smaller leaves. Native to New Zealand. Height 30 ft (10 m) x width 15 ft (5 m). ZONE 9.

Tetraptera = having four sides, referring to the seed pods.

Spiraea

BRIDAL WREATH
Rosaceae

Spiraeas are cherished in colder climates, but often considered boring in warmer ones, as they can be rather common. There are basically two types—those with white flowers on last year's wood and those with pink or red, flat, terminal flowers on the tips of the current growth. They are all deciduous, but rarely have any showy fall color.

Spiraeas are typical rose-family plants. They are tough, resilient and easy to grow. Any soil will do, including difficult, drafty sites around buildings. Full sun is best, but a little shade is fine. They handle summer heat and harsh winter cold as well as windy sites. Most are happy in dry or wet climates, and they've become a standby in many regions because of their resilience.

Spiraea = from the Greek "speira," meaning garlands.

Spiraea cantoniensis

A big, arching, deciduous bush with style and grace that is festooned in spring with sprays of pure white, pompom-like flowers. Thankfully, they shed the petals before the flowers fade so the bush always looks terrific in bloom. Prune immediatley after flowering to allow a whole season's growth to produce next year's flowers.

It sends strong sucker-like new growths up through the plant and you can thin out the old growth to prevent overcrowding. If the plant has a fault, it tends to hold its leaves through winter in warm places and these tatty old leaves, often half burnt brown, are still hanging on at flowering time, though you'd hardy know it with the mass of flowers.

The wood is quite thin and almost cane-like—brittle and easy to break off by hand—yet they are remarkably tough plants and not easily broken by the wind. China. Height 6 ft (2 m) x width 10 ft (3 m). ZONE 5.

Cantoniensis = from the city of Canton, China, where it was first seen by travelers from the West.

Spiraea japonica

JAPANESE SPIRAEA
A small, upright, deciduous bush with a dense thicket of thin, wiry stems and narrow, jagged-edged leaves. Each stem is topped by a flat head of rose-pink flowers up to 8 in (20 cm) across in late spring. There is a slight scent, reminiscent of just-cleaned houses or a linen cupboard. The light green leaves are nothing exciting to look at, but this robust little shrub will grow almost anywhere. Named clones like **'Anthony Waterer'** have bigger, stronger-colored flowers. China, Japan. Height 6 ft (2 m) x width 5 ft (1.5 m). ZONE 4.

The form **Spiraea japonica alpina** is a compact plant with small, neat heads of rosy pink flowers. Height 2 ft (60 cm) x width 3 ft (1 m). ZONE 4.

Japonica = from Japan; *alpina* = alpine.

Spiraea nipponica 'Snowmound'

A delightful selected form of a very good shrub for any garden. Like its sister spiraeas, it is tough and will perform for you wher-

Below left: *Spiraea cantoniensis*

Below right: *Spiraea japonica* 'Anthony Waterer'

Above: *Stachyurus praecox*

What a fine flowering plant this is, and yet it only seems to be appreciated by cut-flower enthusiasts. It is a superb cut flower, lasting for several weeks in a vase. The creamy white, bell-shaped flowers contrast well with the smooth, purple-brown stems and unopened purple buds. They appear in chains 4 in (10 cm) long on the last six or eight leaf buds near the tips of the stems, and although each individual bell is like a small pea, the overall effect is very showy. Each chain has 30 to 40 flowers opening from the top down in sequence. Underplant it with a groundcover of purple-flowering *Ajuga*. The combination of pendulous cream flowers and the upright spikes of purple *Ajuga* is a sight to behold.

The leaves look just like cherry leaves, with serrated edges and pointy tips. The bush itself is a big, open, arching plant around head-high, but easily twice as wide. An older specimen looks like an opened umbrella with its arching stems. The stems are purply black with prominent bumps called lenticels. These are the breathing holes for the stem and are not very obvious on most plants.

These plants are easy to grow in sunny places, but look thin and sparse if shaded or crowded. Any soil will suffice and it handles cold, some moderate winds, and is free of pests. It is also easy to transplant.

There are six species of hardy shrubs in the family, but this is the best by far. Japan. Height 6–9 ft (2–3 m) x width 12 ft (4 m). ZONE 7.

Stachys = spike; *oura* = tail; *praecox* = early.

Stewartia, syn *Stuartia*

Theaceae

Stewartias are small, unassuming trees with white, papery flowers, each with five petals and a central boss of stamens. They tend to flower in succession over a period of weeks rather than one big display so they don't make a big statement, but I wouldn't be without them. Even if I lived in a small town garden, I'm sure I could find room for at least one, probably *Stewartia sinensis*. They usually have a tidy, open structure, often with scintillating trunks and red-stemmed twigs, as well as excellent fall colors in purples and bronze, often with a hint of orange to liven it up.

So the combination of flowers, handsome trunks and fine fall colors means they are good value every day of the year. And they are easy to grow in poor or clay soils, and generally not fussy providing the soil is not too alkaline. Although, like most plants, they will grow much better if given good loam and a mulch, they are much tougher than is generally supposed. They also have a reputation for being difficult to transplant and large specimens should not be moved. However, I shifted a 12 ft (4 m) bush without any ill effects.

They have a good natural shape and don't need pruning, but won't complain if you do. If I was tempted to prune them, it would be to open them up more and create layers Japanese-style. They love hot summer climates, but handle cool and moist climates too. They cope with full hot sun, drought, hard soils and city pollution. And there are no pest problems on the deciduous species.

Stewartia = named after Sir John Stewart (1713–1792), an amateur botanist who was involved in the founding of Kew Gardens, London, England.

ever you choose to plant it. As a young plant, it forms an open, arching bush, filling in to become a dense mound of small, smooth leaves topped in frothy white flower heads in midsummer. They have a smell of new-mown hay or a linen cupboard. The species is native to Japan. Height x width 6 ft (2 m). ZONE 4.

Nipponica = from Nippon, old name for Japan.

Stachyurus

Stachyurus praecox
Stachyuraceae

It is amazing how differently plants perform in different climates. *Stachyurus* is a case in point. The species name *praecox* means "early," and, true to its description, it is one of the first shrubs to flower in the spring in cool climates. I first came across the plant in London and cherished its early blooms. However, if you grow this plant in a warm zone, it will flower later on in the spring, after the magnolias and azaleas have finished. Somehow it loses a lot of its appeal because it doesn't have the stage to itself. It still grows and performs well in these warmer zones, and has better fall color, which seems a contradiction. Cool-climate gardeners don't rate it as a fall-color shrub, whereas it is as good as the best of any cherries, with rich orange and reds in a warm zone.

Above: *Stewartia malacodendron*

Stewartia malacodendron
SILKY STEWARTIA

A wondrous plant with big, white, saucer-shaped flowers 4 in (10 cm) across highlighting the whiskery black stamens in the center. The flowers appear in the latter part of summer, but are certainly worth waiting for. Undoubtably this species has the best flowers of the genus. The upright, almost column-like shrub has purply bronze fall colors. It hails from the warmer southeastern states of the U.S.A. and needs summer heat to thrive. Height 20 ft (6 m) x 10 ft (3 m). ZONE 7.

Malacodendron = mallow tree.

Stewartia monadelpha
TALL STEWARTIA

An undistinguished shrub for most of the summer, the dull, dark green, alternate leaves are shiny beneath, oval, pointed and about 4 in (10 cm) long. The mass of small, white, buttercup-sized blooms in the spring create a froth of flowers attractive to bees. The trunks have smooth, peeling bark, but are not as good as its close relative *Stewartia sinensis*. In the fall it suddenly becomes the most stunning thing in the garden with rich purple-bronze dashed with orange fall color. From Korea and Japan. Height x width 20 ft (6 m). ZONE 6.

Monodelpha = stamens in one bundle.

Stewartia ovata
MOUNTAIN STEWARTIA

Another exciting *Stewartia*, somewhat like *S. malacodendron*, only the central stamens are orange or yellow. The upright habit is similar and the fall colors are usually vivid oranges and reds. **S. ovata var grandiflora** has even larger white flowers at 3–4 in (8–10 cm), but is otherwise the same. This Appalachian mountain shrub is outstanding, but as so often happens is often not appreciated in its homeland. Height 20 ft (6 m) x width 12 ft (4 m). ZONE 5.

Ovata = ovate leaf.

Stewartia pseudocamellia
JAPANESE STEWARTIA

The charming crepe-paper flowers of this species give an impression of frailty, as each flower has crinkled, gossamer-thin, white petals. The four large petals have very serrated edges and a boss of yellow stamens in the center and thus have a likeness to a single

Right: *Stewartia pseudocamellia*

camellia, hence the name *pseudocamellia* (false camellia). The blossoms open in succession over several weeks and so there is never a single stunning flowering display, but the individual flowers and length of flowering make it a good choice.

The leaves are glossy, green and heart-shaped, with a serrated edge leading to a point. New stems and leaf stalks take on a red tinge if exposed to the sun. The bush is best grown in a sunny spot in a woodland garden, though semi-shade will be fine. The shrub has a very upright habit, but is not dense like a camellia. In fact this deciduous shrub has a light, open appearance enhanced by the peeling brown and gray trunks. The fall colors include strong yellows and reds. Japan and Korea. Height 30 ft (10 m) x width 20 ft (6 m). ZONE 5.

Pseudocamellia = false camellia, referring to the similarity of the flower to a camellia flower.

Stewartia sinensis

If you look at the hundreds, if not thousands, of spiky, starry seed capsules on the bare branches in winter, you'll realise just how floriferous this deciduous bush is. And yet when it is in flower, it is easy to pass by as the flowers are nestled among the new leaves. The tips of the branches come into leaf first, and the lower branches open before the upper. When the dainty white flowers appear in early to midsummer they come out in succession over several weeks. The flowers are never a mass display because of this succession and they are never on the same plane as each other, so

Above: *Stewartia sinensis*

from any one angle you only see a portion of the open flowers. They are coin-sized, creamy white, open cups with the added bonus of a pleasant scent of tea. It does tend to be biennial bearing, meaning it flowers well one year and has a rest the following year. Many shrubs do this because in the good flowering year they put all their strength into producing seeds and so there is less energy left for next year's flowers.

The smooth fawn-brown trunks have an obvious appeal and a portion of each trunk loses its top surface, displaying pink new bark, so even in winter this plant is attractive. The fall color is pretty too, in a range of rich reds and crimson.

This relatively small tree is ideal for situations near a house or a building as there are no invasive roots. We planted one just 5 ft (1.5 m) from the house and it caused no problems. The shade is not dense enough to block out the light, though I should add it is on the shady side of the house. It is the kind of plant that every

keen plantsperson seems to rave over, while the general garden-center buying public continue to ignore. Originates in China. Height x width 20–30 ft (6–10 m). ZONE 6.

Sinensis = from China.

Styrax

Styracaceae

Styrax are beautiful small trees and I have grown well over a dozen different species in this genus. Though, when I show visitors around our garden, it is often hard to justify my attraction to them. They would not top anyone's hit parade for foliage, flowers or trunks alone, but in combination they are a very pleasing plant. All have dainty, white, bell-shaped flowers appearing in spring and summer. As an aside, the more I learn about gardening, the more I appreciate white flowers. They blend with everything and look so pure and natural.

This group of plants is easy to grow in any free-draining, acidic or neutral soil. The cultivated species are all deciduous trees but have no special fall color. However, they will grow in climates that are wet or dry, cold or warm. Most are ideal for small town gardens, with the bigger species better placed in woodland gardens. They like an open, sunny situation and need protection from strong or cold winds.

Most *Styrax* are from Asia, with a few from North America and just one, *S. officinalis*, growing in Europe.

Styrax = from the compound storax, once used in medicine, which is extracted from this tree.

Styrax japonica
JAPANESE SNOWBELL
This species is probably the most well-known of all the *Styrax*. It forms a bigger tree than most, with a wide, spreading, pyramid habit. It makes a great shade tree if you can cut off the lower branches. The branch structure tends to be a tidy and horizontal. The small, shiny leaves are a cool shade of deep green and clusters of pretty, white, bell-shaped flowers hang below the branches in midsummer. As a bonus, the flowers are slightly scented. Try and site the plant where you can walk or sit beneath the tree at flowering time. The cultivar **'Pink Chimes'** has rosy pink flowers. Native to China, Japan and Korea. Height 30 ft (10 m) x width 25 ft (8 m). ZONE 6.

Japonica = from Japan.

Styrax obassia
FRAGRANT SNOWBELL
A superb plant for small gardens as it grows very upright when young. Its fabulous peeling trunks and big lush leaves are a bonus. The leaves are covered in soft down when they are young and are nice to touch. All this is topped off with chains of white fragrant flowers 8 in (20 cm) in early to midsummer. It was awarded a First Class Certificate by the English Royal Horticultural Society in 1888, a mere nine years after it was introduced from Japan by Charles Maries, which illustrates what an excellent garden plant it is. From Korea, China and Japan. Height x width 25 ft (8 m). ZONE 6.

Obassia = a Japanese name for this plant.

Left: *Styrax japonica*

141

Above: *Styrax wilsonii*

Styrax wilsonii

An upright, dainty bush with small leaves and thin gray stems, rather like a species lilac. It's one of the first *Styrax* to flower in the spring, when clusters of flowers emerge from the creamy white teardrop-shaped buds. The petals reflex backward to show five starry pure-white petals with a small center of yellow stamens. The flowers hang down in typical *Styrax* fashion. This is one of the best species for small gardens (as long as it has shelter, because the stems are brittle). It is from western China and was named after the great plant hunter E. H. Wilson (1876–1930). Height x width 8 ft (2.5 m). ZONE 7.

The American species, **Styrax americana** (American snow-bell), is very similar in flower though it tends to forms a wide, spreading bush, and is not so easy to accommodate in a garden. Height x width 15 ft (5 m). ZONE 7.

Syringa

LILAC
Oleaceae

Wherever we live, we always miss people and places from the past. This also happens with plants. Here I am with a 10 acre (4 ha) garden and over 3000 different plants and I'd swap virtually any one of them for a common old lilac like the one my grandmother grew in her garden. The cold winters and heavy clay limestone soil of the Mendip Hills in Somerset, England, is just perfect for lilacs. Just a whiff of their

heady fragrance and I'm back as a boy in her garden. Now I live in possibly the best climate in the world and I can't grow lilacs: it is too warm, the soil too acidic and when we do try, they get ringbarked by borer grubs and gradually fade away.

From this, you'll gather that lilacs like alkaline or neutral soils and cold winters, though they will cope with hot summers given a proper winter. They are deciduous shrubs found from eastern Europe right through to Asia, often growing in severe climates with extreme cold and/or drought and baking hot summers. They need good drainage, full sun and preferably some shelter, though this is not essential. Being deciduous, they can be shifted in winter without any difficulty.

Generally they form a good, upright, slightly open shape and don't need any pruning, but if you ever need to, they can be thinned after flowering. Some will tolerate and regenerate from more rigorous pruning.

Lilacs are a worthy addition to any mixed border or shrubbery and the fragrance of the flowers is a heady bonus. Most have large pointed panicles packed with tubular flowers in a range of colors from whites and creams through to strong reds and purple.

Syringa = from the Greek "syrinx," meaning pipe or tube, which could refer to the tubular flowers, but some suggest it is for the hollow stems that were used for tobacco pipes.

Syringa x hyacinthiflora (S. oblata x S. vulgaris)

Large cones of fragrant flowers 5 in (13 cm) long appear in spring, in colors ranging from white to pink to purple, on this upright shrub that spreads with age. The leaves often have a bronzy tinge when they first emerge and it is one of the few lilacs to have any fall color, with hints of purple. The heart-shaped leaves have that typical clean look we associate with lilacs. Height x width 15 ft (5 m). ZONES 3 TO 8.

Hyacinthiflora = means the flowers are like a hyacinth.

Syringa meyeri 'Palibin', syn S. palibiniana
DWARF KOREAN LILAC

A small, amenable shrub ideal for small gardens and even for patios. In mid-spring the surprisingly large (4 in/10 cm) panicles of flowers appear. Each individual flower is a tiny tube of lilac-pink, and the overall effect is very showy. The scent is a bonus, but really two things set this plant apart: it is small enough to grow in any garden and it is quite happy in warm, mild climates. The neat, little, rounded leaves have a smooth, clean appearance and look good all summer. Height x width 5 ft (1.5 m). ZONE 4.

Meyeri = named for the famous American plant explorer Frank Meyer (1875–1918), who spent many years in the colder regions of China and Korea, mostly searching for edible plants.

Syringa oblata

A hardy, upright shrub from north China and Korea, and typical of the plants from this region in that it needs a climate with hot summers and cold winters. Given the right conditions, it is a handsome, clean-leafed bush, often with a hint of purple in the leaves, and lovely, fragrant, lilac-blue flowers in wide, showy panicles 5 in (13 cm) long. Height x width 15 ft (5 m). ZONES 4 TO 8.

Oblata = widened, referring to the broad leaves.

Syringa x prestoniae (S. reflexa x S. villosa)
PRESTON LILAC

This beautiful group of hybrids was developed by Isabella Preston in Ottawa, Canada, in the 1920s. They are handsome upright shrubs or small trees with hanging cones of scented flowers up to

Above: *Syringa meyeri* 'Palibin'

6 in (15 cm) long appearing in late spring and early summer. They come in a variety of colors, from pink to lilac and deep purple. These hybrids are super-hardy and being late-flowering any risk of frost damage to the flowers is reduced. Height x width 12 ft (4 m). ZONES 2 TO 8.

Syringa x prestoniae cultivars
'Elaine' Single, white flowers.
'Hiawatha' Pale pink, single flowers open up from purple buds.
'Isabella' Single, pinky purple flowers.
'Leon Gambetta' Double flowers in lavender shades. A good, strong plant.
'Miss Canada' A tough hardy plant with rosy flowers.
'Royalty' Single, purple-red flowers.
   All height x width 12 ft (4 m).

Syringa vulgaris
COMMON OR FRENCH LILAC

This wonderful plant has one of the most exquisite combinations of flowers and perfume. Flowers appear late spring and early summer in big terminal cones. They come in singles and doubles, in colors ranging from white to cream, purple-pink and red. There are literally hundreds of cultivars.

Typically it is a tall, upright bush or small tree with gray stems and a clean, tidy habit. No pruning is needed apart from shaping in the early years. Lilacs don't have a central leader, as they produce twin buds on the top of each stem and so naturally fork into two shoots. The smooth, heart-shaped leaves add to the manicured

Above: *Syringa vulgaris* 'Sensation'

appearance and it is one of those rare plants that look as luxuriant at the end of summer as it did at the beginning. It is almost the perfect boundary bush as it's unlikely to upset your neighbor—if you plant one on your boundary it will be appreciated by both parties, as it doesn't get too big or cast too much shade and it doesn't have messy leaves or flowers.

Lilacs like heavy soil, including clay, and full sun to ripen the wood and produce more flowers. Most plants for sale are grafted on lilac seedlings or on privet. Remove any suckers that may arise from the rootstock or they will take over the plant. Native to eastern Europe. Height x width 25 ft (8 m). ZONES 4 TO 8.

Vulgaris = Latin word meaning common or plentiful.

Syringa vulgaris cultivars
'Hugo Koster' A true purple-lilac flower.
'Katherine Havemeyer' Double fragrant flowers open as lavender and fade to pink.
'Madame Lemoine' Pure white double flowers. An old but still popular cultivar.
'President Lincoln' Purple opening to almost blue. Very fragrant.
'Primrose' An unusual shade of primrose yellow in short tight heads. A strange color for a lilac.
'Sensation' An unusual twin-color flower with reddish purple base and white edging.
'Souvenir de Louise Spath ' Red wine to purple, scented blooms.

Telopea

WARATAH
Proteaceae

*T*elopea comes from the Greek *telopas* meaning seen at a distance, and what better name could be devised. The dazzling red flowers look like they were designed on another planet. Each terminal flower head is made up of thin, tubular, scarlet or red flowers, clustered together like a pin cushion. The flowers bend round and up, like holding your hand palm up with your fingers curved toward the sky. These delectable flowers are pollinated by nectar-feeding birds and each one produces fresh nectar every day. They are very long-lasting; even as a cut flower they last for three to four weeks in a vase.

Telopeas insist on good drainage and acidic to neutral soil, and are very prone to root rot if poorly drained. Full sun and plenty of air are the next requirements. They seem quite happy near the sea and enjoy a breezy site. The big, synthetic-looking leaves are actually very wind-resistant but the bush can get top-heavy and topple at ground level in severe storms.

Once established, they handle drought and don't seem to mind competing roots from neighboring trees, as long as the bush isn't shaded. Like most of the Protea family, telopeas hate fertilizers and manures, especially phosphates and animal manures, so a poor, sandy soil is best.

It pays to plant them young from pots, as they hate being shifted, and never try to move a plant to another location.

Ideally, shade the roots and don't disturb them again. Don't even disturb the soil around the plant if you can avoid it. Lay a mulch of bark or stones over the soil surface and leave well alone.

Pruning is a good idea, and prune either at, or just after, flowering to keep the bush compact and prevent it getting top-heavy. By taking stems for a vase you prune the bush. Surprisingly for a Protea family member, they cope with hard pruning and even regenerate from stumps. They do get attacked by scale insects and mildews, as well as the more lethal root rot.

They will tolerate mild frosts, the more so in a hot summer climate. Being evergreen with such showy flowers, it is a great impact plant. We have three in our drive and visitors always want to know what they are. They don't blend easily with other shrubs and don't like being crowded anyway, so choose an isolated spot to really show them off.

Telopea = from the Greek "telopas," meaning seen at a distance.

Telopea oreades
VICTORIAN WARATAH, GIPPSLAND WARATAH
Usually seen as a head-high, upright bush, it can become an upright tree with the habit and shape of a *Clethra arborea* or the related *Embothrium*. It is reasonably hardy and easy to grow. In late spring and summer, the tubular red flowers appear on flower heads that are relatively small for this genus, about the size of a small hand (3½ in/9 cm across). They can be easy to overlook at the top of a tall bush, but the birds seem to enjoy them. Australia. Height 10–30 ft (3–10 m) x width 5–10 ft (1.5–3 m). ZONE 8.

Oreades = mountain loving, referring to their homeland in the hills of Victoria, Australia.

Left: *Telopea speciosissima*

Telopea speciosissima
SYDNEY WARATAH, COMMON WARATAH

A stunning plant with crimson flowers in spring. It forms a big, upright bush with a large flower head 6 in (15 cm) across on the top of each stem. The name says it all—speciosus means showy or beautiful, and speciosissima means extra showy. From New South Wales, Australia, and is the state flower. Given a hot summer it will live through a light frost. It is a superb cut flower. Height x width 10 ft (3 m). ZONE 8 if hot summers, otherwise zone 9.

Speciosissima = extra showy.

Telopea truncata
TASMANIAN WARATAH

This Tasmanian native is traditionally thought of as the most hardy species of this genus. So if you are gardening in a cooler climate, you might like to try this species. It makes a large, dense, evergreen shrub with flattish crimson flower heads. The dark leaves and red heads are impressive, but it is hard to match *T. speciosissima*. Tasmania, Australia. Height 6–15 ft (2–5 m) x width 6–10 ft (2–3 m). ZONE 8.

Truncata = truncated or cut off, referring to the cut-off or blunt ends to each leaf.

Viburnum

Caprifoliaceae

Viburnums have become classic garden standbys and most gardeners know at least a few viburnum species. They can be tricky to recognize, however, because they vary so much. Some are evergreen, while most are deciduous and hardy. The leaves vary from soft, maple-like, palmate versions to glossy, smooth or even corrugated, rough types. Even the flowers are inconsistent; some have a simple cluster of starry flowers, but we are probably more familiar with either the pompom heads or the hydrangea-like flat lacecap versions, where the larger sterile flowers surround the smaller true flowers. Some have the advantage of being scented, and even deliciously so. Some are grown for their attractive berries.

They are content in any soil, including very acidic or alkaline soil. Some, like *Viburnum opulus* and *V. sargentii*, will grow in swampy places. In fact, if you have a very wet, boggy area these are two of the best choices to grow in such a site. Most viburnums prefer full sun, but will cope with a little shade. They tend to look sparse and don't flower as well if too shaded. Most are easy to transplant in winter and even quite large specimens of the deciduous types can be shifted.

Viburnums are for the most part an excellent choice for a shrubbery or mixed border, and some are suited to narrow borders around the house. The added bonus of fragrant flowers always helps when planting near to paths and windows.

Viburnum = from the Greek word "vieo," to tie, because of the flexible shoots.

Viburnum opulus
GUELDER ROSE, EUROPEAN CRANBERRY BUSH

Scented, flat, white, lacecap flower heads 3 in (8 cm) across appear in late spring and early summer. These are followed by clusters of delicious-looking red fruits. It is a European native with an upright habit and cane-like stems. The canes are quite pithy and

Above: *Viburnum opulus* 'Sterile'

Above: *Viburnum plicatum* 'Sterile'

can be brittle. The big maple-like leaves have a dull surface and take on purple tints before dropping in fall. Height x width 12–15 ft (4–5 m). ZONE 4.

A smaller version, known as **'Compactum'**, has the same white flowers as the species, but is slow-growing and dense and better suited to smaller gardens. Height x width 5 ft (1.5 m). ZONE 4. The form **'Sterile'**, syn 'Roseum' (snowball bush) has white or green-tinted white pompom-like flowers 2½ in/6 cm in diameter. and is becoming popular as a cut flower. As the name suggests, the flowers are sterile and so there are no fruits. ZONE 4.

Viburnum plicatum, syn V. tomentosum
DOUBLEFILE VIBURNUM

Imagine a drift of white, lacecap flower heads balanced like snow on spreading, horizontal branches and you have an idea of how lovely this deciduous bush can be. The leaves are corrugated, or bullate, and shaped like a cherry leaf. They look fine through summer and take on reasonable fall tints, but it's those lovely spring flowers that set people's hearts alight. The bush itself gets very wide and needs plenty of room. It looks splendid in isolation, and it is not often I recommend that for any shrub. There are several named forms, including **'Mariesii'** (syn *V. mariesii*), which has distinctly layered branches and better fall color than the species. Originates in China, Japan. Height 10 ft (3 m) x width 12 ft (4 m). ZONE 4.

Plicatum = folded together, referring to the contoured leaves.

Viburnum plicatum 'Lanarth'

If ever a bush deserved the title of "dusting-of-snow," this is it. A large bush in full flower has all the horizontal branches laden with a covering of white flowers. On closer inspection, the flat "flower" is made up of smaller flowers arranged lacecap fashion, so-called because of the resemblance to the lacy caps servant girls wore in Victorian England. Each outer, or sterile, flower has five scalloped lobes and these surround the true flowers, which are the tiny seed-producing flowers in the center. These are also creamy white, but have little impact in terms of color as it's the larger sterile flowers that everyone notices.

The rough-textured, furrowed leaves are a delicious grass-green and appear with the flowers, providing a perfect foil. These cherry-like leaves harden up and become almost invisible once the bush has flowered. The aforementioned horizontal habit is a large part of the appeal of this bush. Within the bush, you'll see several upright branches that hold the horizontal ones and the plant sends up several new canes every year. The bush can be pruned, but who would want to ruin the perfect natural shape? Height 10 ft (3 m) x width 12 ft (4 m). ZONE 4.

Viburnum plicatum 'Roseace'

From the time the first new leaves appear in spring, you know this is going to be something special. Each new leaf has a strong bronzy sheen and these become the backdrop for the wonderful sterile pompom-like flower heads. The rounded heads start a creamy color. When the heads are fully open they are the most fantastic shade of pink and suddenly everyone wants one in their garden. Opposite pairs of flowers can be so closely packed they look like pink cream buns. The form **'Roseum'** is similar and *V. plicatum* **'Sterile'** is the beautiful pure-white form introduced from China by Robert Fortune (1812–1880) in 1844, long before the true or wild species was found. Height x width 10 ft (3 m). ZONE 4.

Viburnum sargentii

SARGENT'S VIBURNUM

Charles Sprague Sargent (1841–1927) was the founder and first director of the famous Arnold Arboretum in Boston. He was also the instigator of E.H. Wilson's later trips to China and classified many of Wilson's introductions. This deciduous species is similar to *Viburnum opulus*, with its big, upright canes and large, maple-like leaves turning to reds and yellows in the fall. The big, white, lacecap flower heads are 4 in (10 cm) across and followed by hanging bunches of bright red berries. The plant has a tendency to sucker and may be too vigorous for smaller gardens. Height x width 15 ft (5 m). ZONE 4.

'Onondaga' is a much improved garden form selected by the Washington Arboretum. The lovely purple-maroon leaves are the

Above: *Viburnum plicatum* 'Roseace'

Left: *Viburnum sargentii* 'Onondaga'

first thing to take your eye but when you see the flowers you'll be even more entranced. The fabulous lacecap flowers have white sterile flowers surrounding the red-purple true flowers and are set off against the bronzy foliage—it is a winner. The bush has a very tidy, upright habit and can be pruned to keep the proportions modest. Height 10 ft (3 m) x width 6 ft (2 m). ZONE 4.

Viburnum tinus

LAURUSTINUS

A super evergreen shrub for cool climates, it forms a dense, compact plant that can be clipped to maintain it at around waist- to

shoulder-high. The leaves are rich dark green and look good all year. The flattened heads of white flowers emerge from pinky purple buds giving the flower head a lovely two-tone effect. The other great joy is that it flowers in winter. It is easy to grow and makes a perfect garden shrub. **'Eve Price'** is a good flower form with pink flower buds and **'Variegatum'**, with its cream-edged leaves, adds another dimension to a border. The species grows wild in southern Europe and the Mediterannean. Height x width 10 ft (3 m). ZONE 7.

Weigela

APPLE BLOSSOM
Caprifoliaceae

A group of arching-stemmed deciduous shrubs from China, Japan and Korea, they tend to be untidy and ungainly when young, but with a bit of judicious pruning can be formed into a pleasing, tidy shape. Weigelas flower on the previous summer's wood so any winter pruning will reduce the number of blooms. Prune immediately after flowering, as this allows the plant the maximum time to grow new wood and thus a new crop of flowers. Ideally they are lightly pruned or thinned each year and then give them a severe haircut if and when they get too big or ungainly.

Weigelas will grow in sun or part-shade and are happy in virtually any soil, including alkaline soil and clays. They are good, robust shrubs coping with summer heat and drought, winter cold and city pollution. Such useful hardy shrubs that perform every year for little or no input on our part are few and far between. In fact, they perform so well, we tend to ignore them altogether, which is a shame as they are very pretty in flower and one or two have lovely foliage too. The luscious new leaves can be as big as a hand but typically are a more modest 3–4 in

Below: *Weigela
florida* 'Variegata'

Above: *Weigela* 'Eva Rathke'

(8–10 cm) long, with a cupped valley down the middle and ending in a strong, pointed tip. The flowers appear in late spring. Apple blossom is the common name because the clusters of flowers are very much alike.

As the bush ages the branches lose vigor and produce fewer and fewer flowers, but the bush puts out strong new canes emerging from within.

Weigela = named for German botanist, C. E. von Weigel (1748–1831).

Weigela florida

The species name *floridus* means rich in flowers, and when you see the mass of soft-pink flowers that cover the bush in spring you'll see why it is so appropriate. The flower buds are furrowed and joined at the tip and look like some weird Irish *shelalagh*, or club. They open out to five-petaled, soft pinky white flowers that gain more color intensity as they age, becoming an almost strident rosy pink. When the bush has been in flower for a week or two, you'll see a mix of new and old flowers and so it is delightfully two-toned with both pale and rich pink blossoms. Native to China and Korea. Height x width 8 ft (2.5 m). ZONE 5.

There are numerous beautiful cultivars with white, pink or red flowers. *W.* **'Eva Rathke'** has lovely bright crimson flowers on an arching shrubs. Height x width 5 ft (1.5 m). *W.* **'Newport Red'** has light red flowers on an upright bush. Height 8 ft (2.5 m) x width 5 ft (1.5m). The variegated form, *W. florida* **'Variegata'**, has a creamy yellow edge to the leaves, sometimes taking on a reddish tinge. It looks good all summer as long as the plant isn't stressed for moisture.

Floridus = rich in flowers.

There is a lovely lemon-lime leaf *Weigela*, *W.* **'Looymansii Aurea'**, which has pinky red, bell-shaped flowers with white throats from late spring to early summer. It seems to perform best in partial shade. Height x width 5 ft (1.5 m). ZONE 5.

Weigela praecox is a similar bush, flowering earlier in the spring. The bonus of fragrance adds to the appeal of the rosy pink

Above: *Weigela praecox*

flowers. Native to Russia, Korea and Japan. Height 8 ft (2.5 m) x width 6 ft (2 m). ZONE 5.

Weigela subsessilis is a Korean shrub with long tubular flowers in harsh pink to purple on an upright, whippy shrub. Flowers appear on the tips of the stems in spring. Height 8 ft (2.5 m) x width 6 ft (2 m). ZONE 5.

Wisteria

WISTERIA
Fabaceae

Wisteria—friend or foe? I've never been quite sure. Some say they are too vigorous and will take over the garden. Others diligently prune them and enjoy more flowers and less unchecked growth. The flowers are stupendous, there is nothing quite like them outside of the tropics. In spring, the elongated chains of blossom hang like flowery curtains. Wisterias are perhaps at their best along the side of the house, hanging down from the verandah or simply across a house wall with their mass of vertical flowers.

Somehow you have to contrive to grow the plant horizontally. This does two things: it slows the growth and induces the plant to flower. The same is true of all plants; if you take a vertical branch and tie it down near to horizontal it will change gear from a growth stem to a flowering stem. This is because you are changing the hormone balance within that branch. Gardeners do this with apple trees to make them flower and fruit, but it works with all woody plants. In the case of wisteria, they are extremely vigorous, and if given a free run up a tall tree they will simply run to the top and have their best flowers way up out of sight. Far better to let nature slow the plant down by training it sideways.

Of course you can always resort to pruning. Wisterias may seem complicated to prune but they are not. They put out long, long stems, sometimes many feet long, looking for new trees to climb, and if you left all these you would have a plant out of control. So early summer, cut all these stems off five buds from where they started. The plant then has another rush of blood and the end two buds grow into more long stems. In late summer or winter, cut off these two long stems as well, leaving just three buds at the base. These three will have fattened up by now and they are going to be next spring's flowers. It is basically the same as training and pruning for grapes and kiwifruit.

When you next see a beautiful wisteria decked in long chains of flowers, and those beautiful gnarly twirling branches like a vine in a fairy story, you'll realise it doesn't just happen like that, some diligent gardener has put much time and effort into this "natural" display. Somehow, when they are at their best, it seems idyllic—a little cottage with wisteria on one wall and roses on another.

Another possibility is to train your wisteria as a standard. Only allow one leader and tie it to a cane. When it has reached the desired height, you cut the top off and allow the bush to send a cascade of weeping stems out like an open umbrella. Keep only the best of these stems and, hey presto, you have a free-standing wisteria bush.

Wisteria like plenty of sun, though the roots can be in shade. The soil must be free-draining, but otherwise any will suffice. It is easy to plant out, but you are unlikely to shift one again once the vine is entwined. Winter cold holds no threat as they are deciduous and hardy. Moderate winds are fine, but don't choose a windy site—you will lose all the fabulous bloom.

Wisteria are one of the many plants linking North America with China and Japan. The American versions were introduced to Europe first, but were overshadowed by the more showy Asian species.

The genus was named by Thomas Nuttall in memory of a German professor at the University of Pennsylvania, Caspar Wistar. Some people spell the plant Wist*a*ria and some as Wist*e*ria, and to be correct nowadays it should be with an "e." Even Nuttall himself wasn't consistent. He used both spellings because apparently the family name was Wüster and some members of the family changed to Wistar, others to Wister. Under the rules of plant naming the first-used name is correct, even if wrongly spelt.

Wisteria floribunda
JAPANESE WISTERIA
The Japanese wisteria was first introduced in 1830 by Philipp von Siebold, an eye specialist who made Japan his home for many years. The stems climb clockwise around wires and supports (as opposed to the Chinese species, that grows anti-clockwise). The name floribunda means lots of flowers, and the long 12 in (30 cm) chains of violet-blue flowers stand testament to that. The flowers also have a pleasant fragrance. The flowers open progressively from the top, or, more accurately, the base, of the raceme, to the tip, thus extending the flowering season. There are numerous named varieties with white, blue or mauve flowers. Native to Japan. Height 30 ft (10 m) or more. ZONE 4.

There is a form called **W. f. macrobotrys** and a cultivar of it called **'Multijuga'**, both with exceptionally long flower chains— longer than your arm. Height to 30 ft (10 m). ZONE 4.

Floribunda = lots of flowers.

Right: *Wisteria floribunda* 'Snow Showers' (syn 'Shiro Noda')

Wisteria floribunda cultivars
'Black Dragon' (syn 'Violacea Plena') Rich, dark purple double flowers and good butter-yellow fall color.
'Issai' (syn 'Domino') Short dense trusses of lilac-blue.
'Issai Perfect' A good free-flowering pale lilac form.

'Rosea' (syn 'Honbeni') Long racemes of pale rose-colored flowers with a touch of purple.
'Royal Purple' Purple flowers.
'Snow Showers' (syn 'Shiro Noda') Lovely long racemes of white flowers with just a hint of lilac.

Wisteria frutescens
AMERICAN WISTERIA
You hardly ever see this plant in cultivation, more's the pity. This is the North American version of wisteria. I saw my first one in North Carolina 30 years into my plant career and was left wondering why it had taken me so long to find it.

The flowers are a lovely rich blue and the chains, although shorter than the Asian versions at 6 in (15 cm), are still stunning. It has the advantage of producing flowers on the new growth in spring, so you can prune it any way you fancy during winter without affecting the flowering display. It is also less vigorous than its Asian cousins. The good forms have rich lavender-purple flowers and are fragrant. There is also a white form, *Wisteria frutescens var alba*. Native to southeast U.S.A. Height 30 ft (10 m) or more. ZONE 5.

Frutescens = shrubby or shrub-like.

Wisteria sinensis, syn *W. chinensis*
CHINESE WISTERIA
This is the Chinese version of wisteria, and this species climbs anticlockwise (the Japanese version climbs clockwise). The flowers appear in late spring. They are fragrant and a super rich blue

Left: *Wisteria sinensis*

Left: *Wisteria sinensis* 'Blue Sapphire'

color, with the advantage that they open all at once, creating a more dynamic display. There are white, purple and blue forms and doubles too. Height 30 ft (10 m) or more. ZONE 5.

Sinensis = from China.

Wisteria sinensis cultivars
'Alba' White, scented flowers.
'Amethyst' Beautiful scented flowers of soft purple. Profuse flowering.
'Blue Sapphire' A lovely traditional blue wisteria. Flowers earlier than many varieties and has a nice perfume.
'Caroline' Beautiful, satiny, purple-lilac flowers festoon the vine in spring.

Xanthoceras

Xanthoceras sorbifolium
YELLOWHORN
Sapindaceae

If only I could grow this wonderful plant. A continental climate with hot summers and very cold winters seems to be a prerequisite, and without a winter freeze and summer baking it is doomed to fail. I have tried hot, dry banks and tough, harsh sites in an attempt to please it, but without success.

The foliage is attractive enough, but it is the flowers that have me drooling. The 8 in (20 cm) long panicles of pretty white faces with reddish throats are very appealing. These appear in late spring and early summer on last season's growth, so don't be tempted to prune it in winter because you will lose the flowers.

It is a small, deciduous tree with dark green, pinnate leaves

but no great fall color. Left to its own devices it looks rather scruffy, and may need some thinning in the early years to make a good shape. It will grow in any soil including alkaline, clays or whatever.

It was first introduced from north China in 1866 and, like most plants from that region, it likes definite winters and summers. It's very cold-hardy, but the flowers are in danger of damage from late spring frosts. The other hazard is coral spot fungus. Height 12 ft (4 m) x width 10 ft (3 m). ZONE 5.

Xanthoceras = from the Greek "xanthos," for yellow, and "keras," for horn, referring to the projecting glands between the petals; *sorbifolia* = leaves like a *Sorbus* or mountain ash.

Below: *Xanthoceras sorbifolium*

Ready-reference table

Color group		Flowering season	
R = reds	B = blues	Spr = spring	F = fall
Y = yellows	W = white	Sum = summer	Win = winter
Pi = pinks	O = orange		
Pu = purples			

Species or cultivar	page reference	hardiness zones	flowering season	flower color	native to North America	height x width
Abutilon hybridum	10	8	Spr/Sum/F	R, Y, Pi, W		10 x 6-15 ft (3 x 2-5 m)
'Ashford Red'	10	8	Spr/Sum/F	R		10 x 6-15 ft (3 x 2-5 m)
'Strawberry Crush'	10	8	Spr/Sum/F	R		10 x 6-15 ft (3 x 2-5 m)
'Golden Fleece'	10	8	Spr/Sum/F	Y		10 x 6-15 ft (3 x 2-5 m)
Abutilon megapotamicum	11	8	Sum/F	R/Y		6 x 6 ft (2 x 2 m)
Abutilon vitifolium	11	8	Sum/F	B, W		15 x 8 ft (5 x 2.5 m)
Abutilon ochsenii	12	8	Sum/F	Pu, W		10 x 8 ft (3 x 2.5 m)
Abutilon x suntense	12	8	Sum/F	Pu, W		12 x 8 ft (4 x 2.5 m)
Aesculus californica	12	7	Sum	W	*	25 x 30 ft (8 x 20 m)
Aesculus x carnea	12	6	Spr	Pi		30 x 30 ft (10 x 10 m)
'Briotii'	12	6	Spr	R		30 x 30 ft (10 x 10 m)
Aesculus x plantierensis	12	3	Spr	Pi		30 x 30 ft (10 x 10 m)
Aesculus hippocastanum	12	3	Spr	W		80 x 70 ft (25 x 20 m)
'Baumannii'	12	3	Spr	W		80 x 70 ft (25 x 20 m)
Aesculus indica	12	7	Sum	W, Pi, R		50 x 50 ft (15 x 15 m)
'Sydney Pearce'	12	7	Sum	Pi		50 x 50 ft (15 x 15 m)
Aesculus neglecta	13	5	Sum	Y	*	30 x 25 ft (10 x 8 m)
'Erythroblastos'	13	5	Sum	Y		30 x 25 ft (10 x 8 m)
Aesculus parviflora	13	5	Sum	W	*	10 x 15 ft (3 x 5 m)
Aesculus pavia	14	5	Sum	R	*	15 x 10 ft (5 x 3 m)
'Atrosanguinea'	14	5	Sum	R		15 x 10 ft (5 x 3 m)
Amelanchier alnifolia	15	4-9	Spr	W	*	12 x 12 ft (4 x 4 m)
'Regent'	15	4-9	Spr	W		4-6 x 4-6 ft (1.2-2 x 1.2-2 m)
Amelanchier arborea	15	4-9	Spr	W	*	20 x 15 ft (6 x 5 m)
Amelanchier asiatica	15	5-9	Spr	W		25 x 30 ft (8 x 10 m)
Amelanchier canadensis	15	3-9	Spr	W	*	10 x 6 ft (3 x 2 m)
Amelanchier x grandiflora	15	4-9	Spr	W		25 x 30 ft (8 x 10 m)
'Autumn Brilliance'	15	4-9	Spr	W		25 x 30 ft (8 x 10 m)
'Ballerina'	15	4-9	Spr	W		25 x 30 ft (8 x 10 m)
'Robin Hill'	16	4-9	Spr	Pi		25 x 30 ft (8 x 10 m)
'Rubescens'	16	4-9	Spr	Pi		25 x 30 ft (8 x 10 m)
Amelanchier laevis	16	5-9	Spr	W	*	10-12 x 6-10 ft (3-4 x 2-3 m)
'Cumulus'	16	5-9	Spr	W		12 x 10 ft (4 x 3 m)
Amelanchier lamarckii	16	4-9	Spr	W		10-12 x 6-10 ft (3-4 x 2-3 m)
Aronia abutifolia	17	5	Spr	W		10 x 5 ft (3 x 1.5 m)
'Brilliantissima'	17	5	Spr	W		6-8 x 6-8 ft (2-2.5 x 2-2.5 m)
Aronia melanocarpa	17	4	Spr	W	*	6 x 10 ft (2 x 3 m)
'Autumn Magic'	17	4	Spr	W		6 x 10 ft (2 x 3 m)
Berberidopsis corallina	17	8/9	Sum	R		15 x 15 ft (5 x 5 m)
Bignonia capreolata	18	6	Spr	R, O	*	30 x 30 ft (10 x 10 m)
Bougainvillea	18	9	Sum	R, Pu, Pi, O		to 30 ft (10 m)
Brachyglottis compactus	20	7	Sum	Y		3 x 6 ft (1 x 2 m)
'Sunshine'	20	7	Sum	Y		3 x 6 ft (1 x 2 m)
Brachyglottis greyi	20	7	Sum	Y		6 x 10 ft (2 x 3 m)
Brachyglottis perdicioides	20	8	Sum	Y		6-10 x 6 ft (2-3 x 2 m)
'Alfred Atkinson'	20	8	Sum	W		10 x 6 ft (3 x 2 m)
Brachyglottis repanda	20	9	Spr	creamy W		10 x 10 ft (3 x 3 m)
Buddleja alternifolia	21	6	Sum	Pu		12 x 12 ft (4 x 4 m)
Buddleja colvilei	21	8	Sum	R		20 x 20 ft (6 x 6 m)
'Kewensis'	21	8	Sum	R		20 x 20 ft (6 x 6 m)
Buddleja davidii	21	6	Sum/F	various		10 x 15 ft (3 x 5 m)

Species or cultivar	page reference	hardiness zones	flowering season	fall color	native to North America	height x width
Buddleja globosa	22	8	Sum	O		15 x 15 ft (5 x 5 m)
Buddleja lindleyana	22	7	Sum	Pu		6 x 6 ft (2 x 2 m)
Calluna vulgaris	23	5	Sum/F	R, Pu, Pi, W		4-24 x 30 in (10-60 x 75 cm)
Camellia japonica	24	8	Win/Spr	R, Pi, W		10-20 x 3-10 ft (3-6 x 1-3 m)
Camellia oleifera	25	6	Win	W		20 x 10 ft (7 x 3 m)
Camellia reticulata	25	8/9	Win/Spr	R, Pi		20 x 15 ft (6 x 5 m)
'Robert Fortune'	25	8/9	Win/Spr	Pi		15 x 10 ft (5 x 3 m)
'S.P. Dunn'	26	8/9	Win/Spr	R		15 x 10 ft (5 x 3 m)
'William Hertrich'	26	8/9	Win/Spr	R		20 x 20 ft (6 x 6 m)
Camellia saluenensis	26	7	Win/Spr	W, Pi		15 x 8 ft (5 x 2.5 m)
Camellia x williamsii	26	7	Win/Spr	Pi		15 x 8 ft (5 x 2.5 m)
'Donation'	26	7	Win/Spr	Pi		15 x 8 ft (5 x 2.5 m)
Camellia sasanqua	26	8	F	Pi, W, R		20 x 10 ft (6 x 3 m)
'Hiryu'	27	8	F	Pi/R		20 x 10 ft (6 x 3 m)
'Mini no Yuki'	27	8	F	W		20 x 10 ft (6 x 3 m)
'Plantation Pink'	27	8	F	Pi		20 x 10 ft (6 x 3 m)
Campsis grandiflora	27	7	Sum	R/O		30 ft (10 m)
Campsis radicans	28	5	Sum	R/O	*	30 ft (10 m)
'Flava'	28	5	Sum	Y		30 ft (10 m)
Campsis x tagliabuana	28	5	Sum	R/O		30 ft (10 m)
'Guilfoylei'	28	5	Sum	R		30 ft (10 m)
'Madame Galen'	28	5	Sum	R		30 ft (10 m)
Cantua buxifolia	29	8/9	Sum	P, Y		6-8 x 6-8 ft (2-2.5 x 2-2.5 m)
Cantua pyrifolia	29	8/9	Sum	Y		6-8 x 6-8 ft (2-2.5 x 2-2.5 m)
Cassia corymbosa	30	9	Sum/F	Y		6 x 6 ft (2-3 x 2-3 m)
'John Ball'	31	9	Sum/F	Y		6 x 6 ft (2-3 x 2-3 m)
Cassia didymobotrya	30	9	Sum/F			8 x 6-10 ft (2.5 x 2-3 m)
Cassia x floribunda	31	9	Sum/F	Y		6 x 6 ft (2-3 x 2-3 m)
Ceanothus arboreus	31	8	Spr/Sum	B	*	12 x 10 ft (4 x 3 m)
'Burkwoodii'	32	7	Sum	B		6 x 6 ft (2 x 2 m)
'Concha'	32	8	Spr/Sum	B		6 x 6 ft (2 x 2 m)
'Dark Star'	32	8	Spr/Sum	B		6 x 6 ft (2 x 2 m)
'Trewithen Blue'	31	8	Spr/Sum	B		12 x 10 ft (4 x 3 m)
Ceanothus impressus	32	7/8	Spr/Sum	B	*	6-10 x 6-10 ft (2-3 x 2-3 m)
'Puget Blue'	32	7/8	Spr/Sum	B		6-10 x 6-10 ft (2-3 x 2-3 m)
Ceanothus papillosus	32	8	Spr	B	*	12 x 12 ft (4 x 4 m)
var roweanus	32	8	Spr	B		5 x 10 ft (1.5 x 3 m)
Ceratostigma griffithii	32	8/9	Sum/F	B		1.5 x 3 ft (45 c x 1 m)
Ceratostigma plumbaginoides	32	6	Sum/F	B		1.5 x 1 ft (45 c x 30 cm)
Ceratostigma willmottianum	33	6	Sum/F	B		3 x 5 ft (1 x 1.5 m)
Cercis canadensis	33	5	Spr	R, Pi	*	30 x 30 ft (10 x 10 m)
'Appalachian Red'	33	5	Spr	R		30 x 30 ft (10 x 10 m)
Cercis chinensis	33	6	Spr	Pi		15-20 x 15-30 ft (3-7 x 3 m)
'Avondale'	34	6	Spr	Pu		10 x 10 ft (3 x 3 m)
Cercis siliquastrum	34	8	Spr	Pi/Pu		30 x 30 ft (10 x 10 m)
Chaenomeles cathayensis	35	6	Spr	W, Pi		10 x 10 ft (3 x 3 m)
Chaenomeles japonica	35	5	Spr	R		3 x 6 ft (1 x 2 m)
Chaenomeles speciosa	35	5	Spr	R		8 x 15 ft (2.5 x 5 m)
Chaenomeles x superba	35	5	Spr/Sum	W, Pi, O, R		5 x 6 ft (1.5 x 2 m)
Chionanthus retusus	36	6	Sum	W		10 x 10 ft (3 x 3 m)
Chionanthus virginicus	36	3	Spr/Sum	W	*	10 x 10 ft (3 x 3 m)
Cistus x corbariensis	37	7	Spr/Sum	W		3 x 5 ft (1 x 1.5 m)
Cistus ladanifer	37	8	Sum	W		6 x 5 ft (2 x 1.5 m)
Cistus laurifolius	37	7	Sum	W		9 x 9 ft (3 x 3 m)

Species or cultivar	page reference	hardiness zones	flowering season	flower color	native to North America	height x width
Cistus x *purpureus*	38	7	Sum	Pi, R, Pu		6 x 3 ft (2 x 1 m)
'Betty Taudevin'	38	7	Sum	Pi		6 x 3 ft (2 x 1 m)
'Brilliancy'	38	7	Sum	Pi		6 x 3 ft (2 x 1 m)
Cistus 'Anne Palmer'	38	8	Sum	Pi		3 x 3 ft (1 x 1 m)
Cistus 'Silver Pink'	38	7	Sum	Pi		30 in x 36 in (75 c x 90 cm)
Clematis armandii	39	7	Spr	W		10-15 x 6-10 ft (3-5 x 2-3 m)
'Apple Blossom'	39	7	Spr	Pi/W		10-15 x 6-10 ft (3-5 x 2-3 m)
Clematis x 'Jackmanii'	39	4	Sum	R, Pu		10 x 10 ft (3 x 3 m)
Clematis montana	40	6	Spr	W		40 ft (12 m)
Clematis montana var *rubens*	40	5	Spr	Pi		30 ft (10 m)
Clematis paniculata	40	8	Spr	W		30 ft (10 m)
Clematis tangutica	40	6	Sum/F	Y		15-20 x 6-10 ft (5-6 x 2-3 m)
Clematis terniflora	40	6	F	W		30 ft (10 m)
Clematis texensis	40	5	Sum	R	*	6-15 ft (3-5 m)
Clianthus puniceus	41	8	Win/Spr	R, W, Pi		12 x 10 ft (4 x 3 m)
Cornus florida	42	5	Spr	W, Pi, R	*	20 x 25 ft (6 x 8 m)
'Apple Blossom'	42	5	Spr	Pi, W		15 x 15 ft (5 x 5 m)
'Cherokee Chief'	42	5	Spr	R		15 x 15 ft (5 x 5 m)
'Ormonde'	42	5	Spr	W		25 x 25 ft (8 x 8 m)
'Rainbow'	42	5	Spr	Y		10 x 8 ft (3 x 2.5 m)
Cornus kousa var *chinensis*	43	5	Sum	W, Pi		25 x 25 ft (8 x 8 m)
Cornus mas	43	5	Spr	Y		15 x 15 ft (5 x 5 m)
Corylopsis himalayana	43	8/9	Spr	Y		10-15 x 6-10 ft (3-5 x 2-3 m)
Corylopsis pauciflora	44	6	Spr	Y		5 x 8 ft (1.5 x 2.5 m)
Corylopsis spicata	44	5	Spr	Y		6 x 10 ft (2 x 3 m)
Corylopsis willmottiae 'Spring Purple'	44	6	Spr	Y		12 x 12 ft (4 x 4 m)
Crinodendron hookerianum	45	8	Spr	R		4-10 x 3-6 ft (1.5-3 x 2-3 m)
Crinodendron patagua	45	8	Sum	W		10-15 x 10-15 ft (3-5 x 3-5 m)
Cyrilla racemiflora	46	5-9	Sum	W	*	4 x 30 ft (1.2 x 10 m)
Cytisus x *beanii*	47	7/8	Spr	Y		2 x 3 ft (60 c x 1 m)
Cytisus x *kewensis*	47	6	Spr	Y		1 x 5 ft (30 c x 1.5 m)
Cytisus multiflorus	47	7	Spr/Sum	W		10 x 8 ft (3 x 2.5 m)
Cytisus x *praecox*	47	6	Spr/Sum	Y		4 x 5 ft (1.2 x 1.5 m)
Cytisus scoparius	47	6	Spr/Sum	Y, O, R		6-10 x 6-10 ft (2-3 x 2-3 m)
Desfontainia spinosa	48	8	Sum/F	O/R		3 x 4 ft (1 x 1.2 m)
Deutzia gracilis	49	5	Spr	W		3 x 3 ft (1 x 1 m)
Deutzia x *hybrida*	49	6	Spr	Pi, Pu		5 x 5 ft (1.5 x 1.5 m)
'Joconde'	49	6	Spr	Pi		5 x 5 ft (1.5 m 1.5 m)
'Magicien'	49	6	Spr	Pu/W		5 x 5 ft (1.5 x 1.5 m)
'Montrose'	49	6	Spr	Pi		5 x 5 ft (1.5 mx 1.5 m)
Deutzia ningpoensis	50	6	Spr	W		6-10 x 6 ft (2-3 x 2 m)
Deutzia scabra 'Candidissima'	50	5	Spr	W		10 x 6 ft (3 x 2 m)
Deutzia scabra	50	5	Spr	Pi, W		10 x 6 ft (3 x 2 m)
Dichroa febrifuga	50	8/9	Spr/Sum	B		6 x 4-6 ft (3 x 2-3 m)
Dichroa versicolor	51	8/9	Spr/Sum/F	B		6-8 x 4-6 ft (2-2.5 x 2-3 m)
Embothrium coccineum	52	8	Spr/Sum	O/R		15-20 x 15 ft (5-6 x 5 m)
Embothrium coccineum var *lanceolatum*	52	7/8	Spr/Sum	O R		15-20 x 15 ft (5-6 x 5 m)
Embothrium coccineum var *longifolium*	52	8	Spr/Sum	O R		15-20 x 15 ft (5-6 x 5 m)
Erica arborea	53	9	Spr	W		6 x 2.5 ft (2 x 80 cm)
var *alpina*	53	8	Spr	W		6 x 2.5 ft (2 x 80 cm)

Species or cultivar	page reference	hardiness zones	flowering season	flower color	native to North America	height x width
Erica australis	53	8	Spr	Pu, W		6 x 6 ft (2 x 2 m)
Erica carnea	54	5	Win/Spr	Pi, W, R, Pu		8-10 in x 22 in (20-25 c x 55 cm)
Erica tetralix	54	3	Sum/F	W, Pi		12 in x 20 in (30 c x 50 cm)
Erica vagans	54	7/8	Sum	W, Pi, R		16-32 in x 32 in (40-80 c x 80 cm)
Erythrina blakei	55	9	Win/Spr	R		10 x 10 ft (3 x 3 m)
Erythrina caffra	55	9	Win/Spr	R		50 ft (15 m)
Erythrina crista-galli	55	9	Sum/F	R		25 x 12 ft (8 x 4 m)
Erythrina crista-galli	55	8	Sum/F	R		5-8 x 5 ft (1.5-2.5 x 1.5m) as woody perennial
Erythrina humeana	55	9	Win/Spr	R		10 x 10 ft (3 x 3 m)
Erythrina x *sykesii*	55	9	Win/Spr	R		50 ft (15 m)
Escallonia bifida	56	8/9	Sum	W		10 x 8 ft (3 x 2.5 m)
Escallonia 'Iveyi'	56	8	F	W		10 x 10 ft (3 x 3 m)
Escallonia rubra	56	8-9	Sum	R, Pi, W		12 x 12 ft (4 x 4 m)
Escallonia rubra var *macrantha*	56	8	Sum	R		10 x 10 ft (3 x 3 m)
Euryops pectinatus	57	8/9	Sum	Y		3 x 3 ft (1 x 1 m)
Euryops virgineus	57	8/9	Win/Spr	Y		4 x 4 ft (1.2 x 1.2 m)
Exochorda giraldi	58	4	Spr	W		3 x 3 ft (1 x 1 m)
Exochorda korolkowii	59	4	Spr	W		15 x 10 ft (5 x 3 m)
Exochorda x *macrantha*	59	5	Spr/Sum	W		6 x 10 ft (2 x 3 m)
Exochorda racemosa	59	4	Spr	W		10-12 x 10-12 ft (3-4 x 3-4 m)
Exochorda serratifolia	59	5	Spr	W		10 x 10 ft (3 x 3 m)
Forsythia giraldiana	60	5	Win/Spr	Y		12 x 12 ft (4 x 4 m)
Forsythia x *intermedia*	60	6	Spr	Y		5 x 5 ft (1.5 x 1.5 m)
Forsythia ovata	60	5-8	Spr	Y		5 x 5 ft (1.5 x 1.5 m)
Forsythia suspensa	60	6	Spr	Y		10 x 10 ft (3 x 3m)
Forsythia suspensa var *fortunei*	60	6	Spr	Y		10 x 10 ft (3 x 3 m)
Forsythia suspensa var *sieboldii*	60	6	Spr	Y		6-10 x 10 ft (2-3 x 3 m)
Forsythia viridissima	60	5/6	Spr	Y		6 x 5 ft (2 x 1.5 m)
'Bronxensis'	61	5/6	Spr	Y		3 x 3 ft (1 x 1 m)
Fremontodendron californicum	61	8	Sum	Y	*	20 x 12 ft (6 x 4 m)
'California Glory'	61	8	Sum	Y		20 x 12 ft (6 x 4 m)
'Pacific Sunset'	61	8	Sum	Y		20 x 12 ft (6 x 4 m)
'San Gabriel'	61	8	Sum	Y		20 x 12 ft (6 x 4 m)
Fremontodendron mexicanum	61	9	Sum	Y		20 x 2 ft (6 x 0.6 m)
Fuchsia arborescens	62	8/9	Spr	Pu		10 x 10 ft (3 x 3 m)
Fuchsia 'Gartenmeister Bonstedt'	63	9	Sum	R		2-3 x 1.5-2 ft (60-90 x 45-60 cm)
Fuchsia hybrida	63	8/9	Sum	W, Pi, R, Pu		3-6 x 3-6 ft (1-2 x 1-2 m)
Fuchsia magellanica	63	7	Sum	Pu, R		10 x 10 ft (3 x 3 m)
Fuchsia riccartonii	63	7	Sum	Pu, R		10 x 6 ft (3 x 2 m)
Fuchsia 'Thalia'	63	9	Sum	O/R		1.5 ft-3 x 1.5-3 ft (50-90 x 50-90 cm)
Garrya elliptica	64	7/8	Win/Spr	gray	*	12 x 12 ft (4 x 4 m)
'James Roof'	65	7/8	Win/Spr	gray		6 x 6 ft (2 x 2 m)
Gordonia axillaris	65	8/9	F/Win/Spr	W		22-30 x 22-30 ft (7 x 7 m)
Gordonia chrysandra	66	9	Win/Spr	W		30 x 15 ft (10 x 5 m)
Gordonia lasianthus	66	8	Sum	W	*	30 x 15-20 ft (10 x 5-6 m)
Gordonia szechuanica	66	9	Win/Spr	W		30 x 15 ft (10 x 5 m)
Gordonia yunnanensis	66	9	Win/Spr	W		30 x 15-20 ft (10 x 5-6 m)
Halesia carolina	67	4/5	Spr	W	*	20 x 15 ft (6 x 5 m)
Halesia diptera	67	5	Spr	W	*	20 x 30 ft (6 x 10 m)
Halesia monticola	67	4/5	Spr	W	*	40 x 25 ft (12 x 8 m)

Species or cultivar	page reference	hardiness zones	flowering season	flower color	native to North America	height x width
Halesia monticola var vestita	67	4/5	Spr	W		40 x 25 ft (12 x 8 m)
'Rosea'	67	4/5	Spr	Pi		40 x 25 ft (12 x 8 m)
Hardenbergia comptoniana	68	9	Spr/Sum	Pu		10 ft (3 m)
Hardenbergia violacea	68	9	Win/Spr	Pu		6 ft (2 m)
Hebe albicans	69	7	Spr/Sum	W		24 in x 36 in (60 c x 90 cm)
Hebe cupressoides	69	6	Spr/Sum	W, Pu		4 x 4 ft (1.2 x 1.2 m)
Hebe hulkeana	69	7/8	Spr/Sum	Pi, Pu		24 in x 24 in (60 c x 60 cm)
Hebe pinguifolia 'Pagei'	70	7	Sum	W		12 x 36 in (30 x 90 cm)
Hebe speciosa	70	8/9	Sum	R, Pu		4 x 4 ft (1.2 x 1.2 m)
Helianthemum apenninum	71	6	Sum	W		16 x 24 in (40 x 60 cm)
Helianthemum canadense	71	5	Sum	Y	*	12-16 x 24 in (30-40 x 60 cm)
Helianthemum nummularium	71	6	Sum	Y		12-16 x 24 in (30-40 x 60 cm)
'Amy Baring'	71	6	Sum	Y		12 x 24 in (30 x 60 cm)
Hibiscus moscheutos	71	5	Sum	W, Pi, R	*	8 x 3 ft (2.5 x 1 m)
Hibiscus rosa-sinensis	71	9	Sum/F	R		8-15 x 5-10 ft (2.5-5 x 1.5-3 m)
Hibiscus syriacus	72	5	Sum/F	B, W, R, Pi		10-12 x 6 ft (3-4 x 2 m)
Holodiscus discolor	73	5	Sum	W	*	10-12 x 10-12 ft (3-4 x 3-4 m)
Hydrangea arborescens	73	3	Sum	W	*	10 x 10 ft (3 x 3 m)
'Annabelle'	73	3	Sum	W		10 x 10 ft (3 x 3 m)
Hydrangea aspera var villosa	74	7	Sum	Pi/Pu		4-12 x 4-12 ft (1-4 x 1-4 m)
Hydrangea macrophylla	74	6	Sum	W, B, Pi, R, Pu		3-7 x 3-7 ft (1-2 x 1-2 m)
Hydrangea paniculata	75	3	Sum	W, Pi		6-10 x 6-10 ft (2-3 x 2-3 m)
Hydrangea petiolaris	76	4	Sum	W		50 ft (15 m)
Hydrangea quercifolia	76	5	Sum	W	*	6 x 8 ft (2 m 2.5 m)
Hydrangea serrata	76	6	Sum	W, B, R		4-6 x 4-6 ft (1.2 - 2 x 1.2-2 m)
Hypericum calycinum	78	5	Sum/F	Y		24 in x 3 ft (60 c x 1 m)
Hypericum 'Hidcote'	78	6	Sum/F	Y		5 x 5 ft (1.5 x 1.5 m)
Hypericum leschenaultii	78	9	any season	Y		6 x 4-5 ft (2 x 1.2-1.5 m)
Indigofera amblyantha	79	6	Sum	Pi		5 x 8 ft (1.5 x 1.2-1.5 m)
Indigofera decora	79	7	Sum	Pi		24 in x 36 in (60 c x 90 cm)
Indigofera dielsiana	80	6	Sum/F	Pi		6 x 6 ft (2 x 2 m)
Indigofera heterantha	80	6	Sum	Pi		6-10 x 6-10 ft (2-3 x 2-3 m)
Iochroma cyaneum	81	9	Sum	B		10 x 6 ft (3 x 2 m)
Iochroma gesnerioides	81	9	Sum	R		10 x 6 ft (3 x 2 m)
Iochroma grandiflorum	81	9	Sum/F/Win	B		10 x 10 ft (3 x 3 m)
Isoplexis canariensis	81	9	Sum/F	O		5 x 5 ft (1.5 x 1.5 m)
Isoplexis sceptrum	82	9	Sum/F	O		5-6 x 5-6 ft (1.5-2 x1.5-2 m)
Jacaranda mimosifolia	83	9	Sum	Pu/B		50 x 30 ft (15 x 10 m)
Kalmia angustifolia	83	7	Spr	Pi, R	*	24 in x 5 ft (60 c x 1.5 m)
Kalmia latifolia	83	3-9	Spr	Pi, R	*	10 x 10 ft (3 x 3 m)
Kerria japonica	85	4	Spr	Y		6 x 8 ft (2 x 2.5 m)
Koelreuteria bipinnata	86	7	Sum	Y		30 x 50 ft (10 x 17 m)
Koelreuteria paniculata	86	5-8	Sum	Y		30 x 30 ft (10 x 10 m)
'September Gold'	86	5-8	Sum	Y		30 x 30 ft (10 x 10 m)
Kolkwitzia amabilis	86	5	Spr	Pi		10 x 12 ft (3 x 4 m)
Laburnum alpinum	87	5-8	Spr	Y		25 x 25 ft (8 x 8 m)
Laburnum anagyroides	88	5-8	Spr	Y		25 x 25 ft (8 x 8 m)
Laburnum x watereri	88	5-8	Spr	Y		25 x 25 ft (8 x 8 m)
Lagerstroemia fauriei	89	6	Sum	W		25 x 25 ft (8 x 8 m)
Lagerstroemia indica	89	7	Sum	Pi, W, R		25 x 25 ft (8 x 8 m)

Species or cultivar	page reference	hardiness zones	flowering season	flower color	native to North America	height x width
Lagerstroemia speciosa	90	9	Sum	Pi, W, R		30-80 x 15-30 ft (10-25 x 5 m)
Lagunaria patersonii	90	8	Sum	Pi		50 x 25 ft (15 x 8 m)
Lantana camara	90	8/9	Sum	O, Y, R	*	3-9 x 3-9 ft (1-3 x 1-3 m)
Lantana montevidensis	91	9	Sum	Pu		1-2 x 3-4 ft (30-60 c x 1-1.2 m)
Lavatera arborea	92	8	Sum	Pu		6 x 5 ft (2 x 1.5 m)
Lavatera assurgentiflora	92	9	Sum	Pi	*	6 x 5 ft (2 x 1.5 m)
Lavatera maritima	92	6	Sum	Pi/Pu		5 x 3 ft (1.5 x 1 m)
Lavatera thuringiaca	92	6/7	Sum	Pi, W		10 x 10 ft (3 x 3 m)
Leonotis leonurus	92	9	Sum/F	O, W		6 x 6 ft (2 x 2 m)
Leptospermum petersonii	93	8/9	Sum	W		10 x 6 ft (3 x 2 m)
Leptospermum scoparium	94	8	Spr	W, Pi, R		6-20 x 6-15 ft (3-7 x 2-5 m)
Leucadendron argenteum	95	9	Spr/Sum	Y		30 x 10 ft (10 x 3 m)
Leucadendron laureolum	95	9	Win	Y		6 x 4-5 ft (2 x 1.2-1.5 m)
Leucadendron salignum	95	9	Sum/F/Win	R, Y		4-6 x 4-6 ft (1.5-2 x 1.2-2 m)
Leucospermum cordifolium	96	9	Spr/Sum	O		6 x 6 ft (2 x 2 m)
Leucospermum reflexum	96	9	Spr/Sum	R		10 x 6 ft (3 x 2 m)
Lonicera x brownii 'Dropmore Scarlet'	97	4	Sum	O/R		15 ft (5 m)
Lonicera x heckrottii	97	5	Sum	O/Pu		15 - 20 ft (5-7 m)
Lonicera hildebrandiana	97	9	Sum	W, O		60 ft (20 m)
Lonicera korolkowii	98	6	Spr	Pi		10 x 15 ft (3 x 5 m)
Lonicera sempervirens	98	4	Sum/F	O	*	12 ft (4 m)
Lonicera tatarica	98	3	Spr/Sum	Pi		10 x 8 ft (3 x 2.5 m)
'Arnold Red'	98	3	Spr/Sum	R		10 x 8 ft (3 x 2.5 m)
'Hack's Red'	98	3	Spr/Sum	R		10 x 8 ft (3 x 2.5 m)
Lonicera x tellmanniana	98	7	Spr/Sum	O		15 ft (5 m)
Loropetalum chinense	98	8	Win/Spr	W, Pi, R		10 x 10 ft (3 x 3 m)
Magnolia campbellii	100	7	Spr	Pi, W, Pu		50 x 30 ft (15 x 10 m)
Magnolia liliiflora 'Nigra'	101	6	Spr	Pu		10 x 6 ft (3 x 2 m)
'Sayonara'	101	6	Spr	W		12 x 8 ft (4 x 2.5 m)
'Susan'	101	6	Spr	Pu/R		10 x 6 ft (3 x 2 m)
Magnolia x loebneri	101	5	Spr	W		30 x 10 ft (10 x 3 m)
Magnolia sieboldii	101	6	Spr/Sum	W		25 x 40 ft (8 x 12 m)
Magnolia x soulangeana	102	6	Spr	Pu/R		30 x 30 ft (10 x 10 m)
Magnolia stellata	102	5	Spr	W, Pi		10 x 12 ft (3 x 4 m)
Malus x arnoldiana	103	4	Spr	Pi/W		15 x 25 ft (5 x 8 m)
Malus floribunda	103	5	Spr	Pi/W		30 x 30 ft (10 x 10 m)
Malus ioensis	103	2	Spr	Pi	*	30 x 25 ft (10 x 8 m)
'Plena'	103	2	Spr	Pi		30 x 25 ft (10 x 8 m)
Malus 'Profusion'	104	4	Spr	R/Pu		30 x 30 ft (10 x 10 m)
Malus sieboldii	104	5	Spr	W		10 x 10 ft (3 x 3 m)
Metrosideros collina 'Spring Fire'	105	9	any season	R		6-10 x 6-10 ft (2-3 x 2-3 m)
'Tahiti'	105	9	any season	R		3-6 x 6 ft (1-2 x 2 m)
Metrosideros excelsa	105	9	Sum	R		70 x 70 ft (20 x 20 m)
Metrosideros kermadecensis	106	9	any season	R		20 x 20 ft (7 x 7 m)
Michelia doltsopa	106	8/9	Win/Spr	W		30-50 ft x 30-50 ft (10-15 x 10-15 m)
Michelia maudiae	107	8	Spr	W		15-25 x 15-25 ft (5-8 x 5-8 m)
Michelia yunnanensis	107	8	Spr	W		6-10 x 6-10 ft (2-3 x 2-3 m)
Mitraria coccinea	107	8/9	Spr/Sum	R/O		6-10 ft (2-3 m)
Neillia thibetica	108	6	Sum	Pi		6 x 6 ft (2 x 2 m)

Species or cultivar	page reference	hardiness zones	flowering season	flower color	native to North America	height x width
Nerium oleander	109	9	Sum	Pi, W, O, R		6-10 x 6-10 ft (2-3 x 2-3 m)
Olearia cheesemanii	110	8	Spr	W		12 x 10 ft (4 x 3 m)
Olearia x haastii	110	8	Sum	W		6 x 10 ft (2 x 3 m)
Olearia ilicifolia	111	7	Sum	W		15 x 15 ft (5 x 5 m)
Olearia phlogopappa	111	8	Spr/Sum	W, B, Pi		6 x 6 ft (2 x 2 m)
Paulownia fargesii	111	7	Spr	Pu		30 x 30 ft (8 x 8 m)
Paulownia fortunei	112	6	Spr	W/Pu		25 x 25 ft (8 x 8 m)
Paulownia tomentosa	112	5	Spr	Pu/B		40 x 30 ft (12 x 10 m)
Philadelphus 'Beauclark'	113	5	Spr/Sum	W		8 x 8 ft (2.5 x 2.5 m)
Philadelphus coronarius	113	5	Spr/Sum	W		10 x 8 ft (3 x 2.5 m)
'Aureus'	113	5	Spr/Sum	W		8 x 6 ft (2.5 x 2 m)
Philadelphus 'Sybille'	113	5	Spr/Sum	W		4 x 6 ft (1.2 x 2 m)
Philadelphus 'Virginal'	114	5	Spr/Sum	W		10 x 8 ft (3 x 2.5 m)
Philesia magellanica	114	7	Sum	R		3 x 6 ft (1 x 2 m)
Phlomis cashmeriana	115	8	Sum	Pu		36 x 24 in (90 x 60 cm)
Phlomis fruticosa	115	8	Sum	Y		3 x 5 ft (1 x 1.5 m)
Phlomis italica	115	9	Sum	Pi		12 x 24 in (30 x 60 cm)
Pieris formosa var forrestii	116	7	Spr	W		10 x 6 ft (3 x 2 m)
Pieris japonica	116	6	Spr	Pi, W		12 x 10 ft (4 x 3 m)
Pieris ryukiensis	117	8	Spr	W		3 x 4 ft (1 x 1.2 m)
'Temple Bells'	117	8	Spr	W		3 x 4 ft (1 x 1.2 m)
Plumbago auriculata	117	9	Sum/F	B, W		10-20 x 3-10 ft (3-6 x 1-3 m)
Potentilla fruticosa	118	2	Sum	Y, O	*	3 x 5 ft (1 x 1.5 m)
Protea cynaroides	120	9	Win	Pi		6 x 6-10 ft (2 x 2-3 m)
Protea neriifolia	120	9	Win	Pi		6-10 x 6-10 ft (2-3 x 2-3 m)
Prunus campanulata	121	8/9	Spr	R		25 x 25 ft (8 x 8 m)
Prunus 'Okame'	121	7	Spr	Pi		15 x 6-10 ft (5 x 2-3 m)
Prunus serrulata	122	6	Spr	Pi, W		25 x 30 ft (8 x 10 m)
Prunus subhirtella	123	5	Spr	Pi		25 x 25 ft (8 x 8 m)
Prunus x yedoensis	123	5	Spr	Pi, W		50 x 30 ft (15 x 10 m)
'Awanui'	123	5	Spr	Pi		25 x 30 ft (8 x 10 m)
'Ivensii'	123	5	Spr	W		25 x 25 ft (8 x 8 m)
Rhaphiolepis x delacourii	124	8	Spr/Sum	Pi		6 x 8 ft (2 x 2.5 m)
Rhaphiolepis indica	124	8/9	Spr	Pi		5 x 6 ft (1.5 x 2 m)
Rhaphiolepis umbellata	124	7	Sum	W		5 x 5 ft (1.5 x 1.5 m)
Rhododendron augustinii	126	6	Spr	B		6 x 4 ft (2 x 1.2 m)
Rhododendron catawbiense	126	4	Spr/Sum	Pi	*	10 x 10 ft (3 x 3 m)
'Album'	126	4	Spr/Sum	W		10 x 10 ft (3 x 3 m)
Rhododendron griersonianum	126	8	Spr	R		6 x 6 ft (2 x 2 m)
Rhododendron impeditum	128	4	Spr	B/Pu		24 in x 24 in (60 c x 60 cm)
Rhododendron johnstoneanum	128	8	Spr	Y		6 x 6 ft (2 x 2 m)
Rhododendron obtusum	130	6	Spr	R		6 x 3-4 ft (2 x 1-1.2 m)
'Amoenum'	130	6	Spr	Pu		6 x 3-4 ft (2 x 1-1.2 m)
Rhododendron schlippenbachii	128	5	Spr	Pi		15 x 15 ft (5 x 5 m)
Rhododendron wardii	128	7	Spr	Y		6-10 x 6-10 ft (2-3 x2-3 m)
Rhododendron yakushimanum	128	5	Spr	W/Pi		3-5 x 3-7 ft (1-1.5 x 1-2 m)
Rhododendron indicum	129	7	Spr	R		3 x 3 ft (1 x 1 m)
Rhododendron kaempferi	129	5	Spr	O, R		3 x 4 ft (1 x 1.2 m)
Rhododendron kiusianum	129	6	Spr	Pu, R		3 x 4 ft (1 x 1.2 m)
Rhododendron simsii	130	9/10	Spr	R		5 x 7 ft (1.5 x 2 m)
Rhodotypos scandens	130	5	Spr	W		5 x 5 ft (1.5 x 1.5 m)
Rosa floribunda	132	6	Sum	various		4-5 x 4-5 ft (1.2 m-1.5 x 1.2 -1.5 m)
Rosa Hybrid Tea	133	6	Sum	various		4-6 x 4-6 ft (1.2-2 x 1.2-2 m)
Rosa climbers and ramblers	133	6	Sum	various	*	30 ft (10 m)
Rubus 'Benenden'	134	5	Spr	W		6 x 6 ft (2 x 2 m)
Rubus pentalobus	135	7	Sum	W		4 in x unlimited (8 cm)
Rubus spectabilis 'Olympic Double'	135	5	Spr	Pu/Pi		6 x 6 ft (2 x 2 m)
Schizophragma hydrangeoides	135	5	Sum	W, Pi		40 ft (12 m)
Schizophragma integrifolium	136	7	Sum	W		40 ft (12 m)
Sinojackia rehderiana	136	6	Spr	W		20 x 20 ft (6 x 6 m)
Sophora davidii	137	6	Spr/Sum	W/B		8 x 10 ft (2.5 x 3 m)
Sophora japonica	137	5	Sum	W		60 x 45 ft (20 x 15 m)
Sophora tetraptera	137	9	Spr	Y		30 x 15 ft (10 x 5 m)
Spiraea cantoniensis	138	5	Spr	W		6 x 10 ft (2 x 3 m)
Spiraea japonica	138	4	Spr	Pi		6 x 5 ft (2 x 1.5 m)
Spiraea japonica alpina	138	4	Spr	Pi		2 x 3 ft (60 x 90 cm)
Spiraea nipponica 'Snowmound'	138	4	Sum	W		6 x 6 ft (2 x 2 m)
Stachyurus praecox	139	7	Spr	W		6-9 x 12 ft (2-3 x 4 m)
Stewartia malacodendron	140	7	Sum	W	*	20 x 10 ft (6 x 3 m)
Stewartia monadelpha	140	6	Sum	W		20 x 20 ft (6 x 6 m)
Stewartia ovata	140	5	Spr	W	*	20 x 12 ft (6 x 3 m)
Stewartia pseudocamellia	140	5	Sum	W		30 x 20 ft (10 x 6 m)
Stewartia sinensis	140	6	Sum	W		20-30 x 20-30 ft (6 x 6 m)
Styrax americana	141	7	Sum	W	*	15 x 15 ft (5 x 5 m)
Styrax japonica	141	6	Sum	W, Pi		30 x 25 ft (10 x 8 m)
Styrax obassia	141	6	Sum	W		25 x 25 ft (8 x 8 m)
Styrax wilsonii	142	7	Spr	W		8 x 8 ft (2.5 x 2.5 m)
Syringa x hyacinthiflora	142	3-8	Spr	W, Pi, Pu		15 x 15 ft (5 x 5 m)
Syringa meyeri 'Palibin'	142	4	Spr	Pu/Pi		5 x 5 ft (1.5 x 1.5 m)
Syringa oblata	142	4-8	Spr	Pu/B		15 x 15 ft (5 x 5 m)
Syringa x prestoniae	142	2-8	Spr/Sum	W, Pi, Pu		12 x 12 ft (4 x 4 m)
Syringa vulgaris	143	4-8	Spr/Sum	W, Pi, Pu, Y, R		25 x 25 ft (8 x 8 m)
Telopea oreades	144	8	Spr/Sum	R		10-30 x 5-10 ft (3 x 1.5-3 m)
Telopea speciosissima	145	8	Spr	R		6-15 ft x 6-10 ft (2-5 m x 2-3 m)
Telopea truncata	145	8	Spr/Sum	R		6-15 x 6-10 ft (2-5 x 2-3 m)
Virburnum opulus	145	4	Spr/Sum	W		12-15 x 12-15 ft (4-5 x 4-5 m)
'Compactum'	145	4	Spr/Sum	W		5 x 5 ft (1.5 x 1.5 m)
Viburnum plicatum	145	4	Spr	W, Pi		10 x 12 ft (3 x 4 m)
Viburnum sargentii	146	4	Spr	W		15 x 15 ft (5 x 5 m)
'Onondaga'	146	4	Spr	W		10 x 6 ft (3 x 2 m)
Viburnum tinus	146	7	Win	W		10 x 10 ft (3 x 3 m)
Weigela florida	147	5	Spr	Pi, R, W		8 x 8 ft (2.5 x 2.5 m)
Weigela praecox	147	5	Spr	Pi		8 x 6 ft (2.5 x 2 m)
Weigela subsessilis	148	5	Spr	Pi/Pu		8 x 6 ft (2.5 x 2 m)
Wisteria floribunda	148	4	Spr	Pu, B, W		30 ft (10 m)
Wisteria frutescens	149	5	Spr	Pu, B, W	*	30 ft (10 m)
Wisteria sinensis	149	5	Spr	Pu, B, W		30 ft (10 m)
Xanthoceras sorbifolium	150	5	Spr/Sum	W/R		12 x 10 ft (4 x 3 m)

Mail-order sources for trees and shrubs

The importation of live plants and plant materials across state and country borders may require special arrangements, which will be detailed in suppliers' catalogs.

American regulations vary according to the country of origin and type of plant. Every order requires a phytosanitary certificate and may require a CITES (Convention on International Trade in Endangered Species of Wild Fauna and Flora) certificate. For more information contact:
USDA-APHIS-PPQ
Permit Unit
4700 River Road, Unit 136
Riverdale, Maryland 20727-1236
Tel: (301) 734-8645/Fax: (301) 734-5786
Website: www.aphis.udsda.gov

Canadians importing plant material must pay a fee and complete an "application for permit to import." Contact:
Plant Health and Production Division
Canadian Food Inspection Agency
2nd Floor West, Permit Office
59 Camelot Drive
Nepean, Ontario K1A 0Y9
Tel: (613) 225-2342/Fax: (613) 228-6605
Website: www.cfia-agr.ca

Angelgrove Tree Seed Company
P.O. Box 74, Riverhead
Harbour Grace, Newfoundland A0A 3P0
Website: www.tree-seeds.com
Mail order supplier of seeds for hardy trees and shrubs.

Arbor Village
PO Box 227
Holt, Missouri 64048
Tel: (816) 264-3911/Fax: (816) 264-3760
Email: Arborvillage@aol.com
Wide variety of common and unusual trees and shrubs. Catalog available.

Camellia Forest Nursery
125 Carolina Forest Road
Chapel Hill, North Carolina 27516
Tel: (919) 968-0504/Fax: (919) 960-7690
Website: www.camforest.com
Flowering shrubs and trees from China and Japan.

Collins Lilac Hill Nursery
2366 Turk Hill Road
Victor, New York 14564
Tel: (716) 223-1669
More than 200 lilacs from Ted "Doc Lilac" Collins.

Eastern Plant Specialties
P.O. Box 226W
Georgetown, Maine 04548
Tel: (732) 382-2508
Website: www.easternplant.com
Catalog available.

Forestfarm
990 Tetherow Road
Williams, Oregon 97544-9599
Tel: (541) 846-7269/Fax: (541) 846-6963
Website: www.forestfarm.com
E-Mail: forestfarm@rvi.com
Good selection of trees and shrubs. Ships to Canada.

Fraser's Thimble Farms
175 Arbutus Road
Salt Spring Island, British Columbia V8K 1A3
Tel/Fax: (250) 537-5788
Website: www.thimblefarms.com
E-mail: thimble@saltspring.com
Order by fax or e-mail. Ships to U.S.

Great Plant Company
Tel: (415) 362 5430/Fax: (415) 362 5431
Website: www.greatplants.com
E-mail: plants@greatplants.com
Catalog available. Does not ship to Canada.

Greer Gardens
1280 Goodpasture Island Road
Eugene, Oregon 97401-1794
Tel: (541) 686-8266/Toll-free Tel: (800) 548-0111
Fax: (905) 686-0910
Website: www.greergardens.com
Catalog available. Ships to Canada.

Heronswood Nursery, Ltd.
7530 NE 288th Street
Kingston, Washington 98346
Tel: (360) 297-4172/Fax: (360) 297-8321
Website: www.heronswood.com
Excellent catalog.

Hortico Inc.
723 Robson Road, R.R. 1
Waterdown, Ontario L0R 2H1
Tel: (905) 689-6984/Fax: (905) 689-6566
Website: www.hortico.com
Catalog available. Ships to the U.S.

Louisiana Nursery
5853 Highway 182
Opelousas, Louisiana 70570
Tel: (337) 948-3696/Fax: (337) 942-6404
Website: www.louisiananursery.org
Wide selection including over 600 different varieties of magnolias. Full-color catalog. Ships to Canada.

Molbaks's
13625 N.E. 175 Street
Woodinville, Washington 98072
Tel: (425) 483-5000
Wide range of plants and seeds.

Select Plus International Nursery
1510 Pine
Mascouche, Quebec J7L 2M4
Tel: (450) 477-3797
Website: www.spi.8m.com
Informative website. Ships to the U.S.

Wayside Gardens
1 Garden Lane
Hodges, South Carolina 29695
Toll-free: 1 (800) 213-0379
Website: www.waysidegardens.com
Wide selection. Free catalog.

Glossary

Acidic Any substance with a low pH. See also pH.

Acuminate Tapering to a point.

Acute Sharp pointed, without tapering.

Adventitious Occurring away from the usual place, e.g. aerial roots on stems.

Alkaline Any substance with a high pH. See also pH.

Alternate With leaves arranged singly on different sides of the stem and at different levels.

Apex The tip of a leaf or organ.

Attenuate Very gradually tapering.

Axil The upper angle between the stem and a leaf.

Bare rooted Trees and shrubs that are lifted from the open ground and sold with their roots wrapped in damp shredded newspaper, sphagnum moss, etc.

Bipinnate A leaf that is doubly pinnate, the primary leaflets being again divided into secondary leaflets, e.g. *Jacaranda*.

Bract A modified leaf or sepal at the base of a flower, often the most colorful part, e.g. *Cornus* and *Bougainvillea*.

Bullate A puckered leaf surface.

Calyx (pl. calyxes) The outer, often decorative, covering of a flower bud, usually consisting of united sepals.

Chlorophyll The green pigment in plants essential for the process of photosynthesis.

Clone An exact replica of an individual plant. Any plant propagated by vegetative means.

Cone The seed-bearing organs of conifers, composed of over-lapping scales on a central axis.

Conifer A plant that bears its seeds in cones.

Container-grown Plants raised entirely in containers, as opposed to open ground or field grown.

Cordate Heart-shaped.

Corymb A more or less flat-topped inflorescence, the outer flowers opening first.

Crenate Having shallow, rounded teeth or scalloped edges.

Crenulate Finely crenate.

Cultivar A botanical term for a variety that has arisen or is maintained in cultivation.

Cuneate Wedge-shaped with a gradual, even taper to the base.

Cyme A type of broad, flat-topped inflorescence in which the central flowers open first.

Dead heading The removal of faded flower heads to prevent the production of seed or to encourage heavier flowering.

Deciduous A plant that sheds all its leaves for part of the year.

Dentate With a serrated or toothed edge.

Denticulate Very finely toothed.

Digitate A leaf shape that resembles the arrangement of the fingers on a hand, e.g. *Aesculus*.

Dioecious Having male and female reproductive organs on separate plants.

Dissected Deeply cut into numerous segments.

Divaricate Spreading widely.

Drip line The circle around the outermost branch tips of a shrub or tree, the limit to which rainwater drips fall from the plant.

Drip tip The tapering, pointed end of a leaf, usually indicating an origin in a wet climate as the drip tip of the leaf helps to shed water.

Endemic Native to a particular restricted area.

Evergreen Retaining foliage throughout the year.

Exotic A plant originating in a foreign country and which is not native or endemic.

Family A group of related genera.

Fastigiate Narrow and upright with branches or stems erect and more or less parallel.

Floret One of many small flowers in a compound head.

Genus (pl. genera) A grouping of closely related species.

Glabrous Without hairs of any kind.

Glaucous A distinct blue or gray tint, especially leaves.

Globose Globe-shaped.

Gymnosperm A plant in which the seeds are not enclosed in an ovary, e.g. conifers and podocarps.

Honeydew The sticky secretion of many sap-sucking insects.

Hybrid The result of cross-fertilization of different parent plants.

Indigenous Native to a particular country or area. See also endemic and exotic.

Indumentum See tomentum.

Inflorescence The flower-bearing part of a plant, irrespective of arrangement.

Internode The length of stem between two nodes.

Invasive Said of a plant that grows quickly and spreads to occupy more than its allotted space, usually to the detriment of surrounding plants.

Juvenile A young or immature plant. Many plants display distinct differences between juvenile and adult foliage and growth habit.

Laciniate Having fine lobes, giving the impression of being cut by hand.

Lanceolate Lance-shaped, long and gradually tapering.

Leader The plant's dominant central shoot or one of several lateral shoots trained to produce a particular growth form.

Leaflet One of the smaller leaf-like parts of a compound leaf.

Leaf scar The mark left after a leaf falls. Very noticeable on some plants, e.g. *Aesculus*.

Legume A plant that produces pea-type seeds attached alternately to both sides of the pod and has root nodules that fix atmospheric nitrogen, e.g. peas, beans and lupins.

Lenticel Breathing hole on a stem or trunk, usually seen as a raised bump.

Lepidote Covered in small scales.

Linear Narrow and short with sides almost parallel.

Monoecious Having male and female reproductive organs in separate flowers on the one plant.

Monotypic A genus containing only one species.

Mucronate With a sharply pointed tip.

Mutant A spontaneous variant differing genetically and often visibly from its parent.

Mycorrhiza A beneficial association between a fungus and plant roots. Some plants, such as *Pinus*, rely on mycorrhizae for proper development.

Native A plant that occurs naturally in the area in which it is growing.

Natural cross A hybrid that occurs between two distinct, but usually related, plant species without human help.

Node A point on a stem on which leaves, buds or branches are borne.

Obovate Egg-shaped, with the broadest end at the top.

Open ground Plants raised in fields and lifted prior to sale, as opposed to container-grown plants.

Opposite Leaves on both sides of the stem at the same node.

Ovate Egg-shaped, with the broadest end at the base.

Palmate Roughly hand-shaped, with three or more lobes radiating fan-like from the petiole.

Panicle A branching cluster of flowers.

Parasite A plant that lives off another plant and which is usually unable to survive without the host plant.

Pathogen An organism, especially a bacterium or fungus, capable of causing disease.

Pedicel The stalk of an individual floret within a compound head.

Peduncle The main stalk of an inflorescence or of a flower borne singly.

Peltate Shield-shaped.

Petiole The stalk of a leaf.

pH The degree of acidity or alkalinity of the soil as measured on a scale from 0 (acidic) to 14 (alkaline), with 7 as the neutral point.

Photosynthesis The process whereby plants use solar energy, through the catalytic action of chlorophyll, to convert water and carbon dioxide into carbohydrates.

Pinnate A leaf form with leaflets arranged on both sides of the stalk, like a feather.

Pubescent Covered, often sparsely, in short hairs.

Raceme A stalk with flowers along its length, the individual blossoms with short stems.

Recurved Bent backward and/or downward.

Reflexed Sharply recurved.

Reticulate A net-like structure or markings.

Rootstock A rooted section of plant used as the base onto which a scion from another plant is grafted.

Russet A rough, brownish marking on leaves, fruits or tubers.

Scandent Having a climbing habit.

Scion A bud or shoot that is grafted onto the stock of another plant.

Sepal The individual segment of a calyx.

Serrate Having a saw-toothed or serrated edge.

Species The basic or minor unit in binomial nomenclature.

Specific name A plant's second name, e.g. *Pinus* **radiata.**

Spike A series of stalkless flowers on a single stem. The lower flowers are the first to open.

Sport A mutation showing distinct variations from the norm, e.g. a different foliage form or flower color.

Stellate Star-like or star-shaped.

Sub-shrub A permanently woody plant with soft pliable stems. Often green barked but woody at the base.

Sucker An adventitious stem arising from the roots of a woody plant, often from the stock rather than the scion of a grafted plant.

Systemic Any substance capable of permeating through the entire plant. Often said of insecticides and fungicides.

Taxonomy The science of plant classification.

Tepal The petal-like structures of a flower that does not have clearly defined sepals and petals, e.g. *Magnolia.*

Terminal bud The bud at the tip of the stem. Usually the first to burst into growth at bud break.

Tomentum The furry coating found on some leaves and stems, e.g. many rhododendrons. Also known as indumentum.

Topiary Trimming shrubs and trees to predetermined shapes for aesthetic appeal rather than growth restriction or function.

Trifoliate A leaf that is divided into three leaflets, e.g. clover.

Triploid A plant with three complete sets of chromosomes.

Truncate Ending or cut off abruptly or at right angles.

Truss A compound terminal cluster of flowers borne on one stalk.

Umbel A group of flower heads growing from a common point on a stem, hence umbellate.

Undulate Having a wavy edge.

Varietal name see Cultivar.

Variety Strictly a subdivision of a species, but often refers to a recognizably different member of a plant species worthy of cultivation.

Whorl A circle of three or more flowers or branches on a stem at the same level.

Bibliography

American Horticultural Society. *A-Z Encyclopedia of Garden Plants*. C. Brickell and J. Zuk (Editors-in-Chief). New York: Dorling Kindersley, 1997.

Bean, W. J. *Trees and Shrubs Hardy in the British Isles*. London: John Murray, 1986.

Benvie, S. *The Encyclopedia of North American Trees*. Toronto: Firefly, 2000.

Bryant, G. (Chief Editor). *Botanica: The illustrated A-Z of over 10,000 garden plants*. Auckland: David Bateman Ltd, 1997.

Callaway, D. *The World of Magnolias*. Portland: Timber Press, 1994.

Chicheley Plowden, C. *A Manual of Plant Names*. Sydney: Allen & Unwin, 1968.

Coates, A. M. *The Quest for Plants*. Studio Vista, 1969.

Harrison, R. E. *Handbook of Trees and Shrubs*. Auckland: Reed, 1981.

Haworth-Booth, M. *Effective Flowering Shrubs*. London: Collins, 1965.

Hillier, H. G. *The Hillier Manual of Trees and Shrubs*. Newton Abbot: David & Charles, 1992.

Johnson, A. T. and Smith, H. A. *Plant Names Simplified*. London: W. H. & L. Collingridge, 1931.

Kim, Tae-Wook. *The Woody Plants of Korea*. Seoul: Kyo-Hak, 1994.

Krussmann, G. *A Manual of Cultivated Broad Leaved Trees and Shrubs*. Portland: Timber Press, 1984.

Krussmann, G. *A Manual of Cultivated Conifers*. Portland: Timber Press, 1984.

Lancaster, R. *Travels in China*. Woodbridge: Antique Collectors Club, 1989.

Lance, R. *Woody Plants of the Blue Ridge*. Self-published, 1994.

Little, E. *National Audubon Society Field Guide to North American Trees*. New York: Alfred Knopf, 1980.

Petrides, G. *Eastern Trees*. Boston: Houghton & Mifflin, 1988.

Petrides, G. *Trees and Shrubs*. Boston: Houghton & Mifflin, 1986.

Pizzetti, I. and Cocker, H. *Flowers: A Guide for your Garden*. New York: Abrams, 1975.

Tripp, K.E. and Raulston, J.C. *The Year in Trees*. Portland: Timber Press, 1995.

van Gelderen, D.M., de Jong P.C., Oterdoom H.J., van Hoey Smith J.R.P. *Maples of the World*. Portland: Timber Press, 1994.

Whittle, T. *The Plant Hunters*. Oxford: Heinemann, 1970.

Index

Page numbers in italics indicate that the plant is illustrated.

Acknowledgements

I would like to thank everyone who helped in any way with the making of this book. Most especially, I would like to thank Pat Greenfield for the fantastic photographs; Gail Church for help, advice and support; Theresa Greally for running my nursery and garden during my absence at the computer; Michael Hudson, the most knowledgable plantsman I know, for being my botanical dictionary; and Graham Smith for leading me onto this book-writing trail.

I would also like to thank Tracey Borgfeldt, Jennifer Mair, Errol McLeary, Brian O'Flaherty and Paul Bateman for editing and producing the book, and for frequent advice.

Thank you to the people who hosted us during research trips and who helped with photographs, especially Garry Clapperton, Michael and Carola Hudson, Bob and Lady Anne Berry, John and Fiona Wills, David and Noeline Sampson, Mr Min Pyong-gal (Mr Ferris-Miller), Peter Cave, Graham Smith, Andrew Brooker, Greg Rine, Gwyn Masters, Mark and Abbie Jury, Ian McDowell, Ian and Sheryl Swan, Tony Barnes and John Sole, Margaret and Richard Hodges, Margaret Bunn, Les Taylor, Alan Jellyman, Frédéric Tournay and Geoff Bryant.

And my thanks to Joni Mitchell, for the music to write to.

Picture credits

All photographs by Pat Greenfield except for the following:
Geoff Bryant p. 70 *Helianthemum nummularium* cultivars; p. 78 *Hypericum calycinum*; p. 86 *Koelruteria paniculata*; p. 95 *Leucadendron argenteum*; p. 131 *Rhodotypos scandens*
Geoff Bryant photo collection/Consumers' Institute p. 61 *Fremontodendron californicum*; p. 83 *Jacaranda mimosifolia*; p. 145 *Viburnum opulus* 'Sterile'
Garden Picture Library/Oceania News p. 36 *Chionanthus virginicus*
Frédéric Tournay; p. 44 *Corylopsis pauciflora*
Peter Cave p. 140 *Stewartia malacodendron*; p. 150 *Xantherceras sorbifolium*